Informed Consent

A Guide to the Risks and Benefits
of Volunteering for Clinical Trials

Kenneth Getz & Deborah Borfitz
With a foreword by Paul Gelsinger

R
853
C55
G47
2002

THOMSON
CENTERWATCH

Informed Consent™: A Guide to the Risks and Benefits
of Volunteering for Clinical Trials
by Kenneth Getz & Deborah Borfitz

Editor	Publisher	Designer
Sara Gambrill	Kenneth Getz	Paul Gualdoni

For more information:
Contact CenterWatch, 22 Thomson Place, Boston, MA 02210.
Visit our Internet site at http://www.centerwatch.com or call (617) 856-5900.

ISBN 1-930624-09-3

THE CLINICAL TRIAL VOLUNTEER'S BILL OF RIGHTS

Any volunteer who gives his or her consent to participate in a clinical trial or who is asked to give his or her consent on behalf of another has the following rights:

- To be told the purpose of the clinical trial
- To be told about all the risks, side effects or discomforts that might be reasonably expected
- To be told of any benefits that can be reasonably expected
- To be told what will happen in the study and whether any procedures, drugs or devices are different than those that are used as standard medical treatment
- To be told about options available and how they may be better or worse than being in a clinical trial
- To be allowed to ask any questions about the trial before giving consent and at any time during the course of the study
- To be allowed ample time, without pressure, to decide whether to consent or not to consent to participate
- To refuse to participate, for any reason, before and after the trial has started
- To receive a signed and dated copy of the informed consent form
- To be told of any medical treatments available if complications occur during the trial

OVERVIEW

CONTENTS

7

FOREWORD

nformed Consent. These two words form the backbone of what clinical medical research should be all about. My personal experience in losing a son, Jesse Gelsinger, in a gene therapy clinical trial in September 1999 exposed many very serious flaws in the informed consent process. This book attempts to inform the average human being what to expect and ask when participating in clinical research. It is a book long overdue in that regard.

We found little wrong with the 45-minute consenting process when we first sat down with one of the principal investigators of the gene therapy clinical trial. Risks were indicated but seemed remote. The benefit to be gained for others was enormous. It was described to us that there would be no benefit to Jesse. We were led to believe that there were signs that the treatment was working in animals and humans. It turned out that the picture of the research presented to us and the reality were far different.

Anyone considering participating in clinical research needs to understand how self-importance and greed can affect the consent process. In Jesse's case the head investigator had a 30% vested interest in the company that stood to gain the most from this research. When I met with this man for the first time two month's after Jesse's death, my first question to him while sitting on my back porch was, "What is your financial position in this?" His response was that he was an unpaid consultant to the biotech company behind the research effort every Friday. Being naïve, I accepted his word. Seven months later I learned that he received $13.5 million in stock for his share in the company. When I testified at a U.S. Senate subcommittee hearing on the problems in gene therapy in February 2000, the representative of the biotech lobby, who also testified, offered her condolences to me for Jesse's death three times. That same person turned out five months later to be the head of the biotech firm that bought out the head investigator's company. The pain of that knowledge still rests within me. That same investigator said publicly that money was not his goal, but he instead intimated that he was in pursuit of the Nobel Prize in Medicine.

Neither of the issues that I just described was covered in the consenting process. How can anyone know the right questions to ask? Our government has regulatory authority in the oversight of clinical research. The Food and Drug Administration (FDA) has had its hands tied by law from being able to publicly disseminate adverse reaction information in clinical research. My search for the truth revealed to me why that is. The companies of the pharmaceutical and biotech lobbies do not want to let each other know the pitfalls of research because it might give an advantage to the competition. They have claimed adverse reactions as proprietary information, and the federal authorities bow to that lobbying pressure. The cost of that is an increased danger to those participating in clinical research: the research subject as well as the scientists doing the research. Another federal body, the National Institutes of Health (NIH), has a large responsibility in gene transfer research. Fewer than six percent of nearly seven hundred required adverse event reports were filed with the NIH in the ninety clinical trials using viral vectors similar to the one given to Jesse. Noncompliance with federal guidelines was widespread. Again, how is a research participant able to be aware of this?

Ours is a system rife with conflicts of interest, but also a system that offers great hope to those in desperate circumstances. Because most of medical research is managed by ethical people, I still support our need for clinical trials. It is the ambitious minority of researchers and the motives of industry of which we need to be most wary. I have discovered that while we as human beings are prone to making mistakes, those mistakes can be put in check if we can get our system to apply the same intent that my son demonstrated…not for recognition and not for money, but only to help. Therein lies our hope of health and true prosperity. Since Jesse's death, I have seen a concerted effort by those who really care about our welfare to reform the system. This book will get us a few more steps down the right path. Please read it with care, attention and with the knowledge that your decision to participate in medical research begins with one critical act: your informed consent.

—*Paul Gelsinger*

ACKNOWLEDGEMENTS

The authors thank the many clinical trial participants who shared their experiences for this book. We wish them many years of good health. Their stories help bring to life what it means to be the subject of medical research. Their experiences simplified our task of creating wisdom from words and insights.

We are especially grateful to Barry Miskin, M.D., clinical research director of Palm Beach Research Center in West Palm Beach, Fla., for his constant willingness to explain the realities of research with candor. Although we often contacted Barry at odd hours and between patient visits, he always took the time to speak with us.

For assisting with the chapter on vulnerable populations, we thank John Niles, MS, MBA, CEO of Pediatric Clinical Trials International at Columbus Children's Hospital; Philip Walson, M.D., director of the clinical pharmacology division and clinical trials office at the University of Cincinnati's Children's Hospital Medical Center; and Otis W. Brawley, M.D., associate director for Cancer Control at Winship Cancer Institute in Atlanta. For the section on women in research, the writers acknowledge the generous assistance of Marilynn C. Frederiksen, M.D., associate professor of obstetrics and gynecology at Northwestern University Medical School in Chicago.

Thank you to Bob Young, vice president of marketing at Invivodata (Scotts Valley, Calif.), who provided helpful insights on the use of electronic patient experience diaries discussed in Chapter Three. Jeffrey Roberts, president and founder of the IBS Self Help Group, offered a useful perspective on how to pursue information and hard-to-find treatments.

We thank Gary Chadwick, Pharm.D., M.P.H., clinical associate professor in the division of humanities at the University of Rochester School of Medicine and Dentistry, for his expertise on IRB and informed consent issues, and Thomas H. Murray, president of The Hastings Center in Garrison, N.Y., for his guidance on ethical disputes.

Thank you to Cynthia McGuire Dunn, M.D., former director of the Clinical Research Institute and Chris DiFrancesco, both at the University of Rochester School of Medicine and Dentistry for their ideas and insights that helped shape this book.

We are grateful to David Korn, M.D., senior vice president of biomedical and health sciences research with the Association of American Medical Colleges, for his help with the sections on accreditation of human research programs and medical information privacy. Thank you to Alan Milstein, a Pennsauken, N.Y., lawyer, for his perspective on the problems inherent in modern research.

Thank you to the many experts who assisted us in understanding clinical trial risk. Among them: Adil Shamoo, Ph.D., co-founder of Citizens for Responsible Care and Research; Arthur Caplan, director of the Center for Bioethics at the University of Pennsylvania; Dan Schuster, M.D., associate dean for clinical research at Washington University in St. Louis, Mo.; Leonard Glantz, professor of health law at Boston University School of Public Health; Joseph Lau, M.D., professor of medicine at New England Medical Center; Myrl Weinberg, president of the National Health Council in Washington, D.C.; and Patrick McNeilly, compliance oversight coordinator in the Office for Human Research Protections (OHRP). A special thank you to John Paling, Ph.D., a Gainesville, Fla.-based risk communication consultant and to Diane Hughes, a Vero Beach, Fla.-based librarian, who assisted with Chapter Eight.

The authors appreciate the many hours contributed to this project by members of the Food and Drug Administration—especially in the midst of a national anthrax scare. Among them: Robert Temple, M.D., associate director for medical policy in the Center for Drug Evaluation and Research (CDER); Diane Murphy, M.D., CDER's associate director for pediatrics; David Lepay, M.D., senior advisor for clinical science in the Office of the Commissioner; Steve Hirschfeld, M.D., Ph.D., medical officer; John Swann, Ph.D., historian; and Susan Cruzan and Jason Brodsky in the Office of Public Affairs. Thanks also go out to Dr. Margaret Miller, manager of science programs, and Susan Wood, M.D., director, in the FDA's Office of Women's Health. The authors are similarly grateful to Michael Carome, M.D., director of the OHRP's division of oversight compliance, and Bill Hall, in the HHS Office of the Assistant

Secretary for Public Affairs, for their prompt response to information requests.

Thank you to the many professionals at CenterWatch whose collective dedication and contribution played an instrumental role in bringing this book from idea to completion. Thanks also to the numerous clinical research professionals—research scientists, investigators, study monitors and research coordinators—who have shared their opinions and experiences with CenterWatch over the years.

Our deep appreciation to Sara Gambrill, book editor, and to Paul Gualdoni, designer, for their care and attention without which this manuscript would not have taken shape into this special publication.

We are grateful to our book reviewers for their valuable insights as well as their welcome corrections. Thank you to Carol Saunders, president and CEO, Center for Clinical Research Practice; Karen Woodin, Ph.D., consultant and Myrl Weinberg, president of the National Health Council in Washington D.C.

Lastly, a special thank you to Paul Gelsinger, for his thoughts on needed regulatory reform and for his willingness to share the courageous story of his son, Jesse.

INTRODUCTION

I n 2002, approximately 80,000 federally and industry-sponsored clinical trials will be conducted in the United States on a wide variety of medical conditions. These trials are sponsored by the government and by pharmaceutical, biotechnology and medical device companies. Clinical trials aren't limited to studies of medical treatments for the desperately ill, and they aren't all conducted at famous universities. Clinical trials are conducted at more than 10,000 locations around the country including physicians' offices, stand-alone clinical research centers, government-owned and -operated hospitals and large academic medical centers.

Clinical trials are only one type of medical research involving people. In 2001, industry and government spent approximately $16 billion dollars on a wide variety of clinical research programs. These are primarily research programs of new medical treatments that have yet to be introduced into the market. Other clinical research programs involve activities such as studying blood and tissue samples and evaluating genetic maps of patients and their families. Research programs may entail testing artificial organs and mechanical devices used in (or in place of) surgery; evaluating human behaviors and the impact of nutrition on disease; and watching the long-term progression of illnesses.

This book looks specifically at clinical trials—those research studies that involve the active participation of people to test the safety and effectiveness of new medical treatments. The majority of clinical trials are sponsored by pharmaceutical, biotechnology and medical device companies.

Nationwide, there is growing interest in clinical trials as treatment options. The patient community and health professionals have become more aware of investigational medicines as important considerations when planning their treatment regimens. Every year, millions of people participate in trials. In some cases, clinical trials may offer access to treatments that can dramatically improve and extend the lives of people suffering from severe and chronic illnesses. But along with promise and hope, there are also numerous risks in clinical trials.

Even the best run clinical trials are not completely free of risk despite the fact that the research process is highly regulated, it is managed by experienced professionals, and it has many built-in safeguards to help protect study volunteers. It is important for you to know the facts about clinical trials before choosing whether or not to participate in one. That is what this book—*Informed Consent*—is all about.

Over the past several years, you may have noticed advertisements seeking clinical trial volunteers in your doctor's office or in a health center, on television, radio, billboards, newspapers and on the Internet. Throughout the country, research centers are looking for new ways to reach the patient community and the general public in order to solicit participation.

At the present time, many people are open to learning about clinical trials, and many people are volunteering for them. You may not be happy with your current treatment and would like to try a new therapy that is only accessible through a clinical trial. You may be interested in volunteering for a clinical trial because you want to help researchers better understand how to treat illnesses in the future. Whatever reason you choose, this book will be an important guide to help you understand the clinical trial process and how you can get involved in an informed and intelligent way.

The purpose of the book is to present facts, information and case examples in order for you to make an informed decision about participating in a clinical trial. What should you expect? What kinds of questions should you ask? How can you minimize your risk? We want to prepare you to the fullest extent possible to participate in a clinical trial. We also want to give you enough information about clinical trials so that you can remove as much risk from the experience as possible. But no book, no brochure, no regulatory body can remove all risk. As a subject in a clinical trial, you are always exposing yourself to risk. You have to decide whether that risk is acceptable to you or not, given all you learn from this book and all that you learn about a particular clinical trial.

The book is organized in a very straightforward manner. It begins with a brief history about the industry, a discussion of the drug development process and what is involved in bringing a new drug to market. We'll then talk about your rights as a study volunteer. What is informed consent, for example, and what are specific federal regulations and guidelines that protect your safety and ethical treatment? Next the book describes the process of participating in a clinical trial: How do you volunteer for a study? How can you identify the appropriate trials for your condition or that of a family member or friend? The book also contains ideas and impressions from people who have actually participated in clinical trials.

In order to make *Informed Consent*™ as valuable a resource as possible, we would appreciate your feedback. After you've had a chance to read the book and to review the appendix resources, please send us an email at **cw.informedconsent@centerwatch.com.** Tell us what you liked and disliked; what should we expand or revise in future editions of the book. Tell us what questions of yours were not answered and what was missing.

The advancement of medical knowledge and the discovery of life-saving and revolutionary new treatments require a partnership between scientists, professionals and patients. Your role as a participant is integral to this partnership, and it begins with your informed consent.

—*Ken Getz & Deborah Borfitz*

CHAPTER ONE

Clinical Trials—
A Very Human Enterprise

"At first, I was depressed and thought I couldn't do it. But my friend kept encouraging me, saying, 'You can do it, you can do it.' He had already been in the trial for one year, so he was a year ahead of me. Before that, he had a round of chemotherapy but was only given six months to live. So I went for the clinical trial and got the vaccine."

— Martha, subject in a stage IV melanoma clinical trial

You or someone you know may be facing a severe and life-threatening illness. You may be dealing with an illness that isn't severe, but is unpleasant and debilitating. You may now be considering a variety of treatments—each of them offering different benefits and risks. Some treatments may only be available through *clinical trials.*

For every conceivable health condition, somebody is probably doing a research study on it somewhere. Most trials test either a new *drug* or new uses for or forms of an existing drug, such as a painkiller given through a skin patch rather than by mouth. Other research studies simply measure the benefits of one drug over another. Many thousands of clinical trials focus on preventing, or more efficiently treating, chronic health conditions like osteoporosis, Parkinson's disease, depression and diabetes. Even for cosmetic conditions like male pattern baldness and acne, research scientists across the country are busily testing what could be next year's medical breakthroughs.

In 2002, the National Institutes of Health (NIH) and pharmaceutical and *biotechnology* companies will spend more than $50 billion on research and development—from the discovery phase to FDA approval—of thousands of potential medical treatments and interventions. Many of the largest pharmaceutical companies, for example, have hundreds of new drugs in development, and many of these drugs are being actively studied among participants in clinical trials.

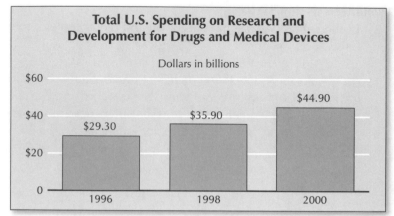

Total U.S. Spending on Research and Development for Drugs and Medical Devices

Dollars in billions

Source: NIH, PhRMA, CenterWatch, 2001

Here is just a sampling of the many types of clinical trials that have actively sought volunteers in recent years:

- Experimental vaccine for urinary tract infection
- Oral insulin for controlling blood sugar in diabetics
- Treatments to prevent restenosis following cardiac surgery
- Topical cream for early-stage skin cancer
- Oral drugs to improve sexual performance
- Cancer screening tests for smokers and people with emphysema and bronchitis
- Non-stimulant drugs for treating attention deficit hyperactivity disorder
- Drugs to prevent joint deterioration in people with rheumatoid arthritis
- Comparisons of treatment options for heart failure patients
- New medications to treat age-related memory loss

Regardless of the disease condition under investigation, no medical therapy is tested in a clinical trial without the approval of the U.S. *Food and Drug Administration (FDA)*—the chief agency overseeing the pharmaceutical and medical *device* research industries. And no new medical therapy is allowed by the FDA to be sold unless it is properly tested according to strict guidelines designed to ensure that the drug works and does no unexpected harm. One of the FDA's top concerns is the safety and ethical treatment of human subjects, or volunteers in clinical trials.

In the United States, pharmaceutical and biotechnology companies sponsor most clinical trials of medical treatments. In total, these companies will spend more than $10 billion on clinical research in 2002. This money is used to pay for the research professionals managing the projects, for equipment and facilities and study grants to research centers conducting the projects. In 2002, more than $4 billion—of that $10 billion—will be paid as grants to *investigators* within these research centers. Investigators are primarily physicians who agree to carry out clinical trials according to a very detailed plan known as the study *protocol*. The protocol safeguards human subject protection and provides direction for research professionals to follow in order to ensure that the study is conducted properly.

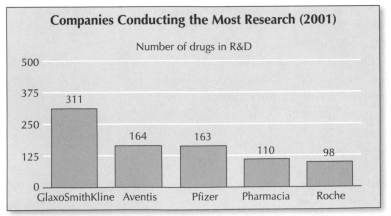

Companies Conducting the Most Research (2001)

Number of drugs in R&D

Company	Number of drugs
GlaxoSmithKline	311
Aventis	164
Pfizer	163
Pharmacia	110
Roche	98

Source: IMS International

The study protocol builds on what is already known about an investigational drug based on results from lab and animal testing

23

and from what is later learned in studies on humans. The protocol establishes the purpose and goals of the clinical trial; who will be included in the trial and who will be excluded from enrolling in it; and what variables will be measured and analyzed. It also spells out other important details, such as when a different dose of the study drug might be tried and how patients will be followed while on study.

When developing a protocol, a company or government agency has to consider dozens of questions. What is to be learned from the study? What outcomes will be measured? How long should the trial last? Who will participate? Should some or all of the volunteers receive the study drug? Is there an existing treatment to compare to the new one? What, currently, is the best standard of treatment? Should some subjects be given a *placebo*? What procedures will be done during research visits? How can the study optimize the potential benefits of a novel treatment while minimizing the potential harm? Under what conditions will the protocol be changed or the study stopped?

The results of clinical trials will not be taken seriously by the FDA unless the protocol follows accepted principles of scientific research. When comparing drug treatments, for example, patient groups must be alike in all important aspects, such as stage and character of disease and age range, and must only differ by the drug that each group receives. Clinical trials must also study different ethnic groups who will eventually be taking a new drug or medical treatment.

The protocol must make sense for the type of trial and condition under study. If the standard medication for an illness is usually ineffective, for example, early clinical trials may involve only the new investigational drug. Worldwide, there are an estimated 10,000 investigational drugs being studied from the discovery phase through the clinical phase.

The number of people allowed to participate in a trial will depend on a host of factors including: how many people have the condition in question; the availability of other treatments; the number of people willing to volunteer; and how much is known about the therapy being studied. This sample size is also arrived at by doing statistical calculations that ensure there are enough participants in studies to answer the research question.

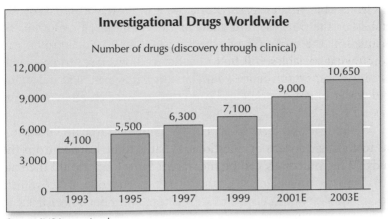

Investigational Drugs Worldwide

Number of drugs (discovery through clinical)

Source: IMS International

The age, health and gender of participants to be recruited also have a big effect on how the study protocol is written. Pediatric clinical trials, for instance, need to consider changing body size and drug absorption rates as children age—and even whether it is appropriate to use healthy youngsters as volunteers. Trials designed for women have to take into account gender differences in behavior and aging and the possibility of pregnancy. Trials designed specifically for pregnant women—and there aren't many—must give careful thought to how patients' vital signs are taken and how medications are given. They must also include a thorough check of the baby after delivery to look for any unintended effects, good or bad. Trials for life-threatening diseases require special stopping rules so that a particularly promising product can quickly be made available to the desperately ill, even before any real clinical benefit has been confirmed. These criteria also serve to identify serious toxicities that would cause the trial to be terminated early.

A clinical trial is sometimes called a clinical research study or a research protocol. But a clinical trial primarily refers to the location where a study protocol is being tested. In other words, a single protocol involves multiple locations across a variety of cities, states and even countries where clinical trials are conducted. Government and industry sponsor more than 80,000 trials in the United States each year, representing as many as 5,000 to 6,000 protocols.

Clinical trials are a human enterprise. Each year, 200,000 research professionals manage and conduct clinical trials; more than 1 million volunteers will complete them.

Many people come together to make a clinical trial happen long before the first person even volunteers to participate. The collective brain power of eminent scientists and statisticians is used to produce drug development plans and study protocols. Often, nurses and doctors will be involved in clinical trial planning and design. Teams of physicians and scientists at the FDA review the protocol to ensure it is safe and ethical for human subject participation. (The official term for a person participating in a clinical trial is *human subject*, although the term participant is also used and will be used more and more.) Local and national review committees—called *Institutional* or *Ethical Review Boards (IRBs)*—must also review and approve study protocols. IRBs are made up of doctors, nurses, and other community members who are responsible for determining if a study is safe, sensible and in keeping with the local standards of healthcare quality.

Once a clinical trial is underway, many more people get involved. *Sponsor* companies dispatch study monitors to assure that research sites are collecting data correctly and treating study volunteers according to the protocol that was submitted to them. The IRB makes sure that advertisements for study subjects aren't misleading and then follows the study's progress, intervening on the subject's behalf if questions or problems arise. The FDA inspects research sites to be sure its rules about trial conduct are followed. It immediately handles any serious safety concerns involving the investigational drug or the conduct of researchers.

FDA rules and regulations help eliminate the temptation of pharmaceutical companies to cut corners in their zeal to get a product to market. They also help ensure that physician researchers, for whom clinical trials can mean prestige as well as income, follow sound scientific practices. Pharmaceutical companies and physician researchers tend to vigorously defend the FDA's watchdog role, even if they feel the agency can sometimes be overly cautious. Some doctors and patient advocates argue that, in this age of genetic research, even more human subject protections are needed.

With every new drug, the mission of the pharmaceutical company is to determine if a product's promising performance in the lab and during animal testing can be replicated in people. The challenge then becomes determining the best ways to administer a new treatment—by pill, liquid, injection, inhaler or patch—and at precisely what dose. Any unintended reactions to the drug during testing must be recorded. If unintended reactions are severe and frequent enough, these *serious adverse events (SAEs)* could immediately end a clinical trial. But if the *adverse events (AEs)* are minor (in relation to the drug's benefits) and the FDA later approves the drug for sale in the market, the information will appear on the drug's label and package insert as possible side effects.

You have probably seen these package inserts in many of the medications that you buy from the retail pharmacy. The wording contained in the package insert—including product warnings and a description of side effects—are reported results from numerous clinical trials that have been conducted.

Building a Support Network

Another important part of the human side of clinical trials is the support network that you create. Study volunteers are not alone in their clinical trial participation. Your decision to participate in a clinical trial is best made with input from the people you know and trust. Your network should include your family physician or specialist who has previously been treating your disease or condition. Your primary care and specialty nurses may be very helpful in sorting out your identification of a clinical trial and the risks and benefits of participating in one.

Perhaps no one has a greater interest in your well-being as a potential study subject than your family and friends. They will want to be actively involved in the decision-making process. Young children rely on their parents or guardians for support and guidance. Parents in their later years may well depend on their adult children. Whatever your support network, you need to draw comfort, assistance and resolve from your family, friends and advocates in order to determine if a clinical trial is right for you. And once you've enrolled in a trial, you need to tap that support network for ongoing encouragement, advice and maybe even transportation to and from visits to the research center.

Many medical conditions have special support groups and communities that can help assist in evaluating clinical trials as treatment options. In the appendix of this book, we have provided information about helpful national health associations and patient advocacy groups. You can also find information about local support groups in the Yellow Pages, your primary care centers, hospitals, the Internet and even your public library. There are also a growing number of online self-help groups that provide up-to-the-minute information on new drugs and treatments, as well as electronic bulletin boards and chat rooms where patients can share their personal stories and experiences with both standard and investigational therapies.

The Clinical Trial Process

For many patients, a clinical trial is an opportunity to gain access to a drug—albeit, generally short-term—as much as five or six years before it becomes commercially available through retail, mail-order or health system pharmacies. Clinical trials are nearly the final leg of a new medical treatment's journey from the laboratory to your medicine cabinet. In all, it may take as much as twenty years and an estimated $800 million to bring a single new drug treatment from its initial discovery through to the market. The chance of a promising drug candidate even reaching the clinical trial stage is very low.

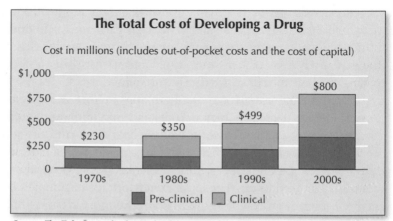

The Total Cost of Developing a Drug

Cost in millions (includes out-of-pocket costs and the cost of capital)

- Pre-clinical
- Clinical

1970s: $230
1980s: $350
1990s: $499
2000s: $800

Source: The Tufts Center for the Study of Drug Development, the Office of Technology Assessment, 2001

A drug making its debut in a clinical trial begins as a molecule discovered by scientists in the research laboratory. It takes approximately 10 years of study in test tubes and laboratory mice to reach the point where a treatment might be tested for its safety and effectiveness in humans.

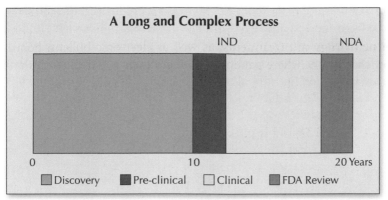

Source: FDA, Tufts Center for the Study of Drug Development

During the discovery phase, scientists find new molecular entities (NMEs) that can be tested for their usefulness as drugs. NMEs are typically extracted from plants or are created by modifying known molecules. Researchers conduct extensive test-tube experiments on NMEs to learn about their effects on human cells. These tests help scientists determine the molecule's role in altering biological processes and may also reveal whether a molecule, when administered as a drug, will be toxic. Scientists at pharmaceutical companies evaluate hundreds of thousands of molecules in order to find a few that have the potential to become a safe and effective treatment. Those few NMEs then advance to testing in animal models.

Testing in animals marks the beginning of *pre-clinical testing* and is a critical step in the process. Animal testing reveals important information about how a drug will behave in a living organism. During pre-clinical studies, researchers will be able to observe how a drug affects the animal's organs (such as the brain, liver, kidneys and reproductive organs) and how it is absorbed and excreted from the animal's body. Scientists set out to answer two fundamental questions during animal studies: (1) Is the drug likely to be safe when administered in humans?;

(2) Is the drug likely to have a desirable therapeutic effect? For example, does the drug lower the animals' blood pressure or does it fight infection? If the answer to both questions is yes, then researchers may decide to begin the process of testing a new drug in humans.

Approximately one in 50 drugs that enter pre-clinical testing prove safe enough and effective enough to be tested in people. And animal studies can only help researchers approximate a drug's safety and effectiveness in humans. But before researchers can begin testing a drug in people, they must submit an application to the FDA that provides the results of the laboratory and animal studies along with a detailed plan for the proposed clinical trials. This request for FDA permission to begin human testing is called an *Investigational New Drug* or *IND application*. If the IND application is not rejected by the FDA, clinical trials can begin.

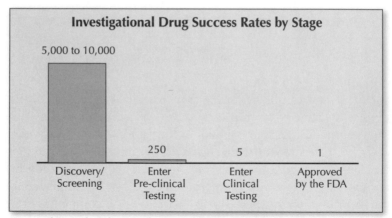

Source: PhRMA, The Tufts Center for the Study of Drug Development

Clinical trials are designed to answer five basic questions about an investigational new drug or device:

- Is it safe?
- Is it effective?
- What side effects does it produce?
- What dosage is most effective?
- Is it more effective than or equally as effective as other treatments already on the market?

Only one in five drugs that enter clinical trials will prove safe and effective enough to receive FDA approval. And some of these drugs end up being most effective for patients with different diseases than those that they were originally created to treat.

It is this long, costly and exhaustive process of clinical research that has brought so many scientific advances and has ultimately saved immeasurable numbers of human lives. Clinical research brought the world vaccines for polio and diphtheria, antibiotics for tuberculosis and pneumonia and medicines to lower cholesterol and control asthma attacks. Today, new drugs continue to be discovered and developed at an ever more frantic pace. More than 120 new remedies get the FDA's stamp of approval every year, including a handful of "breakthrough" drugs that provide the first effective treatment ever for a variety of medical conditions.

Average Time to Develop Drugs by Disease Category

IND filing to NDA submission (years)

Therapeutic Area	Fastest Companies	Industry Average	Slowest Companies
CNS	2.1	7.7	14.1
Oncology	3.2	7.1	16.9
Pulmonary/Respiratory	2.6	7.0	11.2
Cardiovascular	2.0	5.0	17.7
Dermatology	1.9	4.7	8.1
Immunology/ Infectious Diseases	1.9	4.1	16.2

Source: CenterWatch, 2000

Clinical trials led to the introduction, in the late 1990s, of the first approved drug for preventing the progression of joint damage in rheumatoid arthritis. They also brought to market an antibody engineered to target and kill cancer cells in patients all but given up for dead. More recently, clinical trials have provided diabetics with a once-a-day glucose-lowering drug and victims of Alzheimer's disease with a pill—derived from the bulbs of daffodils—to keep their memory longer. Clinical trials have also given us another new cancer drug that literally "turns off" the signal of a protein that causes certain types of leukemia. Virtually no disease category has escaped progress as a result of clinical trials.

Even relatively small improvements to existing drugs, which represent over 40% of new drugs approved by the FDA each year, provide important health benefits to patients. Newer drugs often have fewer side effects, are safer and more effective, and are taken more easily and conveniently. Not surprisingly, these top the list of drugs physicians mostly commonly prescribe. A new drug form—tablets instead of liquids or a pill taken once-a-day versus two- or four-times-a-day—can be a major benefit to individuals who have trouble chewing, swallowing or remembering to take their medications. If you or someone you care about is taking a relatively safe and effective—yet inconvenient or invasive—treatment, there is a good chance that better treatments are being tested.

Examples of the Size and Scope of Clinical Trials

Drug Name	Treatment for	Years in Clinical Trials	Number of Study Volunteers
Allegra	Seasonal allergy relief	2	3,600
Celebrex	Rheumatoid arthritis	3	13,000
Prilosec	Ulcers	4	3,100
Viagra	Erectile dysfunction	2.5	3,000
Vioxx	Osteoarthritis	4	10,000
Zocor	High cholesterol	3.5	20,000

Source: CenterWatch, 2000

Clinical Trial Phases

There are four clinical trial phases, each with a different set of objectives and requirements—from simple outpatient studies requiring only a couple of hours a month to situations requiring overnight or extended stays at medical facilities.

The Clinical Development Phases

Study Phase	Number of Patients	Duration	Primary Purpose
Phase I	20 to 100 healthy, normal patients	Up to one year	Safety
Phase II	Up to several hundred patients	One to three years	Safety, efficacy
Phase III	Several hundred to several thousand patients	Two to four years	Safety, efficacy, cost benefits
Phase IV (Post-marketing)	Several hundred to several thousand patients	Two to ten years	Safety, cost benefits, outcomes

Source: CenterWatch, 2000

During *phase I studies,* a drug is tested for the first time in small numbers (20 to 100) of healthy volunteers—often college students. Phase I trials typically last from several months up to one year. The goal of these trials is to learn about safe dosage ranges in which a drug can be administered, the method of absorption and distribution in the body and the possible toxicity of a new treatment. Researchers start by giving volunteers a single dose of the drug. Then they gradually increase the dosage level until minor side effects like nausea or headaches start to occur. That's how researchers learn about the more common side effects that limit the treatment dosage levels. Payment to participants in this phase of the process is also common because it's often the only way to get enough volunteers.

Only certain new, very toxic treatments for cancer and infectious diseases are tested on actual patients in phase I trials. And only in terminally ill cancer patients—where there are often no other options available—is the dosage amount increased until it is literally intolerable. For these cancer patients, the greatest hope of survival lies in destroying the highest possible number of cancer cells in the body just short of death. Researchers are usually leading experts in their field.

Until 1993, mostly males were enrolled as study subjects in phase I clinical trials because it was considered unethical to allow women to do so. Researchers were concerned that women might become pregnant during a clinical trial and put both the subject and her child at risk. Today, however, more women are allowed to make that decision for themselves. But they must not get pregnant while participating in a clinical trial. During the trial, female study subjects are typically expected to use some form of birth control—contraception or abstinence.

Phase I studies are conducted in numerous locations—frequently in academic settings or in private, specialty centers. Participants are often confined for 24-hour periods to a special inpatient unit—complete with kitchen and recreational facilities—where they may undergo frequent blood and urine tests. These tests help researchers understand how the investigational drug is absorbed, distributed, metabolized and excreted by the human body. This will assist researchers in determining if a new drug will have to be given one, two, three or more times a day. But how safe the drug truly is remains a mystery because so few people have taken it. Due to safety and toxicity problems, many investigational drugs are abandoned during phase I testing. According to the FDA, approximately 70% of new medical treatments pass this testing stage.

In *phase II studies,* researchers begin to understand how safe and effective an investigational drug will be for patients for whom the drug is intended. Similar to phase I, safety is still the primary goal. Phase II studies are conducted on a relatively small number of volunteers—usually 100 to 300 patients who have the disease or condition targeted by the new medical therapy. Clinical trials in this phase take between one and three years to complete. Phase II studies look to answer such basic questions as "Do patients improve?" and "What are the usual side effects?" Researchers also learn if the treatment dosage needs to be lowered or raised.

Eligibility requirements tend to be strict in phase II trials. These scientifically demanding studies are usually "randomized," meaning that volunteers are assigned to different groups—of which only a subset will receive the investigational drug. The *control* group will get another *standard treatment* or a placebo for part of, or perhaps throughout, the entire study. This method helps take the bias out of study results due to human choices or other factors unrelated to the treatments being tested. Typically, the study is *double-blinded,* meaning that neither the patient nor the researcher knows who is getting the investigational drug and who is getting the placebo or standard treatment.

A phase II study may measure something that isn't the drug's ultimate clinical value, such as improving survival after a heart attack. It would instead look at how well the drug opens blood vessels after a heart attack. Overall, it's shorter than the final (phase III) test and involves a smaller population of people. Phase II trials are also the period when researchers look at the body's response to different doses of a drug.

Only about one-third of drugs that enter clinical testing ever successfully complete phase II and progress to larger-scale *phase III studies*. This stage provides hard, statistical facts about a drug. Phase III clinical trials involve extensive testing to assess safety, *efficacy* and dosage levels in a large group of patients facing a specific illness. The study drug is tested on as many as several thousand people over a period of two to five years. Often, "real world" results—such as how long a person can sit at a basketball game, write a letter, or hike up and down stairs—are seen as equally important as clinical findings (lower blood pressure or higher white cell count, for example) in measuring a drug's usefulness. Phase III trials are most often conducted in a doctor's office.

The goal in this research phase is often to have an investigational treatment evaluated by practicing physicians who might one day prescribe it. These trials often involve a more diverse patient group for whom the treatment is initially intended. The number of volunteers needed for a phase III study depends on how many people have the targeted disease. Compared to studies of medications designed to prevent heart attacks, those for asthma would be smaller because researchers can learn something from every single participant, and every enrollee will actually have the disease.

Phase III studies almost always involve a relatively large number of participants with similar *demographic* characteristics. At this stage, researchers may also look to compare the drug's safety and effectiveness in different subsets of patients—men versus women, blacks versus whites, elderly versus young—and how well the treatment works in mild, moderate and severe forms of the same disease. Researchers are also able to test different dosage levels of the drug so that they know, quite precisely, how much of it most people need to get the good effects with as few bad effects as possible.

Drugs tested in phase III clinical trials may include remedies already approved by the FDA to treat a different medical condition—

such as a study of a multipurpose antimicrobial to treat a specific opportunistic infection in AIDS patients. Phase III studies usually test a new drug in comparison with a placebo or an existing treatment.

Therapies that have reached phase III have already passed toxicity testing and have proved to be at least somewhat effective. But subjects in phase III trials still usually have no better than a 50% chance of getting the investigational treatment versus a placebo or standard therapy. About 80% of drugs that enter phase III will successfully complete this stage.

Once clinical trials are completed and the results are analyzed, the company sponsoring the research may submit a *New Drug Application (NDA)* to the Food and Drug Administration if there is enough positive information about the safety and effectiveness of the treatment. The NDA is given to one of two groups within the FDA: (1) The Center for Drug Evaluation and Research (CDER) and (2) The Center for Biologics Evaluation and Research (CBER). The former review group is responsible for evaluating prescription and over-the-counter drugs. The latter group is responsible for evaluating blood and blood products, vaccines, allergenics and medical treatments made from living organisms. The FDA will also look to advisory committees made up of medical experts to assist in determining whether a treatment should be approved for sale on the market. Applications for new medical devices are submitted to the Center for Devices and Radiological Health.

The FDA review period usually lasts about one year for most NDAs. The FDA also has an expedited review process for priority drugs—usually lasting under six months. Priority drugs are those that represent a notable treatment benefit for critical and severe illnesses. FDA review and approval doesn't always happen as quickly as pharmaceutical and biotechnology companies would like. The FDA recently withheld its approval for an effective nasal flu vaccine aimed at toddlers, for example. The agency asked the company to conduct more studies looking at how well the new treatment combines with other vaccines and whether there's a rare risk of pneumonia or asthma among certain children.

The FDA would also be skeptical, for example, if a high blood pressure medication caused a higher-than-expected rate of facial swelling among a minority population. It wouldn't matter if researchers believed they could fix the problem by changing the dose. To prove it to the FDA, the pharmaceutical company would have to conduct a large-scale study of the drug specifically targeting that population. Approximately 60% of all NDAs are approved by the Food and Drug Administration.

After pharmaceutical companies receive FDA approval to market a drug, they will sometimes conduct *phase IV studies*. These clinical trials are performed—often at the FDA's urging—to uncover additional information about a new treatment. What is the long-term safety and effectiveness of a drug? What impact does it have on improving patients' day-to-day lives? When do physicians decide to prescribe the new treatment relative to others in the market? How does the new treatment compare with other similar treatments available to patients? Phase IV clinical trials typically involve large numbers of patients who are routinely taking the medical treatment under investigation. In some cases, phase IV studies are conducted to see if a drug causes unique problems for a certain patient subgroup. The results of these studies may be used to revise product labeling or to further support claims and comparisons that pharmaceutical companies make in package inserts and product advertisements. The offices of community-based physicians are particularly well suited for phase IV studies because they provide routine care for patients and they administer prescriptions regularly.

If you or a loved one is looking to gain access to a novel, investigational treatment not yet available on the market, then you should primarily consider phase II and III studies; however, your participation in any clinical trial is dependent upon your meeting stringent inclusion and *exclusion criteria*, as described in the protocol. Not only are you looking for trials that are right for you, but you must also be the right subject for the trial.

Outside of clinical trials, there are unique situations where desperately ill patients may gain access to medical therapies yet to be approved by the FDA. A *treatment IND* may be issued if an investigational drug has provided enough data to suggest that the drug may be effective without posing unreasonable risk. Under a treatment IND, seriously ill patients—not participating in clinical trials—can begin to receive a drug from their physician before the drug receives FDA approval. Investigational drugs can also be administered in an urgent situation in which there isn't enough time for the sponsor company to submit an IND. In these instances, the FDA may authorize shipment of the drug to health providers for a specific emergency use.

There are occasions when clinical trials have ended and patients are allowed to continue taking the investigational medication while awaiting FDA approval. The FDA may grant Compassionate Use when a study drug is already being marketed in another country and when the drug is the only reasonable treatment available.

Importance of Diversity in Clinical Trials

Fifteen to twenty years ago, research used to be limited primarily to white males, 30 to 40 years old. These days, virtually everyone—men, women, children, the elderly and minorities—has an opportunity to participate in clinical trials. This is largely a result of regulatory pressure from the FDA to spread the benefits and burdens of research participation equitably. It has also become clear that drugs behave differently in people, depending on their gender, age and ethnic group.

The National Institutes of Health—one of the government's largest sponsors of clinical research—specifically requires that its clinical studies include women and minorities. The FDA, through regulation and regulatory guidelines, expects the same.

The FDA also requires that children participate in all clinical trials for new medications that will be or could be used to treat conditions or diseases in children. And the FDA provides incentives for drug companies to conduct similar studies on certain marketed drugs now used to treat pediatric conditions. Medicare has recently eliminated a key barrier to participation by the elderly. Medicare will now cover care required during clinical trials. This includes payment for all services normally covered in conventional care settings and for services provided during clinical trials that wouldn't otherwise be provided free of charge. The chief requirement is that the clinical trials involve a study drug that intends to treat a specific condition such as high blood pressure or migraine.

Women in Clinical Trials

Whereas gender mix in clinical trials appears to be relatively balanced, there is no question that protocol designs have historically addressed disease as it manifests in adult males. During the past decade, public pressures have fueled stricter government requirements for gender-specific studies in both NIH- and industry-sponsored research projects. Pharmaceutical and biotechnology companies have also sought ways to increase the market potential for new and existing drugs by gathering clinical data to make specific claims about drug safety and effectiveness among women. As a result, clinical trials are increasingly being designed to assess gender-specific medical treatment safety and efficacy.

Many diseases behave differently in women than in men. Risk factors, symptoms, clinical course and response to treatment can all be gender-specific. Among a long list of differences, men and women vary by:

- body size, composition and metabolism
- the ways their bodies change during the aging process, e.g., puberty and midlife
- endogenous hormones
- exogenous hormones

Due to these differences and other factors researchers have discovered over the years that:

- Lung cancer kills more women than other cancers do.
- Alzheimer's disease is twice as prevalent in women.
- Men and women experience pain differently.
- Women are two to three times more likely to experience depression—due to less serotonin uptake in the brain.
- About 75% of autoimmune diseases occur in women—most frequently during childbearing years
- Cardiovascular disease kills approximately 250,000 more women each year than all forms of cancer combined, accounting for 58% of all deaths. Within a year of the first myocardial infarction, 44% of women die, compared to 27% of men.

Although the FDA recommended in 1993 that clinical studies include enough women to understand the unique ways in which their bodies respond to drugs, nearly a decade later, women are still under-represented in small, phase I safety trials. And when eligibility is restricted by age, older women are disproportionately excluded from studies of diseases that are more common in women at older ages. The possibility of becoming pregnant also excludes most women in their childbearing years.

Generally, a woman capable of conceiving a child won't be considered for a clinical trial unless she's not pregnant and agrees to use birth control. Many studies require that women of childbearing age use two forms of contraception during participation. Pharmaceutical companies don't want their drugs tested among women who are—or might get—pregnant, mostly because the risk of a lawsuit by the mother is too high. Even in normal pregnancies, 1% to 2% end with an abnormal birth. Many parents are quick to blame poor birth outcomes on drugs. Some doctors erroneously believe that certain drugs cause fetal abnormalities. But genes and chromosomes are the primary culprits, according to Marilynn C. Frederiksen, M.D., associate professor of obstetrics and gynecology at Northwestern University Medical School.

All of this presents a major barrier to clinical trial participation by women who don't want, can't afford or are religiously opposed to contraception. Things aren't bound to change unless the National Institutes of Health (NIH) comes up with the funds to conduct special dosing studies in pregnant women, said Frederiksen. And that probably won't happen quickly or easily. The NIH doesn't have any institutes that devote research dollars specifically to female health issues.

As a direct result of the 1993 NIH Revitalization Act, NIH-sponsored clinical research now routinely includes sufficient numbers of non-pregnant women. Pharmaceutical companies following FDA guidelines, however, pay for most clinical trials. The FDA recommended back in 1977 that premenopausal women capable of becoming pregnant be excluded from early drug trials. In practice, the participation of women in all phases was affected. The FDA's current stance—that a "reasonable" number of women be included in all clinical trials—hasn't fully addressed participation inequities.

In trials where women are included, the Government Accounting Office recently reported that about one-third of pharmaceutical companies fail to present gender-specific safety and efficacy data in their new drug application (NDA) summaries, as required by the FDA. NDAs also frequently arrive at the FDA without any recommended dose adjustments based on sex. Similarly, investigational new drug annual reports routinely leave out the number of study participants by gender.

The participation of women in clinical trials is essential. Real-world experience has proven that some drugs that work well in men may be ineffective or more dangerous to the opposite sex regardless of body size. Women respond in varying ways to drugs during different stages of their menstrual cycle. Hormonal contraceptives and hormone replacement therapy in menopause may even have their own effects. Women also experience pain differently than men and are far more likely to die within a year of a heart attack.

The exclusion of women from early-phase studies, in particular, delays the discovery of sex-specific dosing requirements and side effects, and may limit the identification of drugs that are useful just for women. The problem is compounded by the fact that animal studies, when scientists learn about many of a drug's potential adverse reactions, also tend to exclude females. Limiting studies to a single gender requires fewer study subjects (animal or human) and, thus, shorter and less costly studies.

Many diseases disproportionately affect women, among them: breast cancer, Alzheimer's disease, rheumatoid arthritis, multiple sclerosis, osteoporosis, diabetes and depression. And there are a multitude of unanswered questions. Why, for example, does heart disease kill more women over 50 years old than men of the same age? And why are eating disorders so prevalent in young women and nearly impossible to cure in some of them?

There are hopeful signs of change. Pharmaceutical companies are devoting a tremendous amount of money to trials focusing on diseases and conditions that only affect women. They're also pushing for more representative patient populations in their non-sex-specific studies. But women can be tough to attract to trials because the protocols written for them tend to involve a lot of time-consuming tests.

There are many ethical issues to consider—especially when a woman is pregnant. Does a mother have the right to expose her unborn child to investigational substances whose side effects are not yet fully understood? And what, if anything, does the father have to say about it? What if the couple is no longer married, or the father of the baby is not her husband? Will babies born to these women later sue their mothers for allowing them to be exposed to a drug while in the womb?

Many of the same types of questions have been raised when children are enrolled in studies by the consent of a parent. Children, like pregnant women, are considered a "vulnerable population" and have therefore been given special protections by research regulators. (See "Vulnerable Populations" chapter.)

"In a very real sense, what is good for mom is good for her unborn child," said Frederiksen. Treating pregnant women with investigational AIDS drugs, for instance, helps prevent prenatal transmission of the virus. Pregnant women who take antibiotics for sinusitis also lower the odds their baby will develop nasal allergies and asthma and, by heading off fever, reduce the likelihood of a pre-term birth. Some conditions are pregnancy-related and can only be treated during pregnancy. "If we don't test drugs then, we'll never know if they're effective."

Minorities in Clinical Trials

Certain minority populations are more likely to suffer from specific diseases, such as diabetes and hypertension, and respond to medications differently. In response, the government has made minority inclusion mandatory for trials that it sponsors. Pharmaceutical and biotechnology companies are following suit. They realize that it is in their best interest to study drugs in the specific populations that will use them most frequently.

The government directly funds many clinical trials. The NIH Revitalization Act of 1993 requires that all studies funded by the National Institutes of Health have representation from different minority groups unless there's a good reason to exclude them. The NIH believes data from these groups ought to be analyzed separately in case gender, race or ethnic origin has some bearing on the research results.

As the overall number and size of clinical trials continue to grow, government agencies and pharmaceutical and biotechnology companies are making greater efforts to ensure that clinical trials see higher levels of participation from racial and ethnic minority groups.

A review of drugs approved between 1995 and 1999, published by the FDA in October 2001, shows that blacks participate in clinical trials to a greater extent than other racial and ethnic groups, but overall participation among all minority groups remains low. Far more data are available on minority participation in trials specifically for cancer. Blacks, for instance, are represented in small (less than 3%) but roughly proportional numbers with whites on clinical trials sponsored by the National Cancer Institute (NCI), according to epidemiologist Otis Brawley, M.D., associate director of the Winship Cancer Institute in Atlanta. But, said Brawley, they're clearly underrepresented on prevention studies needing people free of the disease.

Participation of a representative group of volunteers helps researchers understand the different ways that people respond to medical treatments. For a variety of reasons, some illnesses occur much more frequently and progress at different rates in certain populations. Among blacks, for example, there is a higher incidence of hypertension, diabetes and HIV infection. There are documented racial differences in the way people respond to a long list of drugs from ACE-inhibitors to antidepressants. Different levels of certain enzymes in Asians, for example, combined with cultural and dietary disparities, can either diminish or prolong their response to a drug. Drug responses depend on a wide variety of factors—many of them related to an individual's racial and ethnic background. The National Pharmaceutical Council is updating a 42-page monograph it published in 1993 that documents some of these important differences.

Clinical researchers typically conduct "Subset Analyses" of clinical trial data in order to draw conclusions about specific racial and ethnic responses to investigational drugs. Under the NIH Revitalization Act of 1993, no phase III study will receive government funding without the inclusion of minorities such that a "a valid subset analysis" of potential racial differences can be conducted. Subset analysis requires statisticians to collect data on as many non-white patients as are needed to draw meaningful conclusions.

The FDA recently received a new set of guidelines that emphasize the need for new drug applications (NDAs) to describe the number of people of various racial/ethnic groups that were given the study drug during clinical trials and how well the data were analyzed for differences between them. Terry Toigo, associate commissioner of the FDA's Office of Special Health Issues said that her office has also started reviewing information on drug approvals between 1998 and 2001 for diseases that disproportionately affect black patients, such as hypertension, diabetes, AIDS, asthma and breast and prostate cancers. The FDA hopes that this review will provide additional guidance to industry when they design their clinical trials.

The involvement of minority physicians has been shown to have a positive impact on minority involvement in clinical trials. At this time, only about 7% of all physicians in the United States belong to a minority group and a very small percentage are actively involved in clinical research. Several medical societies and associations are now looking for ways to encourage minority physician involvement in clinical trials.

CHAPTER TWO

Why People Participate

"I didn't enter the studies for relief, because there were other things I could take. Even if I found something better, it would-n't be approved for public consumption right away. The main reason I did this was because I had several friends who died from prostate involvement—in their case, cancer. Any trial with 300 people is just a small step and being one part of 300 is an even smaller step, but it's necessary. It's the way the system works in this country, and it protects people. I saw it as an opportunity to do something for science."

— Robert, a subject in three Enlarged Prostate clinical trials

I t is a common misconception that receiving treatment in clinical trials is the same as receiving treatment as a patient. The hard reality about a clinical trial is that it is designed to answer a scientific question, not to provide medical treatment. Someone thinking about participating in a clinical trial needs to understand the difference between research and medical treatment. When you're a research subject, you often feel like a patient. You usually make visits to a doctor's office where you're examined by a doctor, undergo lab tests and receive a medication. In many ways participating in a clinical trial seems just like visiting with your doctor to receive medical care. But your doctor's primary goal is to help you feel better. The principal investigator's primary goal is to see how you will react to a new drug in order to determine whether that drug will be medically useful.

This truth doesn't change the fact that many people feel better while on an investigational drug. Many investigational products prove to be far superior to the older drugs they will one day replace. Drugs given in clinical trials have not only improved, but have also saved thousands of lives.

Patients in clinical trials are treated with drugs for everything from ulcers to strokes years before the FDA approves them. Even people with common illnesses, such as sinusitis or sore throat, are often very motivated to enroll in a clinical trial when other drugs have failed to relieve their suffering. People with AIDS and certain cancers are particularly anxious to sign up for a trial because it gives them access to investigational drugs that may offer their only hope of survival. About 95% of children with leukemia are in clinical trials.

The kinds of benefits people may receive depend not only on the specific study in which they participate, but also on which part of the study they are randomized into. Subjects who get randomized into the control group will, at best, get a standard treatment that is already available at pharmacies and drug stores. But they may also get free screenings and exams, the camaraderie of people dealing with the same medical condition, the opportunity to be an active player in their own health care and the knowledge that they're helping to answer questions that can improve the health care of future generations.

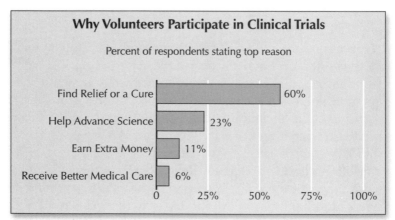

Source: CenterWatch Survey of 1,050 Study Volunteers, 2000

A surprising number of people participate in clinical trials even if they personally have little, if anything, to gain by doing so. Some volunteers get involved because they want to contribute to the advancement of medical knowledge or to help people suffering from an illness. A few do it out of simple curiosity or because they believe study volunteers get better medical care. An altruistic spirit offers no special protections or guarantees. Altruism—unless it's balanced with a healthy dose of skepticism—can leave people vulnerable. Smart patients ask questions and get second and third opinions even if they expect little or no medical gain for themselves.

People who participate in clinical trials often learn a great deal more about their illness and about other conditions (including underlying heart disease and diabetes) they may not have known about. Study-related x-rays, lab tests and physical exams have picked up unsuspected cases of many types of cancers early enough to be successfully treated by specialists. For some participants, the best end result of a clinical trial is that they start taking better care of their own health.

Another common benefit of volunteering for clinical trials is that participants get to meet research professionals who can help introduce them to other patients suffering from similar illnesses. Volunteers also may meet scientists and professionals who can help them better understand their illness and can tell them about new treatment options under development. The many people whom you meet in a clinical trial can greatly enrich your knowledge.

For individuals diagnosed with a severe and possibly life-threatening illness, the greatest benefit of clinical trials is that they offer hope. At its best, a clinical trial is an enlargement of—not a substitution for—a patient's regular medical care team and support circle.

Some people participate in clinical trials because they don't have health insurance and need help covering medical treatment costs. Drugs for cancer and AIDS can run upwards of $1,000 a month. Volunteers in clinical trials almost always get free medication, as well as physical exams and other medical services like blood tests and EKGs (a tracing of the heart's electrical activity) that help researchers monitor the drug's effects. Often, they also get treated at no charge for other minor illnesses that happen to develop during the clinical trial. The free drugs and medical care are primarily provided to ensure compliance with the study protocol and to help the volunteer remain in the study.

A number of study volunteers participate primarily to earn extra money. Payment is most often used as an incentive to recruit healthy volunteers who derive no direct benefit from the research, such as in most phase I studies. Depending on the trial, testing phase and the company sponsoring the research, this can be a significant amount—from $100 to more than $1,500.

There are even some people who make a profession out of being a clinical trial volunteer. They may only earn several thousand dollars a year, but their participation doesn't involve hard labor and it doesn't require much mental work. Professional volunteers feel that they are treated well and that they are needed. But along with the common risks in clinical trials, professional volunteers also face another risk: The long-term, cumulative effect of consuming investigational drugs. Professional patients tend to be young and to feel invincible.

The volunteer compensation on most clinical trials primarily covers the costs of participation. These costs might include time, transportation, babysitter and lunch. Some studies simply hand out money to pay for parking. For other types of trials, a flat fee of between $25 and $50 per visit to the study site is pretty typical. But payments can vary considerably from city to city and from study to study. Research institutions may also have their own unique payment policy. Some institutions limit how much a person can earn during a given time period.

Other factors can influence the amount of compensation that a volunteer will receive. Clinical trials competing for volunteers, requiring numerous procedures and visits, or involving some discomfort—such as wearing a 24-hour blood pressure monitoring device or involving an invasive procedure—often pay more. Compensation would be higher for a phase III vaccine trial requiring a five-night inpatient stay, for example.

In Florida, a recent sinusitis study involving four visits, x-rays, CAT scans and tubes up the nose was paying $500 for participants whose sinus passages were sufficiently blocked. A two-month study of an investigational medication for GERD (gastroesophageal reflux disease) was paying $1,700. But it involved having an endoscopy—an inspection of the digestive tract using a tube-like viewing instrument fed through the mouth—on three different visits. By comparison, a recent clinical trial that involved taking several pills for a week paid each volunteer $150.

Typically, the research center writes each volunteer a check as the study progresses—usually on a per-visit basis. A small bonus may also be paid to volunteers who complete the entire study. In some cases, study doctors may dispense approved medication samples and provide additional care free of charge after the trial to show their appreciation to study volunteers.

Most people who participate in a clinical trial have a positive experience. In exit interviews with volunteers, the majority report that they received high quality care, high levels of professionalism and that they would participate again.

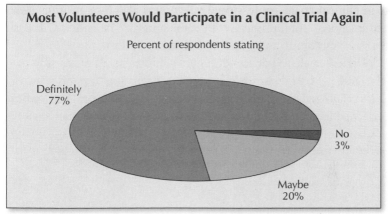

Most Volunteers Would Participate in a Clinical Trial Again

Percent of respondents stating

Definitely
77%

No
3%

Maybe
20%

Source: CenterWatch Survey of 1,050 Study Volunteers, 2000

The reason people initially enroll in a clinical trial is not always the same reason they remain in a clinical trial. The experience is an ever-changing one and, unfortunately, the changes aren't always for the better. When that happens, the temptation to drop out of the study can be very strong. Waning interest in a clinical trial—or sudden, mixed feelings about the whole ordeal—is understandable and completely natural. These feelings should not be disregarded. There may be good reasons to drop out of a clinical trial. There may also be good reasons to stick it out.

No more than one third of all people who come in for a screening end up completing a clinical trial. The reasons for leaving a clinical trial are as varied as the number of study volunteers. Some participants never pass the eligibility criteria. Others drop out because the drug isn't helping them or the side effects are too unpleasant. Some volunteers get too busy to make visits to the research center or they grow tired of the study procedures and having to complete a detailed diary. Some volunteers may move out of the area. Some simply don't like the location of the research center or they don't like the study staff. Some volunteers find another clinical trial.

When you have conflicting and ambivalent feelings, you might begin by talking with the investigator or *study coordinator* at the research center to find out if other study volunteers are feeling the same way. You may also want to speak with your specialist, primary care physician or nurse. Dropping out of a study—at any point and for any reason—is always an option. But it should not be a decision based solely on a bad mood or misinformation. The mood will pass and answers to questions and problems may be forthcoming.

A clinical trial is a partnership between study staff and study volunteer and it's based on informed trust. Dropping out on a whim betrays that trust. Study staff deserve the courtesy of being approached later if something feels wrong.

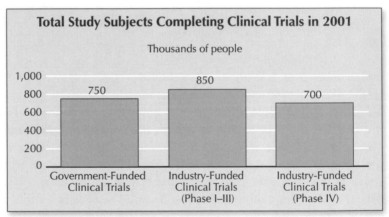

Source: CenterWatch, NIH, 2001

If there are serious problems that can't be corrected or evidence that the investigator or study staff can no longer be trusted, you should most certainly drop out. *You have the right to quit a trial at any time, for any reason—or no reason at all.* Researchers may not like it if you drop out of a study for seemingly trivial reasons, like a headache, because investigational drugs must be tested in volunteers who remain in a clinical trial to the end. A research doctor, however, may well make the first move to drop participants from a trial if a drug appears to be endangering their health.

No ethical investigator would ever try to penalize study subjects—however subtly—for making the decision to quit on their own. But study dropouts should be aware that their financial compensation, if offered, will probably be lower than that had they stayed in the experiment until the end.

Factors to Consider Before Participating

The reasons people choose to participate in clinical trials are compelling: (1) To gain access to new therapies; (2) To advance science and help others who are trying to cope with illnesses; (3) To earn extra money; and (4) To receive free medical care. But there are many reasons why people choose not to participate.

In fact, only about 2% of the American population get involved in clinical research each year. Among people who suffer from severe, chronic illnesses, only 6% participate. As a result, an increasing number of clinical trials are delayed because too few people are willing— or even knew they had the opportunity—to get involved.

Most people appreciate the value of clinical research and say they are likely to participate in a study. Yet no more than a third of those who identify and qualify for a clinical trial choose to enroll. There are a number of reasons for their reluctance. You may share some of these concerns:

They don't want a placebo. They want a guarantee that they'll receive a drug meant to treat their disease, not an inactive pill. For medical conditions for which there is already an effective, FDA-approved drug, such as high blood pressure, this may not be a concern. The investigational drug may be compared to a standard one for the entire study. In other cases, a "crossover" study may be done that rotates study subjects through equal periods on the new drug, the standard one and a placebo. Unfortunately, the best (and sometimes only) way to figure out how well some medications work is to compare people who take them with people who don't. The problem is that patients receiving a placebo are essentially not being treated. Therefore, they may have increased pain and discomfort. Their condition may even worsen, making it more difficult to treat later on. But, some subjects do improve with a placebo because they believe they *are* being treated. That is why a placebo component is included in many protocols—to study how effective the investigational drug is, compared with how effective the placebo is.

They worry about side effects and potential risks. Previous testing, on animals and other people, never completely rules out new, unexpected reactions to a drug. Side effects, also called adverse events, can be minor, such as those associated with drugs already on the market. Volunteers are told of new side effects identified during a clinical trial. Serious side effects, also called serious adverse events, such as anaphylactic shock or liver failure, would require immediate investigation and could stop a study. The research center would cover the cost of any ensuing medical bills for study-related illnesses, but the center may not cover all the bills that might pile up during a participant's recovery.

They're concerned about losing access to the drug when the trial stops. Very little of a drug is made until a pharmaceutical company has clearance from the FDA to sell it. But volunteers with serious or life-threatening illnesses who have completed a phase III study may be rolled into an "open label" study, allowing study subjects to take the investigational drug, for free, until the FDA approves it.

On rare occasions, a life-saving drug will be so popular among study participants that the pharmaceutical company literally can't make enough of it and has to divvy up what it can produce by means of a "lottery." This didn't quite work out as planned for the AIDS drug AZT. Because half of the subjects requesting the drug from every research site were randomly given a placebo, patients ended up dumping their pills together and sharing from a common supply. That way, they figured, everyone at least had some chance of getting the actual drug. Drugs that effectively treat a serious or life-threatening condition and have the potential to address an unmet need are now put on a "fast track" through the FDA approval process, limiting the wait for the product outside the clinical trial environment.

A standard therapy is already available. Some people would rather not take a chance on a new drug if treatments offering even small benefits are already available. Often it is simply inconvenient to change treatments. And, the small benefits of a standard therapy are better known than those of a novel therapy. Patients who are on a helpful medication run the risk of relapse in their illness because testing a new drug requires that study volunteers withdraw from their current treatments. If study participants become too ill, researchers may shorten the "washout" period, which is the period of time when a study participant cannot take any medication in order to "wash out" any drug effects. But there's still the possibility that they they'll receive a placebo. FDA-approved "rescue medications" (Tylenol, for example) might also be used to reduce discomfort.

They're inconvenient. The requirements to participate in some trials might also be viewed as unreasonably burdensome. Some people can't be paid enough to endure repetitive blood draws, rectal exams, needles, or even to temporarily quit smoking, drinking beer, or having sex. Some people do not have the time to fill out a diary of their symptoms and experiences several times a day or week. Some potential volunteers cannot make numerous visits to research centers that are far away or travel tens of miles to perform a test procedure.

They can't afford unexpected costs. Although most of the volunteer's costs in a clinical trial are paid for, some people choose not to participate because they may have to pay for certain routine care costs while they're in the study. These costs can include doctor visits, hospital stays and blood tests. Medicare now covers beneficiaries' healthcare costs while they are in a trial, but only a handful of states require commercial health insurance plans to cover even part of the cost of care during a clinical trial.

In Florida, an enrollee in a phase III antibiotic study was stunned to receive a hospital bill for thousands of dollars simply because of her treatment choice for a severe hand infection. Her insurance company wouldn't pay because the treatment was "experimental." And the study sponsor wouldn't pay because the study medicine is what healed her wound—not what landed her in the hospital.

At the present time, a growing number of health maintenance organizations (HMOs) and other insurers are getting involved in clinical research to offer their patients more treatment options. These are likely to be later phase III and IV trials that are a better fit with their philosophy of covering only treatments that are scientifically proven as both safe and effective. Some health insurers now willingly pay for the routine healthcare costs of patients enrolled in FDA-approved trials for investigational cancer drugs.

Are You Ready for a Clinical Trial?

Before volunteering for any clinical trial, the first question you need to ask is: "How far am I willing to go?" For patients and their families facing a serious, life-threatening illness, the question is often easy to answer. But for less severe though unpleasant illnesses, the answer is more difficult. Your answer to this question dictates how hard you will push yourself to gather as much information as possible about the clinical trials actively seeking volunteers with your illness. Clinical trials are not only time consuming, but also they require an unprecedented commitment from you to intelligently and carefully pursue appropriate trials and the professionals conducting them, to possibly forego using medications with known benefits and to have potentially uncomfortable procedures performed. And, in the end, you may receive a placebo.

The research center isn't the only—and may not even be the best—source of information about a particular clinical trial. Research centers recommend specific clinical trials for a variety of reasons—scientific, political and even economic factors are all influences. Some clinical trials bestow professional prestige and monetary rewards, for example, on researchers and research centers. Often these rewards may cloud otherwise sound medical decisions. Some research centers may overly promote clinical trials that are having trouble finding study volunteers.

It's a good idea to seek second opinions—medical or otherwise. Doctors and health professionals should not discourage you from seeking clinical trials when appropriate and should provide you with the information you need to make an informed decision.

Each person's experience in a clinical trial is unique. Two people with similar conditions—the same diagnosis, the same stage of disease and complicating factors, receiving the same active drug at the same place and time—will not always react the same way to an investigational drug. The human body responds differently to illnesses and illness-fighting drugs due to many factors. The best that researchers can do is seek to do what is best for most people most of the time based on the best available knowledge.

CHAPTER THREE

Doing Your Homework

"Every visit took a long time. I'd eat lunch, read a couple of chapters in a book and fill out surveys. We had to go to different places on the campus, and it's a huge place and my mom didn't walk very well. It would take us a half-hour to walk from neuropsychiatry to the neurology lab. Our days there were a three-to four-hour affair. After two years in the study, it finally got to be too much. We dropped out of the study. My daughter had just been born and I had no time."

– *Karen, daughter of a subject in an Alzheimer's disease clinical trial*

Your decision to participate in a clinical trial requires that you do your homework. You, your family and friends need to play the role of dogged detectives to learn as much as you can. In order for you to evaluate whether a given clinical trial is—or is not—right for you, you need to gather objective answers to the following questions:

What is known about my specific disease or medical condition? Even well educated people usually have at least a few misconceptions about their particular illness. Purging these misconceptions from your mind involves a lot of reading and a lot of listening. Among the most trusted sources of information are your primary care and specialty-care physicians and nurses, current medical encyclopedias and reference books, top medical journals, professional medical societies and associations, other board-certified medical doctors, pharmacists and other allied health professionals. Hospitals frequently choose some of the top medical minds in a community to lead lecture series on different health topics. It may be worthwhile for you to attend a medical conference. Local and national support and advocacy groups may be excellent sources of information about your illness. Often there are useful articles published by your health provider, major health magazines and reputable newspapers. There's also a great deal of information available on the Internet, but the quality of the content is mixed. You might do best to stick with major, well-known web sites like WebMD, the National Library of Medicine and iVillage. Listings and directories of valuable and reputable resources are available in the appendix of the book.

You might even contact research centers and ask if they can help you understand more about your illness or if they can refer you to someone who can. A list of more than 750 active clinical research centers, organized by disease condition, is available on the CenterWatch web site at www.centerwatch.com. Contact information is provided in the listings for you to phone or email research center professionals.

What are ways that people like me are currently being treated? Medical knowledge is not distributed equally around the country, or the world. Reputable medical journals, health references and Internet sites may do a good job of keeping up with common knowledge. But there is a lot of information that has not been published. Your primary care and specialty care physicians and nurses may have information for you. They may also know medical experts and thought leaders—across town, out of state or in another country—who specialize in researching and treating specific illnesses. Chances are very good that someone belonging to your local support group or frequenting an online chat room dedicated to your disease will have already gathered some information. They will willingly share their experiences with you. And it never hurts for you to ask.

Once you've learned about current treatments for your illness, you need to determine if these treatments have any significant drawbacks. Many medications may be only marginally effective and may have bad side effects—such as nausea, drowsiness and diarrhea. Depending on the medical condition, people will search for something—maybe anything—that will bring better relief. Some treatments may be too expensive, they may be administered in an unpleasant or uncomfortable way (e.g., by injection or taken several times each day.)

You may find an available treatment that works well, is reasonably priced and is easy and convenient to take. In this case, you will have to think seriously about what, if any, reason exists to try an investigational treatment. Perhaps you have a genuine desire to volunteer solely to help advance science. But you need to recognize that you are trading a known treatment for an unknown treatment, and you may gain no personal health benefit from participating in a clinical trial.

Compared to treatments available, are clinical trials an option for me? Some clinical trials will offer you potential therapeutic benefit for your illness. But all clinical trials will carry a degree of risk. In considering a clinical trial, you have to weigh the benefits and shortcomings of known treatments with the inherent risk and potential benefit of an investigational treatment.

Your primary care and specialty care physicians and nurses may be helpful sounding boards in thinking through the pros and cons of clinical trials relative to those of other treatment options. Should a clinical trial be considered? You will want to include your physicians and nurses in the early stages of your decision-making process. They may have, or know professionals who have, some specific information about drugs being tested in clinical trials.

Your family and friends can also be good advisors. If they're not convinced that a clinical trial is an appropriate and reasonably safe treatment option, they may be right. It also makes sense to talk over the particulars of the trial with them because they may well be involved in the process. If the study drug causes nausea, will a family member be there to assist you? If you can't drive to the research center, will a friend be taking time off from work to do it? If the trial becomes hard for you to endure, who will be listening to your complaints and providing needed comfort and encouragement?

Narrowing the List of Prospects

With 5,000 to 6,000 different study protocols and approximately 80,000 government- and industry-sponsored clinical trials to be conducted in the United States in 2002, there will likely be many trials to choose from. But choosing the "best" clinical trials will require a lot of deliberation. Some trials may involve a new drug to treat a specific illness, others may be testing a novel drug taken in combination with other therapies already available. Some clinical trials may be evaluating new therapies that help patients cope with disease symptoms. Other clinical trials may be testing new medications that prevent disease or slow its progression.

If a clinical trial sounds like it might be a good option, you need to identify specific trials that are best suited for you. In Chapter Eight, we'll describe in detail the many approaches that you can use to identify clinical trials that target your disease. Sometimes clinical trials will find you—often when you first receive a diagnosis. If you are dealing with a serious, life-threatening illness, you may not have a lot of time to evaluate clinical trials. Depending on the time you have available, some of the factors that you'll need to weigh include:

Study phase. Both phase I and phase II drugs are heavily focused on safety testing. By phase III, however, appropriate doses and uses of drugs are generally established and common side effects are known.

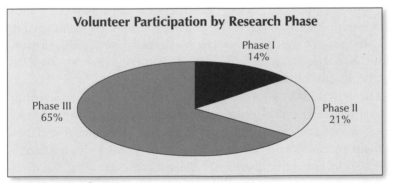

Source: CenterWatch, 2001

Time commitment. Trials can last a month or continue indefinitely, but most fall somewhere in between. It's important that you decide up front how long you're willing to be a study subject, and under what terms. How often will you be expected to visit the study site? How long will each visit take? What kind of procedures will you have to undergo? Can the visits be scheduled for any time of the day or night? What about weekends? What study-related activities will you be required to do at home? When will the study end?

Overnight stays. Depending on your underlying medical condition, you may be required to stay overnight in a hospital or special research facility. Drugs targeting serious conditions like cancer and heart failure frequently involve patients already in the hospital. Many phase I studies also require an overnight stay, regardless of the condition being targeted. Overnight stays could be a problem for single parents or anyone who would have trouble taking time off from work.

Location and access. You need to think about how convenient it will be to get to the research center on a regular basis. What's the drive time? Is it located in a safe neighborhood? Will parking be a hassle? Does public transportation cover this part of town? If a spouse is coming along, are there things for him or her to do (eat, shop, visit a museum, etc.) while waiting? Are office hours convenient?

Research center reputation. Research centers earn a reputation, good or bad, over time. Newspaper articles—not advertisements—can be good sources of objective information about certain centers. Friends and acquaintances may have had experience with a specific center. Your physician or nurse, and a variety of community health organizations, may also have an informed opinion on research centers to consider and to avoid.

The FDA audits research centers and clinical investigators from time to time—especially if there is cause for concern. This audit information is available online at the FDA web site (www.fda.gov). From the main page, under FDA Activities, go to Clinical Trials/Human Subject Protection. From there, click Related Web Sites. That will open a column of information options, including Investigational Human Drugs Clinical Investigator Inspection List. The link will open a large database of names, addresses, and other information gathered from research center inspections since 1977. Also available is a list of 100 or so investigators who have been blacklisted for repeatedly or intentionally disobeying federal regulations or submitting false information to study sponsors. Other investigators are named because of special research restrictions placed on them. If you don't have a personal computer, you should log on at your local public library. Printed versions of the FDA's audit information are available through the Freedom of Information Act. But obtaining a printed copy of the audit is likely to be a long and slow process.

Research environment. Are you comfortable and confident with the center and its staff? Your answer to this question may require that you visit the research center. The following checklist may assist you in evaluating the research environment:

- Are the receptionist and research staff friendly and professional?
- Is the waiting room clean and comfortable?
- Are exam rooms and consultation areas clean and well equipped for the research that is taking place there?
- Are check-in procedures private and confidential?
- If a child is to be the study subject, are there people on staff with experience and skill in dealing with their special concerns?
- Is the center experienced in conducting trials among elderly and physically or mentally disabled volunteers?
- Are there accommodations for family members to accompany you?
- Do the research doctor and staff invite questions?
- Do they seem to genuinely care about the welfare of their volunteers?
- Do they treat volunteers in a culturally appropriate manner?
- Are researchers involved in educating the community about the impact of disease on patients and options other than clinical trials?
- Do they offer literature about their clinical trials and the rights of study volunteers? Is this literature professional and understandable?

Are you eligible to participate? All clinical trials have certain requirements that may make you ineligible to participate. Potential volunteers on certain medications, with history of an uncontrollable disorder, pregnant or breast-feeding, may be excluded from a trial. A recently advertised study on a heartburn treatment, for instance, would consider only people 18 to 65 years old having symptoms at least two days per week. There are a number of characteristics that will exclude you from participating in most clinical trials, including:

- Participation in another clinical trial within the last 30 days
- Drug use or alcohol abuse
- Elevated liver function enzymes
- Serious disease processes, such as renal (kidney) failure or coronary heart disease
- Cancer (excepting clinical trials targeting cancer-related illnesses)
- Pregnancy
- Refusal to use any form of standard birth control (females only)
- Known allergy to ingredients in the study drug

Pre-existing health conditions and current medications being used may—or may not—disqualify you from a particular study. It all depends on the clinical trial—its objectives and requirements.

Many people are deemed ineligible for one reason or another during a brief "pre-screening" over the telephone. The remaining potential volunteers may need to have an EKG, a blood or urine test, their blood pressure checked, or a combination of tests—before they can be formally accepted into a clinical trial. Test results can also be useful as a "baseline" measure against reactions to a study medication. Some clinical trials require would-be volunteers to track the frequency of their symptoms in a diary before determining if they would make suitable candidates for a particular trial.

The criteria for being enrolled in some studies can be hard to meet. Some trials, for example, may require that volunteers have no prior treatment—even if certain drugs are readily available. Coming close to meeting the eligibility criteria isn't good enough to get you into a clinical trial. After all, the purpose of a trial is to determine if an investigational drug works while protecting study participants from harm.

In some cases, research professionals may modify eligibility requirements after a trial is under way. If you were originally ineligible, you may want to periodically check with a research center to determine if you might later qualify.

In clinical trials for "acute" conditions that come on quickly the enrollment process may be less than a one-hour affair that happens on the day a patient shows up at the doctor's office for treatment. For more "chronic," long standing problems, like migraines or high blood pressure, the enrollment process can last hours, days, or even weeks. Trials occasionally get canceled before enrollment even gets under way for a variety of reasons. For example, there may be new findings about an investigational drug's safety, or too few people may be interested in participating.

The Study Staff

Principal investigators, the people who supervise clinical trials, may only meet with you briefly to do a physical exam and required medical procedures. With the exception of dental studies, principal investigators are usually medical doctors. Research visits with physicians can seem like a routine doctor visit with added paperwork. But principal investigators do a great deal of behind-the-scenes work that study participants rarely see, including trial design and monitoring of results. Protocols developed by pharmaceutical companies and research consultants, can be hard to qualify for and grueling to be in. Some principal investigators spend a significant amount of time reworking these trials to be more "patient-friendly." Subinvestigators—including other doctors, graduate students, residents, and lab staff—may conduct study-related procedures under the supervision of the principal investigator.

With few exceptions, the professional whom you will interact with directly and frequently is the research nurse—called a study coordinator. Study coordinators are frequently registered nurses. They essentially run the clinical trial. Among their long list of duties are recruiting and screening patients, obtaining your written consent to participate in a study, monitoring your progress at home and reporting any bad drug reactions. Study coordinators are the individuals whom you likely will first meet with to discuss what you can expect during a clinical trial and the potential risks and benefits of the investigational therapy. Coordinators can, in many ways, make or break the clinical trial experience for you.

Both study investigators and coordinators usually make themselves available 24 hours a day to answer questions about the study and any unexpected reaction—or non-reaction—to the investigational medication. This also allows them to respond quickly to a serious adverse event, if one occurs.

Many research centers will go to great lengths to assist you in feeling comfortable and well cared for. The center may provide transportation services, on-site day care, after-hour appointment times, waiting rooms stocked with refreshments, friendly administrative staff, special dinners and birthday cards. Some research centers even offer valet parking. Patients who repeatedly volunteer for drug trials targeting their particular illness are sometimes supplied with free medications and treatments between studies.

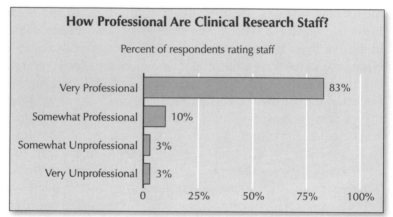

Source: CenterWatch Survey of 1,050 Study Volunteers, 2000

What you should expect from study staff

You should expect that the clinical trial will be conducted in a safe environment. If a trial involves the administration of an intravenous medication, there may be a higher risk of an allergic reaction to the drug. Therefore, the research center should have the necessary medications and emergency equipment on hand to be able to manage serious allergic reactions. The doctors and other personnel at the site should be trained in handling such emergencies. If the study involves any invasive procedure, or if anesthesia is required, it should be performed in a hospital or clinic setting that is fully equipped to manage complications.

You should expect that you will not be charged for any study medication or for study visits. It should not cost you anything to participate in a clinical trial. During a clinical trial, study-related medications and office visits are paid for by the study sponsor. These costs should never be passed along to you.

You should expect to be notified of any safety issues that arise during the trial. Occasionally, during the course of a clinical trial, new information may be learned about a drug's safety. For example, a study drug may be found to cause an unexpected side effect such as drowsiness. If this happens, the study staff are required to inform you because it may change the risk/benefit balance of the study. After you receive the new information, you may wish to continue in the study. In this case, you will be asked to sign an amendment to your consent form indicating that you understand the new information and have consented to continue in the study. If serious safety problems are discovered, however, the study may be suspended until the problem can be better understood.

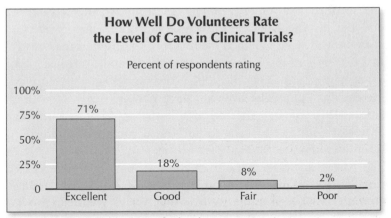

Source: CenterWatch Survey of 1,050 Study Volunteers, 2000

You should expect to be able to withdraw from the study at any time without any negative impact on your care. If for any reason you decide that you want to drop out of a clinical trial, you should feel entirely free to do so. If you elect to withdraw from a trial, the researcher may want to discuss the situation with you to see of there are any problems that can be addressed which would make it acceptable for you to remain in the study. However the study staff should not pressure you in any way to remain in a study if you still wish to withdraw.

If a clinical trial involves an investigational medication for a disease or condition that required you to take a prescribed medication, your doctor will probably ask you to stop taking your medication before starting the trial. After you've completed the trial or if you're withdrawn from the study, your doctor may ask you to start taking your original prescription again.

It is helpful to discuss alternative treatment options before you agree to participate in a clinical trial. That way you will know in advance what treatment options will be available should you decide to withdraw from the study.

You should expect that your confidentiality will be maintained. No one beyond the medical personnel directly involved in your care should have access to your medical records without your knowledge and consent. There are two exceptions to this rule: Your insurance company may have limited access to your medical records so that they can verify the treatment that you received and determine whether it is covered under your insurance plan. And inspectors from regulatory agencies that monitor the care provided by doctors and hospitals may be permitted to view your medical records to ensure that the care being provided is appropriate. Other outside parties cannot obtain your medical records, and cannot be given any information from them, without your knowledge and consent. Your employer, for example, cannot call your doctor's office or hospital to find out if you are taking medication for depression.

As part of any clinical trial that you may participate in, detailed personal information about you and your illness will be collected and maintained in written study records that are very similar to your medical records. Just as you would expect a doctor or hospital to treat this information as confidential, you should expect the researchers conducting the study to do the same.

In addition to the researchers who are directly involved in the clinical trial, your records may be reviewed by the Institutional Review Board, which may conduct periodic reviews to ensure the safety and ethical conduct of the research studies it oversees. In some cases outside agencies such as the Food and Drug Administration or the National Cancer Institute may conduct similar reviews for regulatory purposes. The sponsor also has access to the medical records and study files. While the results of the clinical trial may be published in a medical journal, your identity will never be revealed in these published reports.

You should expect to have any questions or concerns addressed promptly at any time during the study. Your ability to obtain information about a clinical trial—and to have your concerns addressed—is one of the fundamental rights that you have as a study volunteer. Your questions should be answered in everyday language, and not in scientific or medical terms that you can't understand. You should always feel completely comfortable asking questions before and during the study.

You should expect to make a time commitment. On one end of the spectrum, there are clinical trials that require no tests and only one brief visit. On the other end are clinical trials that require hourly checks of vital signs, diary entries, uncomfortable tests and procedures over the course of many visits, and overnight stays in a hospital or research lab. Trials for life-threatening conditions, such as AIDS, often have no finite ending. Some volunteers may take a life-lengthening drug their entire lifetime as part of an informal, *open-label study.* Most clinical trials fall somewhere in the middle, often requiring a handful of study visits.

Frank enrolled in a 12-week double-blinded, placebo-controlled study for his Irritable Bowel Syndrome:

> *"I had to call in once a day and answer multiple choice questions over an automated telephone setup. There were maybe 15 questions, like 'Have you had a bowel movement today? How often? Have you had any cramping? If so, was it mild, moderate or severe? It was the same questions each time. At the end, I could get through it in about two minutes."* Frank only had to go to the research center about once a month to repeat the same tests he had during his initial screening—blood, urine and stool—as well as checks on his blood pressure and weight. The study coordinator also asked if he had experienced any side effects. *"The visits weren't long, maybe 25 minutes,"* he said.

Not all research visits are short and routine. Some clinical trials involve regular trips between a research center and a doctor's office, where required tests—such as endoscopies—may be performed.

Martha, suffering from melanoma, had to make the 500-mile trip to Bethesda 18 times over two years, running between tests at the National Cancer Institute campus and doctor visits at Bethesda Naval Hospital. Then she would rest at a nearby motel room for several days at a stretch. The investigational vaccine was delivered, by injection, to alternating spots on her thighs and right arm once a month during the first year. Thereafter, Martha returned every few months for follow-up visits when the principal investigator reviewed a copy of her latest CT scan taken back home. The first few times she got the vaccine, she had to stick around for several days in case she had a bad reaction.

"You were supposed to swell up like a huge bee sting and have a lot of redness," said Martha. "I had to measure that every day with a tape measure, as well as keep a diary of any other effects," she said. Every so often researchers had to draw some of her blood, remove selected components, and then re-infuse it to see how the vaccine was behaving. It was an all-day procedure, two hours of which was spent weighed down by sandbags to stop the bleeding. "I just got tired of lying in bed," said Martha.

Down time in a study is not necessarily unpleasant. Volunteers generally aren't required to lie flat on their back at any point. For some people, participation can bring some relaxation.

Jill, 41 and self-employed, had to stay at a research center for two, 24-hour observation periods as a participant in a three-month arthritis study. After receiving an injection of the study drug, researchers drew blood from her every three hours.

"It wasn't bad," she said. "They fed me well and had a TV and tapes. It was a relaxing day." She also had to make shorter outpatient visits to the center every two weeks, as well as a follow-up visit a day or two after the study ended. "The best part was that it helped my arthritis. I had no pain whatsoever for six months."

Visits during a clinical trial take on additional challenges when the visits require the involvement of a parent or spouse. Disability, in particular, can make every research visit a tiring one for the driver and caretaker. Simply navigating from test to test can take enormous effort and a great deal of patience. Patient and caregiver experiences are bound to change as a result of technological innovation. Use of electronic rather than paper diaries, for instance, may reduce the number of in-person research visits volunteers need to make in order to deliver self-reported data. New hand-held devices use beeps and on-screen messages to remind study volunteers to answer questions when prompted. Some even pick up on inconsistencies and double-check responses, much like a human researcher would do.

CHAPTER FOUR

Giving Your Informed Consent

"Unless you've studied medicine, you don't know what you're signing. It was Greek to me. No one ever really explained anything to me. They handed me the papers and gave me a lot of time to look them over. I just asked a few questions, then went ahead and signed it. That was probably a stupid thing to do, but I had suffered with this IBS for so long."

— Frank, subject in an Irritable Bowel Syndrome trial

"They wanted to make sure I knew exactly what the terms involved were. They explained everything very well and said what the risks were and side effects might have been. And they were forever reminding me that if I had any problems to call immediately. They also made it clear that I could ask questions at any time."

— Robert, subject in three Enlarged Prostate trials

FDA rules require that every adult volunteer must agree to participate—in writing—before he or she can enroll in a clinical trial. This is no small matter. By giving your consent to be in a clinical trial, you are saying that you understand and accept the risks involved. This doesn't take away the responsibility of the principal investigator and the rest of the study staff to protect your safety and to provide ethical and professional care. Your consent doesn't take away your right to file a lawsuit if something goes wrong. But consent does provide a certain degree of protection to investigators, research sites and drug companies against later accusations of negligence in explaining study risks. And consent ensures that you take the proper steps to fully understand the clinical trial for which you are volunteering to be a subject.

The process of *informed consent* is not so much about signing a piece of paper as it is about reading brochures, listening to instructions and asking lots of questions. You can't very well agree to take any medication—available or investigational—until you know what to expect. The consent form is a contract between you and the investigator.

In a very real sense, your informed consent might best be described as your bill of rights. These rights were formally recognized in 1979 in what is well known among research professionals as "The Belmont Report." Informed consent, the report stated, demands three basic things:

1. Research subjects are told everything about the study, including risks.
2. The information must be easy to understand.
3. Research subjects who agree to participate must do so voluntarily—they must not be pressured or swayed into it.

How the consent process is handled depends on the individual clinical trial, the volunteer and the *standard operating procedures (SOPs)* of the research center. But in no case should investigators simply be handing people a consent form to read and sign. If you are handed a consent form to sign on the spot without discussing its content with the research staff and without having your questions answered, do not participate in that trial. It is often a very complicated document that even the well schooled have trouble deciphering unassisted.

Investigators—and more often the study coordinator—review the consent form document with you, line by line, and have you initial every page. For more complex studies, such as those targeting cancer and AIDS, the investigator tends to do most of the explaining.

The initial visit, during which the informed consent form is reviewed with you by the study coordinator and/or principal investigator, can last more than an hour. Screening tests and study procedures are often done on subsequent visits. Patients who do not have a chance to read the informed consent form in advance are asked to give it an initial read-through at the research site. They are often left alone to do so in a waiting area or a private consultation room. If your first chance to read the informed consent form is at your initial visit, you should consider taking it home before signing it. It's important that you think very clearly about your participation in a familiar environment and also give a chance for family and loved ones to raise questions.

Alternatively, if you know you are very interested in a particular trial, you may want to telephone the research center to request that a consent form be mailed to you before your initial visit. That way, you have time to discuss the specifics of the clinical trial with your family and loved ones beforehand. When you go to the center for a face-to-face visit with a research professional, you will have had time to prepare your list of questions and concerns. Having the consent form ahead of time in no way takes away your right to consider it afterward as well. You may want to take home the answers you received to your questions and discuss those with your family and loved ones.

Your principal investigator and study coordinator want you to thoroughly understand what you're signing. Some research professionals will even ask you to verbalize your understanding of the clinical trial's purpose, procedures to be conducted and the potential risks and benefits before moving forward. The details of a clinical trial can be difficult to recall—even an hour later. You should always keep a copy of the consent form and your notes close at hand. This way, you can refer to them to refresh your memory.

Inside the Consent Form

The consent form spells out the study procedure, how long the study will last, side effects that could happen and how much you will be paid for your participation, if anything. The form also states the reasons for various research steps, hoped-for benefits and other available treatment options. Many other important details are also provided, such as screening tests that you will be expected to take and other medications that you'll be required to stop (or start) taking. Every foreseeable risk—including the remote possibility of infection from a routine blood draw—is covered.

Elements of Informed Consent
From the Code of Federal Regulations Title 21, Section 50.25

Basic elements of informed consent

- A statement explaining the purpose of the research, the procedures to be followed, the duration of participation and any investigational treatments or procedures
- A description of foreseeable risks and discomforts to volunteers
- A description of benefits that the volunteer can reasonably expect
- A disclosure of any alternative treatments or procedures that might be advantageous to volunteers
- A statement about how volunteer confidentiality will be maintained
- An explanation of compensation and whether medical treatments are available if injury occurs
- A list of contacts to answer study-related questions and to help with research-related injuries
- A statement that participation is voluntary and that there is no penalty or loss of benefits for refusing to participate

Additional Elements on Informed Consent Forms When Appropriate

- A statement of unforeseeable risks to the volunteer, embryo or fetus—if the volunteer is or may become pregnant
- A list of anticipated circumstances under which the investigator may terminate a volunteer's participation
- A description of additional costs to the volunteer
- An explanation of the consequences and procedures if a volunteer decides to withdraw
- A statement about informing volunteers of significant new findings that might affect their willingness to participate
- A description of the number of volunteers participating in the study

Among the many promises made in a consent form is that study volunteers will be told anything new learned about the study drug that could affect their willingness to continue participating. The consent form also gives the name and telephone number of at least one person at the Institutional Review Board (IRB) or a patient advocate. The IRB is made up of professionals and lay people charged with ensuring that the clinical trial follows FDA regulations and protects your safety and ethical treatment. The IRB answers questions about the trial and the rights of study volunteers. The IRB also helps in shaping the specific information to be covered in the consent form.

Research professionals have an ethical obligation to: review with you your right to withdraw from a study at any time without penalty; encourage you to drop out if you do not wish to continue; and help you access alternative treatments. A signature on a consent form represents neither an ethical nor a legal obligation from you to participate. It signifies your permission to be a study volunteer for as long as you choose. Some states, such as California, require by law that consenting individuals receive a copy of an "Experimental Subject's Bill of Rights." This document outlines what study subjects can expect to be told, their right to refuse to participate and to change their mind, and their right to a copy of the signed and dated consent form. It is required by federal law that all clinical trial participants in every state get a copy of their informed consent form.

Consent forms can be long and complicated. And unfortunately, they can also be poorly written. Others can be more straightforward and clearly written such as the one in the example below. Many experienced clinical trial participants say researchers make a very big deal out of the process and go to extra lengths to be sure they understand what's in the paperwork before they sign.

Evaluating the Consent Form

The consent form contains a lot of information for you to evaluate and understand. Here is an actual consent form used for a clinical trial. This form is clearly written and intelligible, but most forms will be difficult to understand. This example will give you an idea of the structure of the informed consent form.

Research Subject Information and Consent Form

Title of Study: An 8-Week, Double-Blind, Placebo-Controlled Trial of Pregabalin (300 mg/day) for Relief of Pain in Patients

With Painful Diabetic Peripheral Neuropathy
(Protocol 1008-13 1)

Protocol No.: 1008-131-114, WIRB 991249

Sponsor: Parke-Davis Pharmaceutical Research
Ann Arbor, MI 48105

Investigator: James Smith, M.D.
(800) 555-1234 (24-hour number)
Sites: 2030 Monroe Avenue
Rochester, NY 14618

This consent form may contain words that you do not understand. Please ask the study doctor or the study staff to explain any words or information that you do not clearly understand. You may take home an unsigned copy of this consent form to think about or discuss with family or friends before making your decision.

This section of the consent form provides the title of the study, which is often too technical for most volunteers to understand. The term "placebo-controlled" means that some patients will receive the drug being studied and other patients will receive a placebo, and the findings of the two groups will be compared. "Double-blind" means that neither the research subjects nor the researchers will know which patients will be receiving the active study drug and which patients will be receiving the placebo.

This section also tells you the number assigned to the clinical trial. The first number, 1008-131-114 is the number assigned by the company sponsoring the study. The second number, WIRB 991249, is the number assigned by the institutional review board that reviewed the safety and ethical aspects of the protocol and the consent documents.

A reminder that you should ask questions is not always included in a consent form, but your right to do so always applies.

Nature and Purpose of this Study
You have been invited to participate in a medical research study. The purpose of this study is to compare the pain relieving effects and safety of pre-

gabalin (300 mg/day) compared to placebo (inactive substance) in subjects with painful diabetic neuropathy.

Pregabalin is an experimental (investigational) drug that is being developed as a pain-relieving drug for patients with diabetic neuropathy. An investigational drug is one which has not been approved by the U.S. Food and Drug Administration (FDA).

You will be one of approximately 140 subjects participating in this study. Sixteen (16) of those subjects will come from this site.

This section describes, in simple terms, the purpose of the study and the number of research subjects who will be enrolled in the study.

Duration of Study
Participation in this study will involve taking study medicine for an eight-week period. During this time you will be required to complete regular office visits so that your medical condition may be monitored. There will be three phases to the study: the baseline phase (lasting one week before taking study medicine), the eight-week double-blind phase (during which you are taking study medicine), and the one-week follow-up phase (lasting one week after you stop taking study medication). If necessary, however, the study may be stopped or you may be withdrawn at any time.

This paragraph tells you how long each phase of the study will last. It also states that the study may be stopped or that you may be withdrawn. This would happen if the drug is found to cause unacceptable side effects.

Description of the Study

A. Baseline Phase
In order to qualify for this study, you must be at least 18 years old and you must have had a history of pain associated with diabetic neuropathy for one to five years. You cannot be pregnant or nursing a baby. If you meet these qualifications, you will be scheduled for a screening visit.

During the screening visit you will undergo a medical history, a physical examination, have your vital signs taken (pulse rate, respiration rate and blood pressure), have blood drawn, and provide urine samples, both for laboratory testing. You will also have an electrocardiogram (ECG—a tracing of the electrical activity of your heart), a visual function test (a test to check your eyes), and a neurological exam (a test of your nervous system function). For females of childbearing potential, a serum pregnancy test will be performed (and must be negative) during your screening visit. You will also have a chest x-ray taken unless you have had one done in the past two years. You will be asked to complete a pain questionnaire. If you are found to qualify and want to participate in the study, you will begin the seven-day baseline phase.

During the baseline phase you will be given a pain and sleep diary. You will be given instructions on how to complete the diary. This diary must be completed daily in order to receive study medicine.

During the baseline phase you will be required to stop most of the pain relieving medicines and possibly other medicines that you may currently be taking. The study doctor will carefully go over with you the medicines you can and cannot take.

This section describes the basic criteria you must meet in order to qualify for the study. Remember, wanting to participate in a study is no guarantee that you will. The study is a scientific experiment. The tests performed at the screening visit are used to collect "baseline" information—that is, information about your physical condition before you start taking the study drug or placebo. For example, your blood pressure will be taken before you start taking the drug so that researchers can determine if your blood pressure increases or decreases while you are taking the study drug. Some of these tests are used to determine eligibility, as well. For example, a pregnancy test is performed. If a woman is found to be pregnant, she would be excluded from the study because the study drug's effects on the fetus are unknown and could be harmful.

The last two paragraphs in this section let you know what will be required of you if you meet the inclusion/exclusion criteria and decide to participate in the study. In this case, you would be required to maintain a diary to record any pain and sleep disturbance. It also informs you of what medications you need to stop taking. In this case, you will probably have to stop taking other pain relieving medications (and possibly other medications, too) during the study.

B. 8-Week Double-Blind Phase

After you have completed the seven-day baseline phase and if it has been determined that you meet all of the entry requirements, you will return to the office (for Visit #2) in order to begin study medicine. At this time your pain and sleep diary will be reviewed and you will be asked to rate your pain and sleeplessness as well as answer some questionnaires and surveys. The study doctor will also examine your current symptoms of painful diabetic neuropathy. You will then be randomly assigned (like the flip of a coin) to one of two treatment groups:

Group #1   pregabalin 300 mg/day; or

Group #2   placebo.

You have an equal chance of being assigned to either treatment group.

You will remain in the same treatment group throughout the remainder of the study. Neither you nor the study doctor or study nurse will know the treatment group to which you were assigned; however, this information is available to the study doctor if needed in an emergency. All study medication will be in the form of pills and you will need to take it three times a day. You will begin taking the study medication the day after Visit #2. As long as you remain in the study you will continue to fill out your pain and sleep diary every day.

Throughout the eight-week double-blind phase, you will be required to attend four more office visits according to the following schedule:

Visit #3   one week after Visit #2;

Visit #4   three weeks after Visit #2;

Visit #5   five weeks after Visit #2;

Visit #6   eight weeks after Visit #2.

During your third, fourth and fifth visits your daily pain and sleep diaries will be collected, you will be given new diaries, and you will be asked to complete a questionnaire. Additionally, you will be asked about other medicines you are taking, and you will receive additional study medicine. Also, during your fourth and fifth visits your vital signs will be taken and some blood and urine samples will be taken to check how your body is responding to the study medicine. The serum pregnancy test will be repeated at Visit #4 (if you are of childbearing ability).

You may also need to attend an extra visit at some point during the eight weeks of the study. During this visit you will be asked about other medications you are taking. Blood and urine samples will be taken to check how your body is responding to the study medicine, and you will be asked about any discomfort and pain you have experienced.

In this section, the consent form describes what will happen in the second part of the study, the eight-week double-blind phase. Especially important here is that the participants in this study will be divided randomly into two groups: one will receive the study medication and the other group will receive a placebo. The consent form calls both groups "treatment groups," but remember that one group will be receiving the placebo or an inactive substance. Some patients will improve on placebo due to what is called a "placebo" or "halo" effect. Some people respond well to any new medication, even inactive substances. For this reason, the study drug must be tested against placebo to determine if the study drug is more effective. If the study drug is not found to be more effective, then it is not considered effective. Because the study is double blinded, neither the participants themselves nor the researchers know which participants are receiving the study medication and which participants are receiving the placebo. The consent form notes, however, that in an emergency (if you develop an allergic reaction, for example) the study doctor can find out whether you are taking the study medication or the placebo.

When a blinded, placebo-controlled study has ended, the study sponsor will usually tell investigators who did and didn't receive the study drug. At that time your investigator can tell you. Keep in mind, however, that a single study protocol is used in many clinical trials over several years. If you were among the first groups testing the drug, you may have to wait years for placebo information to be "unblinded."

The double-blind phase of the study ends on your sixth visit. At this time you will no longer take study medication unless you choose to continue with the pregabalin open label study (a study without a placebo where both you and the study doctor know which study medicine you are taking). If you choose to be in the open label study, you will need to sign a new consent form.

This paragraph tells you that after this phase of the study, you will be able to receive the study medication by participating in another study in which no placebo is used. All participants will receive the study medication. This type of trial is called an "open label" study, meaning that it is not blinded. Both the researchers and participants know that all of the study participants are taking the study medication.

During your sixth visit you will have a physical exam, a neurological exam, an ECG, a visual exam, blood and urine samples will be collected, a serum pregnancy test will be given, and you will be asked about other medicines you are taking. Your daily pain and sleep diaries will be collected and you will be asked to fill out the same surveys and questionnaires you completed during Visit #2. Also, you will be asked to give your overall opinion of any change in your symptoms during the entire study.

During the sixth visit, the investigator will examine study participants. They will have tests performed and will be asked to complete questionnaires and surveys. This information is gathered to help researchers assess how the study medication has affected participants.

At any time, if you wish to take additional non-study pain medication, you must inform the study doctor (or study nurse). At this time you will discontinue the study and begin taking the alternative medication.

Because this study is designed to test the effectiveness of a pain medication, the researchers don't want you to take any other pain medications during the study. If you did, researchers wouldn't be able to distinguish the effects of the study medication from the effects of the other pain medication you are taking.

C. Follow-up Phase
If you do not continue into the open-label study, you will be asked to complete a seventh, follow-up visit one week after your sixth visit. At this time

additional blood and urine samples will be taken and you will be asked about other medicines you are taking. The study doctor or study nurse will review any medical conditions that may have begun during the study.

Risks, Inconveniences and Discomforts

The side effects seen with pregabalin include headaches, dizziness, light-headedness, sleepiness, euphoria (an unrealistic feeling of well-being), nausea, impaired concentration, drowsiness, blurred vision, tingling sensations and impaired coordination. In addition, this study drug can cause tremors, clumsiness, confusion and seizures. Mild elevations in some liver function tests have been observed. These have returned to normal levels after stopping medication. Your study doctor will discuss these with you.

This section discloses the risks and problems that can sometimes arise after taking the investigational medication Pregabalin. The first paragraph describes the side effects that other people have experienced after taking the study medication. If you were to participate in the study, you would want to ask the investigator detailed questions about known side effects and how they may affect your life—your ability to work, to function, to sleep and to eat, for example.

A two-year study of pregabalin in mice has shown an increased number of a type of tumor called hemangiosarcoma. This type of tumor tends to occur in mice spontaneously. It is unknown if this indicates an increased risk for cancer in humans.

This paragraph informs you of a finding from earlier animal studies of the drug: Some mice developed a type of tumor called hemangiosarcoma. You may want to ask the investigator to explain what hemangiosarcoma is. You may also want to ask how big a dose the mice received and how much time elapsed before hemangiosarcoma developed. Then ask how that compares to the dose that you will receive.

Because of potential interactions between medications, you should not start taking a new medication or change the dose of an existing medication without first discussing the new medication or medication dose change with the study doctor or a member of his study staff. Medication interactions can have serious, even fatal, consequences.

Drug interactions pose an important risk in clinical trials. If your doctor were to prescribe an already approved medication, information would exist on how that drug interacts with other commonly prescribed drugs. But because the investigational drug in a clinical trial is new and has been taken by few people, little may be known about its interactions with other drugs. If you are in a clinical trial, never begin taking another medication without first discussing it with the study doctor.

> There may be side effects which are unknown at this time. Serious allergic reactions that can be life-threatening may occur. You should exercise special caution when driving or using machinery since the study medications may cause drowsiness, lack of coordination or slowed reaction time. Obtaining blood can cause pain, bruising or redness where the skin is punctured. Fainting sometimes occurs and infection rarely occurs.

This paragraph tells you that the study entails risks beyond the risks of the investigational drug. Sometimes tests that are done as part of a clinical trial have risks. It's possible, for example, that you could develop an infection in your arm where blood was drawn. This is a small risk, and one that you always face when you get your blood drawn whether or not you are participating in a trial, but the researchers are acting ethically by informing you about it.

> Your pain may not improve or may worsen while participating in the study. The study drug must be taken only by the person for whom it has been prescribed, and it must be kept out of the reach of children and persons of limited capacity to read or understand.
>
> *If you are a woman of childbearing potential:* If you are or become pregnant, the treatment involved in this study may involve unknown risks to you or the fetus. Therefore, you must be using an effective method of birth control before, during and immediately after the study. Acceptable methods of birth control include being post-menopausal or surgically sterile; using oral contraceptive implants or injections; ITUD; diaphragm or cervical cap with spermicide; abstinence; condoms with contraceptive foam/gel/cream; or male sterilization. If you suspect that you have become pregnant you must notify the study doctor immediately.

Because the study drug is new, the risks to a fetus are unknown. The researchers will want to be sure that women enrolled in the study are not pregnant and will not become pregnant during the study.

You will be notified of significant new findings that may affect your willingness to continue in this study.

During the course of the study, if the investigational drug is found to cause side effects that had not been anticipated, this new information must be conveyed to you. In light of this new information, you may want to reconsider your decision to participate in the study.

Safeguards
For your own safety, you must tell the study doctor all your past and present diseases, allergies you are aware of; and all drugs and medications you are presently using.

Benefits
Your participation in this study may decrease the pain you feel from diabetic peripheral neuropathy. However, you may not receive direct benefit from your participation in this study and no direct medical benefits are guaranteed. Your participation in this study may provide knowledge that may be of benefit to you or to others.

Costs
There will be no cost to you for the study doctor's time, procedures, and supplies related to this study. The study medication will be provided to you without charge.

This paragraph describes the benefits that you may gain by participating in the study. It is careful to point out that you may not benefit at all. Typically you should not have to pay for any costs associated with your participation in a clinical trial.

Alternative Treatments
You do not have to participate in this study to receive pain medication. Instead, you may choose to receive standard treatment as prescribed by your doctor.

If you are considering participating in a clinical trial because the medication you are taking for your condition isn't helping you, there may be other drugs available that have been tested and approved by the Food and Drug Administration. Participating in a clinical trial usually isn't the only option available to you. Researchers should be able to tell you more information about these alternative treatments.

Confidentiality

Information from this study will be gathered and submitted to Parke-Davis Pharmaceuticals (sponsor) and to the U.S. Food and Drug Administration (FDA). It may be submitted to governmental agencies in other countries where the study drug may be considered for approval. Medical records which identify you and the consent form signed by you, will be inspected and/or copied by the sponsor and an agent for the sponsor, and may be inspected and/or copied by the FDA, the Department of Health and Human Services (DHHS) agencies, governmental agencies in other countries; the University of Rochester; and the Western Institutional Review Boards (WIRB).

Because of the need to release information to these parties, absolute confidentiality cannot be guaranteed. The results of this research study may be presented at meetings or in publications; however, you will not be identified by name in any publication or presentation.

This section informs study participants about who will have access to the information collected as part of the clinical trial. Absolute confidentiality cannot be guaranteed. But research information, as a rule, is very tightly secured and will be even more so once sweeping federal privacy regulations go into effect February 26, 2003. Results of investigational treatments will go into your medical record and they will be as well protected as any other part of your medical history. Clinical trials are generally designed to protect study participants from loss of privacy and breach of confidentiality. This includes the removal of names and other identifying information about illnesses and behaviors, limiting access to the data, and hiding the personal identities of study participants when research results are presented at meetings and in medical publications. Investigators can get a Certificate of Confidentiality that provides protection even against a court subpoena for data from any FDA-regulated research. The provision was initially designed to shield the identities of study participants who use illegal drugs or commit crimes. Today, it is considered equally important in preventing the leakage of genetic information about study participants that could threaten their employment, health insurance or social standing.

The new privacy regulations contained in the Health Insurance Portability and Accountability Act (HIPAA) will substantially limit access to archived medical records, which researchers insist they need for the design of safe and sensible clinical trials. Protected health information is also to be "de-identified" by removing key information like your name and social security number. Waivers for unauthorized access are to be granted only if a strict set of criteria is met, including disclosure of information that involves no more than "minimal risk" to you and research that would be impractical to conduct without access to that information. Chances are, clinical investigators will need to obtain not only your consent to participate in a trial (as is currently the case), but also your permission to use and disclose personal health information in your past and future medical records.

Questions

If you have any questions concerning your participation in this study, or if at any time you feel you have experienced a research-related injury or a reaction to the study medication, contact:

Dr. James Smith at (800) 555-1234 (24-hour number).

If you have questions about your rights as a research subject, you may contact:

Western Institutional Review Board (WIRB)
Telephone: (800) 562-4789.

Do not sign this consent form unless you have had a chance to ask questions and have received satisfactory answers to all of your questions. Do not sign this consent form if you do not wish to participate in this study.

There should always be two people for you to contact in order to discuss your questions and concerns. The first contact is the principal investigator. The second contact is a representative from the institutional review board (IRB) or a patient advocate that is responsible for ensuring the safety and ethical treatment of volunteers in the study. This section also reminds you again not to sign the consent form until you have had your questions answered.

Consent

I have read and I understand the information in this consent form. All my questions regarding the study and my participation in it have been answered to my satisfaction. I have been informed of the risks involved and my rights as a research subject.

I voluntarily agree to participate in this study. I understand that I will receive a signed and dated copy of this consent form. I authorize the release of my medical records to Parke-Davis, Kendle, the FDA, DHHS agencies, governmental agencies in other countries, the University of Rochester, and WIRB.

By signing this consent form, I have not waived any of the legal rights which I otherwise would have as a subject in a research study.

_____

Subject's Name (Printed)

_____

Subject's Signature   Date

The above-named subject has been fully informed of the study.

_____

Signature of Person Conducting   Date
Informed Consent Discussion

_____

Investigator's Signature (if different from above)   Date

At the conclusion of the consent form, you provide your consent in writing. And the study staff involved in this process also sign. This completes the contract that you have now entered into with the investigator and the research center.

Exceptions to the Rules

If the study participant is a child or an individual under the care of another person, a parent, caregiver or legal guardian will usually sign the consent form. This would be the case with most Alzheimer's disease patients.

"My mom participated in the decision as much as she was able to. But the Alzheimer's made her pessimistic," Karen said. "She worried about everything. What if she flunked the [screening] test? What if we got lost on the way there? Are you sure you have time to do this? If left to decide on her own, she would have said no. She hates doctors. I just told her we were going to do this; we were going to go get this new medicine. The only drug [then] on the market...was effective for fewer than half the people who took it. So I thought, 'Why not try something new?' It took me maybe 10 minutes to decide, although the doctor made me take home the consent papers to read through them before I signed."

In special circumstances, FDA regulations allow doctors to provide "emergency" research before informed consent is obtained from a volunteer or caregiver. A trauma patient who shows up in a hospital emergency room in shock, for example, might be immediately placed on a resuscitation study. This would happen only because the patient is physically unable to give consent at the time the investigational treatment must be given to potentially save his or her life. The patient, or a family member, generally signs consent papers a short time later.

Take Your Time

Unlike study volunteers, investigators have usually gone through the informed consent process countless times before. Research staff may zip through explanations and give you too little time to think of questions that you might want to ask. They may also explain things in a way you don't understand. There is absolutely nothing wrong with asking a researcher to slow down and repeat something. It is also not out of line to ask them to explain something in another way, using everyday words. If English is not your first language, you need to speak up. Research centers can, and should, produce documents in your first language upon request.

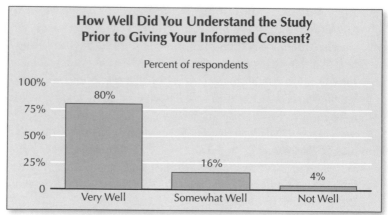

Source: CenterWatch, NIH, 2001

It is the principal investigator's responsibility to make sure that you completely understand everything that you've read in the consent form. It is also the investigator's responsibility to give you enough time to think of any questions that you may still have. This is not necessarily going to happen in a single visit. When given time to think over your decision, you may raise important concerns that no one else ever thought to bring up.

Questions to Ask Before Participating in Clinical Research

Following is a comprehensive list of questions for you to consider asking. More than anything else, this checklist of questions may assist you in beginning your conversation with research center staff. You may want to invite along a friend or relative for support—and to help you recall answers to your questions. You may even want to record answers to these questions so you can replay them at a later date.

About the Clinical Trial

- ☐ What is the main purpose of the study?
- ☐ Why is this study important to me?
- ☐ What are the chances that this drug will work?
- ☐ Is the drug already being used in other countries?
- ☐ How long will the clinical trial last?
- ☐ What kinds of risks are involved?
- ☐ What are the eligibility requirements?
- ☐ What kinds of medical problems would prevent me from participating in the study?
- ☐ What kind of screening do I have to go through to qualify as a study subject?
- ☐ Where is the study being conducted?
- ☐ Who else is participating in the study?
- ☐ How much of my time will this take?
- ☐ Does the study involve a placebo or a treatment already on the market?
- ☐ What are my chances of getting a placebo?
- ☐ Have other studies already been done on this drug?
- ☐ What has been learned about this drug so far and where have those results been published?
- ☐ How many adverse events have been associated with this drug to date?
- ☐ What kind of side effects have other people (or animals) experienced?
- ☐ (If pregnant) What kinds of effects might this drug have on my unborn child?
- ☐ Who will be watching out for my safety?
- ☐ What other kinds of treatments are available to treat my condition?
- ☐ What can you tell me about the drug company sponsoring this study?

□ Who has reviewed and approved this study? How can I contact them?

□ Will I be able to find out the results of the study?

About Your Care

□ How will the treatment be given to me?

□ What kind of tests will be done? Will they hurt? If so, for how long?

□ How will the tests in the study compare to tests I would have outside the study?

□ Will I be able to see my own doctor?

□ Will the research staff work with my doctor while I am in the clinical trial?

□ Will I be able to take my regular medications during the study?

□ If the study drug doesn't work, will I be able to take anything else for my symptoms?

□ Will everything be done on an outpatient basis, or will I have to be hospitalized?

□ What if I miss a dose of the study drug?

□ If I have side effects, can they be treated during the study?

□ Is it possible my condition will worsen during, or after, the study?

□ Will I receive any follow-up care after the study ends? Who will provide it?

□ Whom can I call with questions and concerns during the study?

□ Who on the research staff will be with me in the event of an emergency?

□ If the treatment works for me, can I keep using it after the study ends? For free?

□ Who will provide my medical care after the study ends?

About Your Personal Matters

□ Can anyone find out if I'm participating in the clinical trial?

□ How might this study affect my daily life?

□ Who will review my information collected during the trial?

□ Can I talk to other volunteers in the trial?

□ What support is available in the community for me and my family?

□ What happens if I decide to quit the study?

□ Can I be withdrawn from the study for any reason?

About Your Compensation and Costs

□ Do I have to pay for any part of the study? If so, will insurance cover these costs?

□ Do I have to talk to my health insurance company before enrolling in the study?

□ How much will I be paid for my participation?

□ Will I be reimbursed for gas, or will transportation be provided?

About the Research Staff

□ Why did the investigator decide to get involved in clinical research?

□ What is the investigator's background and training?

□ What sort of research training and certification have the investigator and coordinator had?

□ How many studies has the investigator done before?

□ Was the investigator involved in the design of the study?

□ Has the investigator or study coordinator ever participated in a clinical trial?

□ Does this facility have any special credentials or experience in research?

□ Do the investigator and study coordinator have any formal training in research safety and ethics?

□ Does the investigator have a financial interest in the drug being studied?

□ Is the investigator or study coordinator paid a bonus for recruiting me into the trial?

If a study involves a great deal of risk and close patient monitoring, for instance, it will probably be very important to the study volunteer (or their legal guardian) to know how much research training and experience the principal investigator has had. Two-thirds of our country's 50,000 investigators have limited experience conducting clinical trials. Being a researcher is a tough job, even for otherwise well-schooled medical doctors.

The U.S. Department of Health and Human Services requires that investigators involved in any of the studies it funds (through the NIH, for example) be instructed on how to conduct research responsibly. Although the FDA intends to become more specific about its educational requirements, the onus is currently on pharmaceutical companies to ensure that clinical investigators are sufficiently qualified with experience and training. Investigators have a medical or professional degree, but it is not always enough because many investigators have not received formal training in clinical research. A pathologist accustomed to working all day in a lab, for instance, wouldn't be well suited for clinical trials with pediatric populations.

Although there are no certification exams for physicians as proof of their competency in conducting clinical trials, there is plenty of accredited coursework being offered by universities, trade associations and training companies. A number of medical schools also offer research training during doctors' internship and residency years. And at this time, 10 medical colleges and universities now offer doctors a two-year program leading to a Master's degree of Science in Clinical Research. Some research institutions require that all investigators undergo a fairly rigorous educational program covering the basics of clinical research. The NIH and several universities (Case Western Reserve University and the University of Rochester among them) make investigators take an online test that demonstrates their knowledge of human research protections before they can seek IRB approval of a protocol.

Study coordinators and other support staff have a wide variety of accredited courses to choose from. Study coordinators can be certified. This distinction adds the letters "CCRC"—Certified Clinical Research Coordinator—to their titles. Coordinators tend to be the ones who handle informed consent discussions. In fact, at some universities, informed consent discussions exclude investigators who are also healthcare providers. This is done to lower the chance that potential study volunteers will be influenced to participate in research simply because it's being done by people they know and respect as healers.

Beginning a Dialogue
When people either blindly or half-heartedly commit to participate in a clinical trial, neither science nor an individual's health may gain

anything. One reason why a high number of volunteers drop out of a study is because many don't fully understand what they're consenting to from the outset. That's why you need to find out all that you can before you give your consent. Informed consent papers and new drug brochures will answer many—but not all—of your important questions.

When it comes to study risks, in particular, you may have to dig for the full story. Families have told stories of needlessly losing a loved one in a clinical trial where earlier deaths and serious adverse events went unreported on informed consent documents because the study's sponsor didn't identify the study drug as the culprit. FDA guidelines say that study volunteers should understand the risks they're taking, but they don't require a drug's complete track record be shared. If you want to know details, such as the number of deaths and serious side effects observed in earlier clinical trials even if the study drug was not implicated, you have to make a point to request that information.

Not everyone has the time, interest or even the capability of understanding everything that is uncovered. You may want to bring some of this information to a trusted, impartial family physician or health professional for their medical opinion. Another good option is to consult with the IRB. They decide whether or not a clinical trial gets done. The IRB is also your chief advocate and troubleshooter throughout the course of the trial.

You need to always remember that you are the one volunteering for a clinical trial. The study drug may make you feel better. And your study visits may seem just like any other visit to the doctor's office, but the main purpose of research is to collect data, not to treat your illness. You should therefore participate in a clinical trial only if you feel that it is in your best interest—not in the interest of your doctor, employer, researchers, college professor or anyone else.

During and After a Trial

Informed consent doesn't stop the moment a form is signed and witnessed. It's something you are entitled to during—and even after—the clinical trial has ended. Experienced investigators and study coordinators will repeat, remind and reassure you frequently about what is happening to you. If they don't (and even if they do), it's okay to ask questions and expect answers from researchers. It's their job.

Any time you feel that your questions and concerns have not been sufficiently addressed, you have the option to seek help from the IRB. The pharmaceutical company sponsoring the clinical trial may also have a consumer hotline that participants can call with any unanswered concerns or general questions specifically about the drug. A list of sponsor companies and their contact information is provided in the appendix.

If a clinical trial gets suspended for reasons unrelated to the study drug, volunteers who have a medical need to continue taking the drug may be allowed to do so. If a trial is suspended due to serious adverse events related to the study drug, or production problems on the part of the pharmaceutical company, then you would be required to stop taking the drug and to seek care from your regular doctor. But the principal investigator and study staff would continue to keep an eye on you, at least until the study drug is out of your system.

Your consent means that you can withdraw from a clinical trial. This is your fundamental right as a study participant. If your withdrawal may prove harmful to you, the investigator and study coordinator must tell you so. Investigators and study coordinators should not coerce you to continue to participate in a clinical trial if your decision to withdraw is final. Informed consent regulations forbid investigators who are practicing doctors from denying future care to their patients who have withdrawn from a clinical trial. If you drop out of a clinical trial, you should still be told anything that is later learned about the investigational drug that could affect your health.

Compassionate Use of Experimental Treatments

For most people, access to a study drug ends when the clinical trial does. But there are some notable exceptions. Study volunteers with serious or life-threatening illnesses who have completed a phase III study are sometimes rolled into an "open label" study, allowing them to take an effective investigational drug, for free, until the FDA approves it or for a fixed time period such as six months or a year.

Such compassionate use, as it is often called, is only occasionally extended to patients with debilitating but not necessarily life-shortening medical conditions. And only then if the pharmaceutical company hasn't abandoned plans to take the drug to market for one reason or another.

Even if a pharmaceutical company is willing to provide compassionate use of a helpful drug, the process doesn't necessarily happen quickly. The research investigator would need to send in a special FDA form to the company, whose attorneys might mull it over for weeks or even years.

In the meantime, patients can check with the FDA or pharmaceutical companies to learn about where investigational drugs are in the development process. If approval of the desired drug isn't far off, the best course of action may be to wait it out. There may even be another drug with a similar composition and action under study. Patients can always ask the pharmaceutical company about other promising trials it is conducting, or start a wider search on their own.

Consent and Your Obligations

By signing the consent form and agreeing to participate, *you* also assume certain responsibilities. Consent is a covenant of trust between researchers and research subjects. It is your responsibility to tell the truth and to comply with the rules of the clinical trial. If you fail to meet these obligations, the data collected during the clinical trial have no integrity.

You should never lie to qualify for a clinical trial. No matter how badly you want to qualify to participate in a clinical trial, you must tell the truth. Some people might neglect to mention things, like a prior medical condition or daily treatment of pain symptoms, which would automatically exclude them from some studies. Others might knowingly participate in two drug studies at the same time—a standard exclusion criterion.

Dishonesty invalidates the study results and it is dangerous. Taking two drugs at the same time, for instance, exposes a person to unknown and difficult-to-detect interactions that can cause serious health problems—even death. One drug also may be mistakenly credited for the action of the other, or mask its harmful side effects. Faulty data lead to faulty conclusions about a drug's safety and, in the end, it may endanger public health.

You should never disregard the study protocol. Protocols are very carefully designed. Failure to comply with the protocol can endanger you and can harm the results of the trial. Study volunteers who are instructed not to drink any alcoholic beverages but do so anyway may skew important lab results. Volunteers who fail to take the study medication as instructed or ignore their promise to use birth control and become pregnant (not to mention the unknown harm done to the fetus) may invalidate the clinical trial results not to mention put themselves at risk. Researchers need to understand how a study medication is working, whether doses need to be adjusted and what side effects you are experiencing.

Maintaining a diary is important if it is required in the protocol. If you aren't willing to devote time to keeping a diary, you shouldn't volunteer to participate. Hastily made diary entries won't benefit the research effort. To help you comply with this requirement, investigators and study coordinators often have to call to remind you to record your experiences in your diary.

Your informed consent is a fundamental right as a participant in a clinical trial. It is a major responsibility that you and your support network must assume when you decide to volunteer to participate in a clinical trial.

CHAPTER FIVE

Historical Events that Have Shaped Human Subject Protection

"During my first studies, I wasn't told very much. I didn't know what kind of medication I was on, where it came from, or anything. Now, doctors tell me how they're going to do the study, who and what they're doing it for and the effects it might have on me—positive and negative. If I see something I don't like, I tell them I don't want to go any further."

– Lillian, 20-year veteran of clinical trials

This chapter offers a brief overview of the evolution of human subject protections. These protections have evolved in response to abuses and atrocities that were carried out against vulnerable members of our population, including children, prisoners, the mentally ill and the poor.

For hundreds of years, children were typically recruited for scientific studies. They were easy to recruit precisely because they were vulnerable. This practice reached its ugliest point in Europe in the late 1930s, when children diagnosed with various defects were sometimes sacrificed because they were deemed too costly for the government to care for.

At the beginning of World War II, Germany was the most scientifically and technologically advanced country in the world and even had a proposed code of research ethics. In the field of medicine, the Nazi government supported midwifery, homeopathy and nutrition programs as well as research into ecology, public health, human genetics, cancer, radiation and asbestos. They were the first to ban smoking in public buildings. Women were denied tobacco ration coupons because of concern about the effect of nicotine on the fetus. German physicians stressed the importance of preventive medicine rather than curative medicine.

The Nazi party, however, exploited people's trust in the medical community and public health by performing unethical experiments and atrocities on populations they discriminated against. The German Air Force, for example, was concerned about the survival of pilots at extremely high altitudes. One question they wanted the answer to was: What was the maximum safe altitude for bailing out of a damaged aircraft? To answer this question, researchers designed a series of experiments involving internees at Dachau. In one series of experiments, researchers placed the victims in vacuum chambers that could duplicate the low air pressure and anoxia (lack of oxygen) at altitudes as high as 65,000 feet (about two to three times the maximum altitude that aircraft were flying). Approximately 200 internees at Dachau were used in these experiments, and about 40% died as a result. Some deaths were caused by extended anoxia; others were attributable to lungs rupturing from the low pressures in the chamber.

The German Air Force was also concerned with survival time after parachuting into the cold water of the North Atlantic. Some victims of this research were immersed for hours in tubs of ice water; others were fed nothing but salt water for days. Still others were penned outside, unclothed and unsheltered in sub-freezing temperatures for 12 to 14 hours. Some of these "freezing victims" were sprayed with cold water. No attempts were made to relieve the tremendous pain and suffering caused by these experiments. Approximately 30% or 100 out of 300 Dachau internees in these studies died.

Experiments involving battlefield medicine included treatment of gunshot wounds, burns, traumatic amputations and chemical and biological agent exposures. In these experiments, the wound was first inflicted upon the victim (by gunshot, stabbing, amputation or other traumatic method) and then treated using various techniques. For example, in a study of sulfanilamide at the Ravensbrueck camp, Polish women were shot and slashed on the legs. The resulting wounds were stuffed with glass, dirt and various bacteria cultures, and sewn shut. The infected wounds were then treated with experimental anti-infective agents.

Nazi experiments on treating exposure to chemical-warfare agents were ongoing throughout the war years. Concentration camp internees were forced to drink poisoned water and to breathe noxious gases. Some were shot with cyanide-tipped bullets or given cyanide capsules. It was not uncommon for one out of every four internees in these studies to die as a result of their involvement in the experiments.

Representatives of the British, French, Soviet and United States governments established the International Military Tribunal in Nuremberg, Germany, in 1945. After the initial Nuremberg Trial of Nazi leaders, a series of supplemental trials was held. The trial, officially known as United States v. Karl Brandt et al., and commonly referred to as "The Nazi Doctors Trial," was held from December 9, 1946, to July 19, 1947. As the title indicates, the judges and prosecutors in this court trial were all from the United States. The 23 defendants (including 20 physicians)—all members of the Nazi Party—were charged with murder, torture and other atrocities committed in the name of medical science.

When the final judgment in the Nazi Doctors Trial was delivered on July 19, 1947, 15 of the 23 defendants were found guilty. Seven were sentenced to death. Four American judges presiding issued a ten point code that described basic principles of ethical behavior in the conduct of human experimentation. This ten-point code is known as the *Nuremberg Code.* The Code is an "ethical standard" and reflects the modern thinking that:

- Informed consent should be obtained without coercion.
- The experiment should be useful and necessary.
- Human experiments should be based on previous experiments with animals.
- Physical and mental suffering should be avoided.
- Death and disability should not be expected outcomes of an experiment.
- The degree of risk to be taken should not exceed the humanitarian importance of solving the problem.
- Human subjects should be protected against even remote possibilities of harm.
- Only qualified scientists should conduct medical research.

- Human subjects should be free to end an experiment at any time.
- The scientist in charge must be prepared to end an experiment at any stage.

In 1953, the World Medical Association began drafting a document that became known as the *Declaration of Helsinki*. This statement of ethical principles, first issued in 1964, defined rules for "therapeutic" and "non-therapeutic" research. It repeated the Nuremberg Code requirement for consent for non-therapeutic research, but it did allow for enrolling certain patients in therapeutic research without consent. The Declaration of Helsinki also allowed legal guardians to grant permission to enroll subjects in research, both therapeutic and non-therapeutic and recommended written consent—an issue not addressed in the Nuremberg Code. In addition, the Declaration of Helsinki requires review and prior approval of a protocol by an IRB. The Declaration of Helsinki is included in the appendix for you to read.

In 1966, following the publication of the Declaration of Helsinki, Henry K. Beecher, M.D., reported in the *New England Journal of Medicine (NEJM)* on 22 studies that had serious ethical problems. Beecher cited various problems related to study design and to informed consent. Probably even more than the Nuremberg Trial/Code, this article (and his other earlier publications) helped to spur debate on research ethics throughout the United States.

As late as the 1960s, few research institutions had heeded requests by the NIH to set up a system for protecting research subjects. Numerous safeguards have since been added, many as a result of what is known as the "thalidomide tragedy." Thalidomide, approved as a sedative in Europe in the late 1950s, disfigured over 10,000 babies worldwide whose mothers took the drug during their first trimester of pregnancy. Congressional hearings in the United States revealed that women were not told the FDA hadn't approved the drug and that they weren't asked to give their consent. In 1962, the NDA for thalidomide was withdrawn by its U.S. manufacturer. The Kefauver-Harris Amendment was signed into law in 1962 and made the following demands on clinical trials:

- Proof of efficacy as well as safety
- Mandated reporting of adverse events
- Disclosure of risks in advertisements
- Required reproduction studies in two species of animal using two dose levels of drug

Long after the Nuremberg Code was announced and informed consent laws were being issued and rewritten, human research subject protection was far from guaranteed. The Centers for Disease Control and Prevention (a Department of Health and Human Services agency), for example, was actively overseeing an ongoing study that involved withholding treatment to more than 400 black sharecroppers diagnosed with syphilis. The experiment, then known as the Tuskegee Study of Untreated Syphilis in the Negro Male, began in 1932 and didn't end until 1972. In the beginning, the disease was untreatable and the prevailing belief was that it behaved differently in black than white men. The men involved were not told they had the disease, the purpose of the study or the fact that the research would not benefit them. Even when penicillin was accepted as a treatment for syphilis, it was purposefully withheld from the study subjects. Not long after the story came to light in *The New York Times* and *The Washington Star*, the study stopped and the men—together with the wives and children who contracted the disease—were given free antibiotic treatment and lifetime medical care. But the damage to their health, as well as their trust in the medical research community, was beyond repair. In a formal White House ceremony in 1997, President Clinton apologized to subjects and their families who participated in the Tuskegee Study and called for renewed emphasis on research ethics.

Sadly, the list of historical abuses is long. Prisoners were routinely coerced into phase I safety testing of drugs until their use as study subjects began to be regulated in the late 1970s. In the 1940s and 1950s, the Atomic Energy Commission secretly fed people breakfast cereal containing radioactive tracers and intentionally released radioactive substances, while researchers at several major universities injected plutonium into unknowing patients to study the effects of the atomic bomb. Institutionalized patients in the 1960s became the victims of CIA brainwashing experiments with LSD. The U.S. Army carried out further experiments with the drug on soldiers as recently as 1970.

In 1974, Congress passed the National Research Act. The Act required regulations for the protection of human subjects that included requirements for informed consent and review of research by institutional review boards (IRBs). IRBs were given the charge to conduct peer review of research involving human subjects. For the first time, individual physician investigators could not make decisions about the use of human volunteers in clinical research without being granted approval by colleagues in the medical community. This Act led to the creation of the National Commission for the Protection of Human Subjects of Biomedical and Behavioral Research. This commission was composed of 11 members, the majority of whom were individuals outside the medical community. Commission members included clergy, lawyers, ethicists and philosophers. In 1979, the National Commission issued the Belmont Report, which is the cornerstone statement of ethical principles upon which the federal regulations for the protection of subjects are based.

In 1982, The Council for the International Organization of Medical Sciences (CIOMS) published the International Ethics Guidelines for Biomedical Research Involving Human Subjects (CIOMS Guidelines). These guidelines were designed to provide direction for researchers from technologically advanced countries when conducting research in developing countries. The guidelines sought to correct perceived omissions in the Nuremberg Code and the Declaration of Helsinki, especially as they applied to cross-cultural research. The CIOMS Guidelines address cultural differences in ethical standards.

Today, there are many overlapping layers of oversight and scrutiny by the FDA, IRBs and by pharmaceutical and biotechnology companies. The federal agency governing clinical drug trials is the FDA's Center for Drug Evaluation and Research and, if federal funds are involved, the Office for Human Research Protections (OHRP). Either agency can temporarily—or permanently—end a study if it believes patient welfare is at risk.

Good Clinical Practice Guidelines

Government laws, regulations and guidelines meant to protect the safety and rights of study volunteers, while ensuring the accuracy of collected study data, are collectively known as *Good Clinical Practices (GCPs)*. They apply to drug companies and their employees, contract review organizations that manage studies for them, Institutional Review Boards (IRBs), investigators and all those who work at research centers.

GCPs essentially follow the Declaration of Helsinki. The latest, most controversial version of the Declaration holds that placebo-controlled trials should in general be used only in the absence of an existing, proven treatment. The change reflects growing fear that, without some type of prohibition, people in developing countries will be exposed to inferior treatments as research moves onto international soil. The World Medical Association recently issued a clarification, saying a placebo-controlled trial may be acceptable even if an effective treatment is available so long as it meets one of two conditions. It must be scientifically necessary. Or it has to be a study for a minor condition in which patients receiving the placebo face no more risk of serious harm than anyone else in the trial.

GCPs continue to recognize that placebo-controlled trials, in certain circumstances, constitute better science. It would be hard to make a case for a placebo-controlled study if, for example, the subjects are people with a life-threatening illness or a raging, deadly bacterial infection and are already taking an effective treatment. But it would be acceptable to test an investigational drug for a chronic illness against a placebo if the standard treatment is only mildly effective. Many researchers believe it is the only way to measure the true effects of drugs used for diseases like chronic fatigue syndrome and depression that have lots of "self-reported" symptoms like low energy or moodiness.

The Belmont Report

The ethical principles upon which human subject protection regulations are based appear in a formal document written in 1979 by the National Commission for the Protection of Human Subjects of Biomedical and Behavioral Research. The report outlines three fundamental principles: (1) Respect for Persons, (2) Beneficence, and (3) Justice.

Respect for Persons. The first principle basically states that individuals should be respected regardless of their age, race, gender and socio-economic status. This principle also recognizes that certain individuals are incapable of making decisions without the assistance of a guardian or caregiver.

Beneficence. This second principle means that the goal of research is to maximize the benefits of a drug under investigation while minimizing the risks to study subjects. Clinical trials should be properly designed to prevent harm—a primary responsibility of the principal investigators. This principle also means that the potential for risks must be justified by the greater good to society—a primary responsibility of the IRB.

Justice. The third principle means that the benefits and risks of research are shared fairly among different types of people. Regulations make both investigators and IRBs concerned about selecting sufficient numbers of men, women, children, and minorities as research subjects. It also makes them cautious when dealing with disadvantaged people—the poor, the sick and the institutionalized—on matters of informed consent.

On April 18, 1979 the commission issued a report of its findings and recommendations. The document, called "The Belmont Report: Ethical Principles and Guidelines for the Protection of Human Subjects of Research," serves as the backbone of the Department of Health and Human Services (HHS) as well as Food and Drug Administration (FDA) regulations governing IRBs.

In 1991, a common set of regulations sprang from these three principles. Although this so-called "Common Rule" applies only to research conducted or paid for by federal agencies, similar FDA human subject protections govern all research with drugs, *biologics* and medical devices. Every clinical trial, therefore, requires review by an IRB, informed consent from study volunteers, and the signed promise of researchers and research sites to comply with human subject research laws.

An up-to-date, and comprehensive, list of patient protection guidelines is outlined in detail in the Code of Federal Regulations. A

1991 revision to the Code spells out federal policy for human subject protection. A summary of the Code of Federal Regulations is provided in the appendix.

The Role of the FDA

The FDA reviews study protocols and study results. It regularly sends out inspectors to research centers to make sure that investigators are following the protocol, treating study volunteers well, maintaining the required records and following standard operating procedures for conducting research. The FDA also inspects sites that it suspects have not followed Good Clinical Practice guidelines. Some investigations are sparked by complaints filed with the FDA by drug companies, IRBs, research staff members and patients.

If fraudulent or deceptive practices are uncovered, investigators can be "blacklisted" by the FDA, preventing them from ever conducting clinical research. Principal investigators can be criminally prosecuted—meaning they can be fined, imprisoned and have their medical license revoked.

The FDA also conducts routine and "for-cause" inspections of IRBs, study sponsors and study monitors to be sure they are fulfilling all their responsibilities. Unless it has been newly formed, an established IRB may be visited once every five years if it is found to be fully compliant.

Regulations require that all adverse events associated with an investigational drug be reported to the FDA. Serious adverse events that occur during a clinical trial must be reported within seven days. If a study drug raises safety concerns, the FDA has the power to either halt the study or require the pharmaceutical company to conduct additional studies to answer questions about side effects and dosage levels. The FDA frequently instructs pharmaceutical companies to conduct a phase IV study as a condition of marketing their drug, and the companies usually do it. *The Food and Drug Administration Modernization Act* requires the FDA to keep lists of these requests and track how well companies adhere to them. That gives the agency the power to enforce compliance.

Whether or not a drug eventually gets the FDA's stamp of approval to be sold is heavily based on the opinion of an advisory committee of scientists who review the study data. To ensure its opinion is unbiased, committee members who have any conflict of interest associated with the clinical trials or company whose product is being reviewed are excluded from these discussions.

The Institutional Review Board

The Institutional Review Board (IRB) that has approved your clinical trial is the primary body protecting your safe and ethical treatment. The IRB—also called a Research Subject Protection board—is your advocate and you can contact them to discuss any questions that you have about your safety and protection.

FDA regulations first began requiring IRB approval of research studies in 1971. IRBs may be created and run by a hospital or university (which generally oversee all studies conducted by its network of faculty and affiliated investigators). Some IRBs are independent for-profit enterprises that oversee clinical trials conducted by independent research centers. By law, an IRB must include five or more people that are representative of the community demographics. It also must have at least one member whose primary interest is scientific, one member whose primary interest is non-scientific (a lawyer, clergyman, or ethicist, for example), and one "public member" who isn't connected with the institution, hospital or business sponsoring the IRB.

Before any clinical trial can begin, the IRB must do a "risk/benefit assessment" to be certain that the trial does not pose a level of risk that outweighs potential benefits. The majority of IRB members must agree that it is ethical—meaning the study protocol follows the highest scientific and medical standards for conducting experiments with humans. This includes the appropriateness of using a placebo, or whether a study should be done at all. The IRB would probably reject a study designed to test a drug on very young children before the drug was tested on adults and older children. The majority of IRB members also must be convinced that the rights of children and other "vulnerable" populations (e.g., prisoners, pregnant women, mentally disabled persons and economically or educationally disadvantaged persons) are given special attention. Finally, the IRB must be convinced that it makes sense to conduct a clinical trial within a particular community.

A well-run IRB spends a great deal of time reviewing the informed consent form. It is the IRB's responsibility to ensure that the consent form truthfully covers all important points about the clinical trial using words that are easy to understand. How well IRBs do their job has become a matter of considerable debate during the past several years. The IRB is also responsible for approving any advertisement that research centers use to recruit study volunteers. The IRB checks these advertisements to make sure that they are accurate and not coercive. One IRB's decision to approve a protocol or advertisement may be countered by another IRB's decision to reject them. What happens is that a large trial will be conducted at many research centers. Each center may have its own IRB reviewing its protocols and advertisements. The committee members on each IRB may have different opinions about a protocol or an advertisement. For instance, a few years ago an IRB for the University of Rochester in Upstate New York pulled a national ad for a breast cancer trial because it was asking women to be study volunteers for their "daughter's sake." To the ears of those IRB members, that sounded coercive. But IRBs in other cities had no problem with the ad and let it run.

IRBs must also make a judgment call on whether the payment offered to study volunteers is reasonable or, conversely, whether it represents "undue influence" on volunteers to participate. The concern is that monetary compensation that is too attractive may blind potential subjects to the risks of participating or tempt them to lie or hide information about themselves that would disqualify them from enrolling in the study. There are no federal rules governing the matter. The idea is to arrive at some "reasonable" arrangement with study volunteers to compensate them for their time.

Of particular concern are people who may be induced to enter a trial even for a $25 payment. Just the prospect of free health care can entice people with major medical problems who are having a tough time making ends meet. IRB members must therefore decide, based on the number of "economically vulnerable" people who agree to volunteer, whether the opportunity to get free care is too large an incentive as to be ethically questionable.

Study volunteers who are unable to give informed consent—including some people who have had a stroke or abused drugs, have Alzheimer's disease and certain psychiatric illnesses, or are in a coma—are usually given special attention by IRBs. As long as these individuals are fairly selected and the study is not abnormally risky, many IRBs will allow consent documents to be signed by a legally authorized representative.

The oversight responsibilities of the IRB last for the duration of the study. Members receive regular updates on the study's progress, approve any needed changes to the study protocol and are among the first to know if any serious, adverse events happen. The IRB also decides which patients are allowed to have open-label, or "compassionate use," of study drugs awaiting approval by the FDA.

The FDA has the right to inspect IRBs and review their records in order to determine if they are following their own written procedures, as well as FDA regulations.

How an IRB Works

Before a researcher can begin a clinical trial, the principal investigator must submit the study protocol to the IRB for approval. The protocol describes the clinical trial in detail including the purpose and objectives of the study and how the study is to be carried out. In a typical clinical trial, the protocol includes:

- The number of volunteers who will participate in the trial
- The eligibility criteria the volunteers must meet in order to be enrolled
- The potential risks and benefits of the trial and how they will be communicated to volunteers
- The informed consent form that volunteers will be asked to read and sign
- The design of the study and whether some volunteers will receive placebo or a standard treatment
- The study drug dosage levels, how often and for how long
- A description of how the effects of the drug will be measured
- A description of all study activities

When the researcher submits the protocol to the IRB for review, the protocol is usually assigned to one member of the IRB. This member is asked to review the protocol and the consent form, and then make a presentation about them at a future IRB meeting. This individual will review the protocol and consent form carefully, usually over a period of several days or more. If any information in the protocol or consent form is unclear, the reviewer may contact the investigator for clarification.

Protocols are not presented to the IRB by the principal investigator because their presence could make it uncomfortable for IRB members to rigorously question and scrutinize the protocols put before them. IRB meetings are conducted privately. No outside observers are allowed to attend IRB meetings. Research investigators may attend IRB meetings to provide information, but they must leave the meeting during the discussion and approval or rejection of their study protocols.

At an IRB meeting, each member gives a presentation to the board members about the protocol(s) that they have been asked to review. The members of the board then have an opportunity to ask the reviewer questions about protocol and the consent form. These questions usually lead to a discussion among members of the group about issues that may affect the safety and ethical treatment of volunteers in the research study. After IRB members have reviewed the protocol and consent form, and the group has had an opportunity to discuss any concerns, the members vote on whether to approve the protocol. Approval by a majority of the IRB members present at the meeting is necessary in order for the IRB to approve a protocol.

It is unusual for an IRB to withhold their approval of a protocol. It is more typical for the IRB to require modifications to a protocol so that the study can be conducted safely, ethically and according to federal regulations. In these situations, the investigator is responsible for making changes that have been requested by the IRB before the protocol can be resubmitted for board approval. Typically, an IRB at a research institution, such as a university or hospital, meets every other week. Some IRBs meet more frequently. The meetings typically last two to three hours.

Once a protocol is approved by the IRB, the IRB sends the investigator a written notification of the approval. The research project is then permitted to proceed and to begin enrolling volunteers.

Monitoring Clinical Trials

Pharmaceutical companies routinely send their own study monitors out to the research centers. Companies do this to be sure that they get good, accurate information about a study drug. And companies do this to ensure that study staff are complying with Good Clinical Practice guidelines. Pharmaceutical companies are very concerned that volunteers enrolled in studies actually meet the inclusion and exclusion criteria, as spelled out in the study protocol. The *inclusion criteria* may include an age range, such as ages 55 to 75, and a disease state or condition, such as "must be diagnosed with a specific type and stage of cancer." The exclusion criteria, or reasons you wouldn't be able to participate, might include if you are taking a certain type of medication or have a disease in addition to the one being studied. The list of inclusion and exclusion criteria is generally fairly long. An investigator who "qualifies" every person screened for a study would immediately draw suspicion and would himself be disqualified from participating in the study if breeches in protocol were detected.

Study monitors—also called clinical research associates (CRAs)—perform a variety of monitoring activities. The CRA's primary role is to help ensure that the investigator and study staff properly conduct the trial and accurately and efficiently collect the results. Study monitors interact regularly with the study staff and they are an important way that pharmaceutical companies promote quality and good clinical practices.

Pharmaceutical companies spend enormous sums developing medicines—it is estimated that companies spend approximately $800 million for each drug that they successfully develop from discovery to approval. This estimate assumes that the cost of failed drugs must be assigned to those drugs that succeed. With so many dollars invested, pharmaceutical companies are eager to learn about their drugs in clinical trials. They want to know about the successes and shortcomings of their investigational medications. Clinical research professionals employed by pharmaceutical companies are scientists and people who want to know all of the facts—both positive and negative.

Pharmaceutical companies are businesses and one of their primary goals is to generate profits and satisfy their shareholders. But it is in a company's best interest to develop safe and effective drugs. Companies have already invested hundreds of millions of dollars before they even begin clinical trials. Unsafe drugs will halt their research and delay the approval process resulting in the loss of significant investment. It is far less costly, over the long term, to quickly end a study and pay for any unintended injuries than to continue testing a marginal drug and risk greater loss.

Concerns about side effects by the FDA have caused pharmaceutical companies to abandon multi-million dollar projects just months before a medication was to make its debut on the market. If the side effect happens very infrequently, or there is question about whether it is even caused by the drug, the risk of having that side effect will instead be recorded and, upon approval of the drug by the FDA, be listed on the drug's label. Physicians would therefore be more cautious when prescribing the drug.

The Most Responsible Party— The Principal Investigator

Physicians get involved in clinical research for many reasons. For some, it's the desire to be on the "cutting edge" of medicine. For others, it's a break from the routine of day-to-day medical practice, the opportunity to become better at treating specific diseases, or simple intellectual curiosity. For still others, it's a way to avoid the restrictions on treatment choices imposed by some insurance companies. Some physicians do clinical studies, at least in part, to make money. Select investigators can earn tens to hundreds of thousands of dollars conducting clinical trials.

But being the principal investigator in a clinical trial requires a major commitment, long hours, hard work and a great deal of patience. It is reasonable that a physician is paid for the time that is dedicated to conducting clinical trials. Physician investigators must review and modify protocols, solicit IRB approval, explain a trial in detail to patients, determine which potential volunteers meet the eligibility criteria, perform required medical evaluations and record and evaluate the findings. After covering the cost of a research nurse and additional testing, many investigators will spend more money than they earn. University-affiliated researchers, who are salaried, don't benefit directly from research profits. The funds all get funneled to the institution. However, they can earn large sums of money lecturing about a drug at medical conferences. But even researchers who do studies mostly "for the money" have a powerful incentive to do it right. Failure to follow the rules almost guarantees that they'll never do another clinical trial and will severely damage their reputation.

The principal investigator on every study is required to complete a 1572 Statement of Investigator Form that the pharmaceutical company files with the FDA. In this form, the investigator promises to strictly adhere to Good Clinical Practice guidelines (GCPs) and the requirements of the protocol. The 1572 Form holds the principal investigator personally accountable for every aspect of the clinical trial. For example, GCPs forbid investigators from changing the study protocol unless a patient's safety is at stake. They demand that investigators explain the clinical trial clearly and honestly to study volunteers. The investigator is required to maintain accurate, detailed records for each and every volunteer. And the investigator is required to promptly report any unexpected or "serious" adverse events—including those that are fatal or life-threatening, permanently disabling, or that result in hospitalization—to the IRB and the sponsor company.

Of growing public concern are clinical investigators who have a financial relationship with a commercial sponsor of a study. Influenced by a financial incentive, a doctor may—even if unwittingly—downplay risks or overstate benefits during informed consent discussions. Being paid a per-participant "recruitment bonus" or a "finder's fee" for referral of potential participants may also color a doctor's judgment or willingness to report adverse reactions and even his or her analysis of research data.

The FDA has had regulations requiring "financial disclosure" for investigators since 1998. But this information has typically only been reported to the FDA—not study volunteers. If an investigator has a financial interest in an investigational drug or the pharmaceutical company sponsoring the research, study participants aren't necessarily going to hear about it. For now, the FDA and its sister agencies are merely saying it's a good idea to make that disclosure part of the informed consent process.

On your behalf, the FDA keeps an especially close watch on investigators with a reported conflict of interest to ensure that conflict doesn't influence your enrollment in a clinical trial or the data collection methods. But the FDA's regulations don't spell out what types of financial interests are "right" and which are "wrong," nor do they instruct IRBs about their roles and responsibilities in this area.

Academic research sites, to their credit, are increasingly and voluntarily making financial conflict-of-interest disclosures about their investigators within the informed consent documents. Many exclude IRB members from decision-making on protocols for which they have a potential or actual financial conflict of interest. Some, but not all, institutions have a policy against accepting funding from pharmaceutical companies in which their investigators have a financial interest. But institutional financial interests in outside commercial businesses are rarely revealed.

There is still no agreement about what kinds of financial interests may by problematic and what should be done about it. The Department of Health and Human Services released a guidance paper on the matter in May 2000 in hopes of better protecting research volunteers. The guidance promotes "openness and honesty" on the part of study sponsors, institutions and investigators. Specifically, it cites the usefulness of a Conflict of Interest Committee—alone or together with the IRB—in managing conflicts. The guidance also notes the wisdom of freeing IRBs from pressures (real or perceived) to okay research activities in which its affiliated institution has a financial stake or other interest in the outcome of the research.

If the research institution itself has a financial stake in the outcome of a trial, The Department of Health and Human Services suggests that the institution either set up "special safeguards" to protect the scientific integrity of the study and its participants or let the trial be carried out elsewhere. A financial stake may be anything from an extra up-front payment to carry out a protocol to part ownership in the pharmaceutical or biotechnology company sponsoring the study.

In November 2001, the U.S. General Accounting Office (GAO) issued a report finding that the Department of Health and Human

Services' regulations and its oversight of financial conflicts of interest in biomedical research have serious limitations for promoting research integrity and protecting human subjects.

Two main limitations exist. One is that both Public Health Service (PHS) regulations, which cover federally funded research, and Food and Drug Administration (FDA) regulations, which cover privately funded and federally regulated research, are not directly linked to the regulations on human subjects protection. According to the GAO report, the result is that "financial interest information may not necessarily be conveyed to institutional review boards (IRBs) for consideration when they review research proposals for risks to human subjects." The other limitation is the difference between PHS regulations and FDA regulations. According to the GAO report, these regulations differ in two areas: "when they require review of investigators' financial disclosures, and in the amounts of their disclosure thresholds." PHS regulations state that institutions must report investigator financial conflicts of interests before research funds are spent. FDA regulations require that the sponsor only submits that information to FDA after the research has been completed. Both sets of regulations are vague in terms of what constitutes a conflict of interest and how it should be managed.

Recent steps to improve oversight and monitoring include the National Institutes of Health's inclusion of a review of financial conflict-of-interest issues in its site visits to institutions. Also, FDA now lists the review of financial disclosures in its guidance to reviewers of drug marketing applications.

Some institutions and independent researchers have established policies against accepting special "payment incentives" from drug companies for recruiting volunteers or referring patients to investigators. Such payments aren't specifically prohibited by federal regulations, but they are on the list of items scrutinized by IRBs. They may also run afoul of certain state medical licensing board regulations and the strict standards of practice set by the American Medical Association against the payment of referral fees. Ethically, incentive fees aren't necessarily a problem. It all depends on why the special fees are being paid. Is the money meant to cover the time needed to fill in special paperwork, prepare a report, or to do preliminary data analysis? Or is it simply to pass on names? These are questions worth asking—especially of doctors who seem anxious to sign up patients for trials.

There is as yet no agreement about how much study investigators should be paid per enrolled subject. Ethicists worry that if the payment per study volunteer is excessive, investigators' financial interests could compromise their judgment of who should and who shouldn't be asked to participate.

There are several ways that you can weed out potential conflicts of interest in your clinical trial: First, if an investigator suggests that you participate in a clinical trial, among the questions you should ask is how he or she is compensated for enrolling patients into the trial. Your investigator should be paid for those services by the company sponsoring the clinical trial just as your insurance company would pay for the doctor's time if he or she were giving you an annual physical exam or treating your for an illness.

If the payment your investigator receives for enrolling you in a clinical trial is substantially more than the payment he or she would receive for treating your illness, this may indicate a conflict. Compensation should also be limited to payment for services. If the investigator or study staff are paid a special bonus simply for enrolling volunteers into the study (in addition to payment for the services provided during the study) this may also signal a conflict.

Clinical researchers can benefit in ways other than direct compensation. For example, if the investigator developed the new therapy under investigation, then he or she may stand to benefit financially once the product reaches the market. Similarly, if the investigator holds stock or part ownership in the company developing the investigational drug or device, the researcher may benefit financially. The lure of profits from the eventual success of an experimental product can unduly influence an investigator to enroll volunteers in clinical studies so that the product can be brought to market as quickly as possible.

Before you agree to participate in a clinical trial, you will want to be confident that the principal investigator is recommending the trial for the right reasons. Discuss ahead of time how your doctor is being compensated for his or her role in the clinical trial. Try to find out if there are other incentives that could be influencing his or her recommendation. If you think your doctor may have a potential conflict of interest, run the information by a physician you trust and ask his or her opinion, or contact the IRB.

Setting New Safety Standards

There are now two national programs that offer their seal of approval—or accreditation—of programs, institutions and organizations that conduct human trials. Although both speak to the necessity of having financial disclosure policies, neither specifically define a "conflict of interest" nor prescribes how to deal with it. But they do offer potential volunteers reassurances that regulatory requirements are being met.

The National Committee for Quality Assurance (NCQA) in Washington, D.C.—the primary watchdog of the managed care industry—has developed a mandatory accreditation program for every Veterans Affairs Medical Center that conducts human research. Accreditation standards cover:

- Institutional responsibilities for human research protection
- Structure and operation of the IRB
- IRB consideration of risks and benefits of research
- IRB consideration of recruitment and subject selection for participation in research
- IRB consideration of research-related risks to privacy and confidentiality
- IRB consideration of informed consent for research participants

VA medical centers, numbering more than 120 nationwide, have until the end of 2004 to meet the new standards. These centers can go beyond federal requirements for "extra credit," but failure to do so won't count against them—at least for now.

The Association of American Medical Colleges (AAMC), together with a variety of other academic organizations, has also just launched a voluntary, education-oriented accreditation program for human research protection. Although aimed at universities, all research sites are welcome to apply. The program, which becomes operational in 2002, goes beyond current regulations and collectively examines the performance of the research center, investigators and the IRB. Accreditation draws from what the AAMC believes are the best features of two draft standards of subject protection measures submitted to the Institute of Medicine, an organization affiliated with the National Academy of Sciences that has spent several years reviewing clinical trial safety. The AAMC also has implemented a Task Force on Financial Conflicts of Interest in Clinical Research to both update its 1990 guidelines and to determine new ways for academic research centers to police themselves.

The Office of the Inspector General (OIG) has been paying a great deal of attention to the clinical trial process. The OIG has found that measures to protect the safety and ethical treatment of human subjects vary considerably from research center to research center. And some IRBs tend to be overworked and under-supported. Due to increased attention placed on IRBs, the protocol review and approval process is becoming more stringent. The FDA is also issuing more warning letters to investigators regarding GCP violations.

While Congress works on legislation to provide greater oversight and strengthen protections for human participants, the FDA has been attempting to clarify the IRB's central role in ensuring that clinical trials are ethically conducted. The FDA supports the idea of both voluntary IRB accreditation and investigator certification. The agency is working with the Office of Human Research Protection (OHRP) and the Veterans' Administration and other federal agencies to make sure all clinical research is governed by a common set of standards. It is also setting up a one-stop informational web site for consumers interested in, and involved with, clinical trials.

OHRP has expanded the number of staff monitoring government-funded clinical research. During the past three years, OHRP has temporarily suspended research at many well-known universities. These suspensions have spurred virtually all university-based research centers around the country to invest millions of new dollars into human subject oversight.

The Office of Good Clinical Practice (OGCP) was opened by the FDA in the fall of 2001 in order to establish consistency in policy. OGCP and OHRP will work closely on some initiatives. OGCP and OHRP have already worked together promoting a voluntary accreditation program for U.S. IRBs as well as other *quality assurance* initiatives. In terms of human subject protection, OHRP has a broader role. It works with OGCP not only on FDA-regulated trials but across biomedical research and across social and behavioral research that does not involve clinical trials.

Human subject protection is just one responsibility of OGCP. This agency is broadly responsible for ensuring FDA's protective role in clinical research, from trial design through trial conduct, trial analysis, trial oversight, data integrity and data quality. One of OGCP's highest priorities will be to bring about GCP compliance globally.

Perhaps these ongoing efforts to set and raise standards of protection will make a difference. "We don't know if study subjects were endangered before or are better protected now," said David Korn, M.D., AAMC's senior vice president for biomedical and health sciences research. Until the concerns surrounding gene therapy studies sprang up a few years ago, almost no one was claiming that study volunteers were being harmed. "I think researchers have always taken human research safety seriously. But more attention, detail and seriousness is now being directed toward the process of oversight to make sure everything is done right and people will be protected."

What You Don't Know Can Hurt You

There is one form of "misconduct" during clinical trials that has yet to be addressed: underreporting of adverse events and deaths to federal regulators. It's human nature to avoid responsibility for hurting others and easy for investigators to place the blame for a bad outcome on an underlying illness or the frailty of a study subject rather than the study drug. So adverse events, when they happen, tend to get underreported and misunderstood. That leaves doctors with a false sense of security about using certain drugs and patients with an incomplete picture about the risk of taking them.

Bioethicists are especially concerned about government-funded studies because of the absence of monitoring by pharmaceutical companies. These studies often take place at a relatively small number of research centers, reducing the number of clinical opinions about whether an adverse event is related to the investigational medicine. IRB members have also had trouble coping with the responsibility of monitoring adverse events that occur during hundreds, if not thousands, of trials at individual institutions each year.

Between 1990 and 2000, "thousands of deaths and tens of thousands of adverse events" during NIH-sponsored clinical trials went unreported to the OHRP, according to Adil Shamoo, a bioethicist at the University of Maryland School of Medicine. Part of the explanation may be that only "unexpected" bad effects are reportable. Also, some investigators only report problems that they consider serious and study-related. Perhaps more disturbing is that a significant amount of human research has limited oversight because it isn't sponsored by a drug or device manufacturer and doesn't receive federal funds. Some human studies are also done before an "investigational new drug" application is filed with the FDA, said Shamoo.

Based on a review of several hundred new drug applications sponsored by industry and approved by the FDA, CenterWatch found a high incidence of adverse events across all disease categories—an average of one adverse event reported for every volunteer. But these events include many minor complaints like headache and diarrhea, some of which investigators couldn't even connect to the study drug.

Among study volunteers, CenterWatch estimates that the chances of dying due to an investigational drug during a clinical trial are low. Approximately one out of every 10,000 volunteers dies in a clinical trial. "That's on par with the odds of a mother dying while giving birth to a single child," according to John Paling, M.D., a risk communication consultant in Gainesville, Fla. The risk probably isn't a bad tradeoff—at least when measured against the possibility of significant benefit, like relief from constant and debilitating pain or an extended lifetime.

The odds of your having a serious adverse event—any reaction that may be fatal, life threatening, permanently disabling or that results in hospitalization—are one in 30. But keep in mind that the majority of these events happen in trials for people with cancer, heart disease and immunology/infectious diseases like AIDS. Volunteers may be willing to take drugs that are likely to have unpleasant side effects because the alternative is worse: almost certain death.

No one knows how risky trials are that never make it past the early phases of testing. But it is very likely that there will be more benefit than harm by the time a drug reaches phase III trials, said Joseph Lau, M.D., professor of medicine at New England Medical Center.

The problem remains that there is no one place to go for comprehensive adverse event and death information and no independent observer making sure the reporting is accurate. Then there's the problem of what the numbers mean. Most people simply trust the judgment of the investigator and the study staff. Most volunteers assume that they have their best interests in mind.

Theoretically, the most important decision-making information—namely, the relative risk of taking a particular drug at a certain dose and specific time and setting—should be divulged during the informed consent process. But "investigators have a conflict of interest," said Leonard Glantz, professor of health law at Boston University School of Medicine. "They want people to be in a study." Someone other than the investigator ought to be talking to potential volunteers. Even consent forms may subtly understate the risks of participation, or may mislead readers with scientific jargon.

Clinical trials are simply getting too complex for all information to flow from a single investigator, said Myrl Weinberg, president of the National Safety Council in Washington, D.C. The best way for patients to understand both the benefits and risks of participation is to get the message through multiple communication vehicles—written words, dialogue and videos—and more than one person. In practice, this rarely happens. Until it does, many research subjects will remain uninformed about the true risk of their participation.

There are inescapable conflicts between medical practice—where the aim is to heal—and medical research—where the goal is to learn. That's a difficult, but very important, thing to remember when an investigator is also a study participant's personal physician, social worker or teacher. The line between practice and research can get very blurry when both happen at the same time. Some diabetics, for example, might get treated as patients for blood sugar and foot examinations and get treated as study participants during blood pressure readings and surveys connected with an investigational hypertension drug they're taking—all within the same visit.

Your doctors' main intent is to gather information when they are wearing their "research investigator" hat and to enhance your well being when they're wearing their "doctor" hat. The aim of some study protocols, after all, is to induce symptoms (often by taking patients off their current prescription) so that the effect of the investigational medication can be measured. Clinical research might best be likened to a journey down a new, unexplored and potentially dangerous path. As pioneering medical ethicist Paul Ramsey once said, investigators need to ask study participants to be "co-adventurers" with them on that journey.

CHAPTER SIX

Vulnerable Populations

"The study coordinator told him he may experience reactions to the medicine, so he would constantly say, 'I have a stomachache.' It was like he thought we were looking for him to get a stomachache and wanted to please us. It was amazing how he'd come to me and say, 'I have a fever,' and I'd say, 'No you don't' and he'd then say, 'Oh, I meant a stomachache.' He'd come up with some reactions we didn't even talk about. We used the cough medicine once, but I was never sure if it was a forced or real cough."

— *Cathy, mother of Josh, a pediatric subject in a cold remedy trial*

For many years, research with children and pregnant women was virtually nonexistent. People living in prisons and institutions, who could not fully participate in the consent process, were disproportionately represented. These vulnerable populations are now given special consideration and, in some cases, extra protection from the federal government.

Children

The Food and Drug Administration has established specific protections for children involved in clinical trials. Several years ago, pharmaceutical companies were not particularly interested in testing their drugs in children because doctors were already prescribing them—*off label*—to youngsters. Almost all pediatric studies were funded by the

U.S. government, and children in those trials were protected under regulations developed during the 1970s and 1980s.

The FDA's Pediatric Rule, which went into effect at the end of 2000, demands that pediatric clinical trials be conducted for all new medications that will be—or could be—used to treat conditions or diseases in children. In March 2002, the FDA announced plans to suspend the Pediatric Rule for two years. During that time period, the FDA hopes to evaluate whether the incentive provision of the FDA Modernization Act is enough to entice pharmaceutical and biotechnology companies to adequately test investigational treatments for children on a voluntary basis.

The Pediatric Exclusivity portion of the FDA Modernization Act of 1997 has prompted pharmaceutical companies to voluntarily put about 165 medicines and vaccines in clinical trials involving pediatric volunteers. The law allowed pharmaceutical companies to extend patent protection on existing drugs by doing safety and dosing studies with children. Extending patent protection gives companies the opportunity to generate more sales without competition. Over three dozen clinical research studies have already been completed on critical drugs used to treat a variety of conditions like gastroesophageal reflux disease, diabetes, pain, asthma and hypertension.

Pediatric Exclusivity is no longer in effect. Passage of the new Best Pharmaceuticals for Children Act in January 2002 is designed to ensure that many more drugs already on the market will continue to be carefully studied in children. The new law not only gives pharmaceutical companies longer patent protection in exchange for conducting pediatric studies; it requires them to share what they learn as a result of those studies, good or bad. If they refuse to do a study that is requested by the FDA, a third party can do it as permitted by a fundraising organization for the NIH. A competitive bidding process for $200 million in funding will be set up through the new NIH office to encourage pediatric clinical trials of older drugs whose patent has expired, meaning that *generic* versions of the drug are allowed to be produced.

Only a small fraction of all prescription drugs marketed in the United States come with instructions on how much to give children and even some of those don't come in a liquid or chewable form. This can make administering treatment to children difficult—almost like a guessing game. If a medicine isn't labeled for children, pediatricians will usually prescribe a dose based on a child's weight. But they never know exactly how effective or safe the drug is when given in a smaller dose to a smaller person.

A lesson has been learned from studies that have already been done: Medications need to be dispensed to children at far different doses than they once were. Researchers are learning that children's age can have a big effect on how they handle a drug. So can their gender, both because of differences in size and body composition and changes that accompany puberty in girls. Simply reducing the adult dose, therefore, is not a medically sound idea.

Pediatric studies of a popular drug for epilepsy found that some children react with aggressive behavior—an adverse event not seen in studies on adults. The drug had to be given at a higher-than-expected dose to be effective in kids under the age of five. A similar discovery was made about an adult anti-depression medication used to treat obsessive-compulsive disorder in kids. When prescribed on a per-weight basis, adolescents were being given a dose that was too low. Conversely, girls ages eight to 11 were routinely being given a dose that was too high. It has also been found that some children need higher or more frequent doses (and sometimes both) of several important antibiotics, including penicillin.

The Pediatric Rule ensures that doctors get the information they need to appropriately and safely prescribe new medications to kids. Generally, the FDA will not even approve products for use in adults until pharmaceutical companies have shared their plans for studying the same drugs in children. The exceptions are for drugs that treat adult diseases, such as prostate cancer, and drugs that are used to treat conditions that manifest differently in adults than in children.

Increasing numbers of children are needed to participate in clinical trials. Their involvement, however, creates a whole new set of concerns and issues. Because of both their size and legal inability to consent to what happens to them, they are the most vulnerable of all vulnerable populations. Is it safe to expose children to potentially harmful procedures and unknown side effects? Are children more easily coerced to participate in clinical trials with the promise of cash, toys and attention? The answers to these issues aren't as clear as parents and researchers would like. It's one thing for parents to enroll their children in studies that could save their life, especially if there are no other options. It's quite another to enroll them for treatment of a cold and flu, or routine ear infections for which there are already available medications.

Children's safety in clinical trials of all types has been exceedingly well protected by federal rules laid out over the past two decades. Until recently, federal protections were so strict that pharmaceutical companies were prohibited from labeling products with known information unless at least two adequate, scientific studies were done. With the exception of clinical trials specifically designed to modify a package insert, pediatric research findings have never translated into prescribing recommendations on medication labels, said Philip Walson, M.D., a pediatric clinical pharmacologist at the University of Cincinnati's Children's Hospital Medical Center. A child's every encounter with a doctor, therefore, became "an uncontrolled experiment" since so few objective, scientific data were readily available to make decisions.

Clinical trials with children have at least three significant shortcomings that researchers aren't apt to share. For starters, the interest in conducting pediatric research exceeds the number of research centers with sufficiently trained personnel to get credible results, said Steve Hirschfeld, M.D., Ph.D., a medical officer with the FDA. Most clinical trials, for example, involve blood sampling to watch the effects of an investigational drug on the body. But a child's small body size limits the amount of blood that can be taken to no more than about one-third a teaspoon—six times less than normally would be taken from an adult. Processing smaller volumes of blood requires special machinery and specially trained staff, which many research sites do not have. Even some hospital emergency rooms lack such expertise, Hirschfeld noted.

Research sites also need to create an environment where a child feels comfortable. Those that specialize in pediatric research have people in their playrooms trained to show children how different procedures are done and get them used to the idea of undergoing the procedures themselves. It's called "medical play" and is credited with helping to make the clinical trial experience for children fun and interesting, said Hirschfeld. It also helps children better understand that the research process is partially, if not solely, about helping other children.

Pediatric research, unlike research with adults, never fits the "ideal" situation for the protection of the study subject, continued

Hirschfeld. Ideally, "the same person who takes on the risk accrues the benefit and gives consent." In reality, the child takes the risk, only sometimes (perhaps even accidentally) accrues a benefit and never gives permission to go into a study.

To ensure a child is protected, the principal investigator should not be an investor in or principal of a company sponsoring the research, or hold the patent on the product. And if the investigator is the same one who takes care of a child's other health needs, another doctor should be given the job of monitoring the study.

The FDA has set forth standards by which institutional review boards (IRBs) can determine if proposed pediatric clinical trials can be safely and ethically conducted. One of the key points in the rule is that kids should assent to participate in a clinical trial—basically, to say they agree to do it—and their parents or guardians should give fully informed consent for them to do so. Recruitment of study participants using "coercive inducements"—financial or otherwise—is deemed inappropriate.

The rule essentially places pediatric research in one of three risk categories, explained Hirschfeld. If the risk is no different than what a child would encounter in daily life, the research is acceptable. But if the risk is any greater than that, additional safeguards are recommended. In the eyes of the FDA, a child is not a "research subject" but a "patient." That's because of the overriding belief that normal and healthy children should not be in research studies. "They're for children who have a disease, are likely to get a disease or have just recovered from it," said Hirschfeld. A good example would be an epileptic child on an anti-convulsive medication who wants to try a new drug.

Studies posing greater-than-minimal risk beg the question: Will there be any benefit to the child? If benefits are likely to occur, there's not much of an ethical dilemma. If benefits are considered unlikely, the child would need to go into a trial with the idea that he won't necessarily feel better but other children with the same condition, one day, might. The child, of course, might also get lucky by stumbling across an effective treatment and being one of the first people to get it. The child's medical condition may also benefit from the careful observation that occurs during a study and his or her own improved understanding of the disease.

IRBs are also expected to consider a host of other factors before allowing a pediatric study to proceed. If the investigational medicine will be treating a serious condition without good alternative therapies, for example, the study would probably be viewed as somewhat urgent. The IRB would look at any pediatric safety concerns about the drug, often based on the experience of adult users. The *formulation*—liquid, suspensions, chewable tablets—would also have to make sense for the age of the children for whom it is intended.

Questions Every Parent Should Ask About Pediatric Clinical Trials

- What are the IRB reviewers' comments and concerns?
- Does the study need to be done? If the information can be gleaned from studies with adults or on animals, is there a need to put children at risk?
- What are the obligations and expectations for child volunteers? Are overnight stays required? Is a diary required? How many visits to the research center are required? How often are the visits?
- What is the "escape rule"? That is, what adverse event or other type of discomfort has to happen for my child to be removed from the study? If that happens, will some alternative therapy be offered?
- Are there "stopping rules" regarding what might prematurely end the entire study? What safety-related events, or frequency of adverse events, would close the study?
- How much evidence is needed about an investigational drug's failure to work before a study is halted?
- If the experimental treatment is for a serious or life-threatening illness, will the study have some kind of special safety monitoring? Will study results periodically be reviewed by an independent third party?
- Are there any alternative clinical trials under way?

As a practical matter, research sites and IRBs try to seek out study protocols that have therapeutic value and may actually help a child get better. They try to avoid protocols that are real "invasive," requiring tubes to be run from the nose to the stomach or an unnecessarily high number of blood draws. They also make every attempt to minimize the overall number of study participants needed.

Any number of strategies may be employed to make the whole experience less distressing to children. These include conducting studies in health settings where they normally receive their care, providing age-appropriate furniture and play equipment in study areas and using research staff who are accustomed to performing pediatric procedures.

Whether or not placebo-controlled trials are appropriate for children is a matter of some debate. But the FDA's pediatric advisors, as well as a group of ethicists and international experts, recently agreed that they're acceptable if there are no approved or adequately studied treatments for children with the condition under study. For serious or life-threatening conditions, special monitoring is recommended along with "stopping rules" for investigational drugs that prove to be either too risky or unquestionably effective. For minor illnesses and conditions with symptoms, they suggest use of studies that minimize exposure to ineffective treatment.

The ways pediatric studies are developed and designed vary by the age category of study volunteers needed. A clinical trial involving pre-term newborns, for instance, would have the input of neonatologists and neonatal pharmacologists because of the unique way their tiny bodies, with their immature organs and small volume of circulating blood, respond to drugs. A study on toddlers would have to consider the great variation in maturity level from child to child. In older children, protocols need to measure the impact of a medicinal product on growth and development. They also need to allow for needed dosage changes once they hit puberty, which can affect the way drugs are broken down by the body.

The hormonal changes associated with puberty can influence the behavior of diseases and, consequently, the findings of clinical studies. Recreational drug use and noncompliance—forgetting to take a drug as instructed or an unwillingness to show up for important tests and visits—are also factors that have to be carefully and thoughtfully planned for.

With few exceptions, such as cancer treatments, most investigational products are not studied in children until they reach phase III or are already being marketed for the same disease in adults. This is a consequence of both FDA guidance and the objectives of the pharmaceutical firm. Once clinical trials on a drug are under way, most companies won't initiate studies in children until they see if it works as intended in adults—a more predictable and viable market.

Pediatric studies touch virtually every category of disease and condition. Clinical trials on new treatments for infectious diseases, attention deficit hyperactivity disorder, asthma and allergies are particularly common. So are vaccine trials, including new "combination" therapies that immunize children against several diseases at the same time. The Exclusivity Provision has also spurred numerous other pediatric studies of hypertension, diabetes and rheumatoid arthritis drugs—so many, in fact, that there often aren't child volunteers to be found.

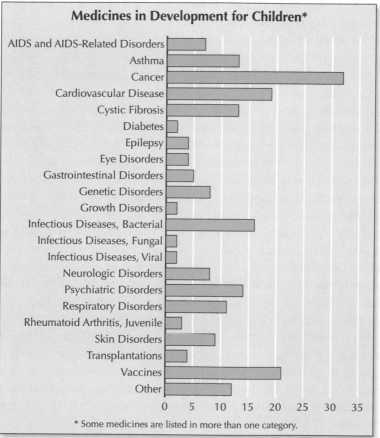

Medicines in Development for Children*

* Some medicines are listed in more than one category.

Source: PhRMA, 2001

The majority of pediatric trials are conducted by well-trained investigators at large academic medical centers with access to kid-friendly radiology and EKG units and labs. Office-based pediatricians, if they do research at all, tend to focus on studies of vaccines, nutritional formulas, infectious diseases and common illnesses seen in the community. A lot of clinical trials are done in conjunction with nearby medical centers.

The Age of Assent

Children aren't expected to give their consent, but they're often asked to give their assent. This will generally be recorded on a simplified form, separate from the longer, more detailed one their parents sign. But older children, depending on their level of maturity, may sign the very same form that their parents do.

The written permission of children's parents or legal guardians is also required before they can be enrolled in any study. IRBs consider parental permission sufficient if the research is going to be done on young children (vaguely defined as somewhere under age seven to 11) who lack the intellectual and emotional ability to understand what they're agreeing to. The "right" age to start asking children for their assent is when they're developmentally able to understand cause and effect, said Walson. But a multitude of other factors come into play, including whether a particular child has been in a clinical trial before, knows what to expect, and knows how to weigh the benefits and risks of participation.

IRBs don't require assent when children have a life-threatening illness, such as leukemia or a heart abnormality, and the study is considered likely to benefit them—no matter how much they may protest the idea. But recruitment of handicapped or institutionalized children is frowned upon unless the study is for diseases or conditions found mostly, or exclusively, in those populations.

For researchers, one of the harder parts of informed consent/assent among children is avoiding medical jargon and not assuming anything is understood. They also have to put themselves in the child's place to understand their motivations, fears and desires. "Personally, the most difficult part for me is dealing with parental fear and guilt," said Walson.

As for a situation that involves a screaming three-year-old, the thoughtful researcher would probably discourage parents from enrolling the child—unless, of course, the child is seriously ill and no other good treatment option is available. It's also the more practical parental decision. Without the hope of great medicinal benefit, it's doubtful that many parents would be able to endure the ranting of an already cranky toddler past his first or second blood draw.

Compensation in Pediatric Clinical Trials

Parents are often pleased that their child's research-related visits, tests and medications are provided free of charge. Children could care less. To reward them for their participation, researchers will often give them gifts and even hourly fees of $5 or more. But whether children should be paid at all remains a matter of debate. The FDA takes no official position on the matter, leaving such matters to the discretion of the IRB.

"It is not wrong to compensate children and their parents for the inconvenience of being in a trial, but it is wrong to make the amount of payment or presents so much as to become an undue influence," said Walson. "Experienced institutions are likely to have unbiased people on the committees (IRBs) that decide what is 'too much.' This is not a simple question. The risks and benefits of the trial determine it. No inducement may be necessary or proper for a life-saving treatment offered nowhere else but through a clinical trial. A study requiring nightly trips to the hospital to test a new flavor of an approved, effective medication might justify a lot of payment for travel, babysitters and missed work."

Many research centers will provide payments for pediatric studies that they believe are proportional to the time required to participate and appeal directly to the child rather than the parent. The "honorarium" might be a savings bond, toy, movie pass, gift certificates for CDs, or cash. But a few university-affiliated research centers have policies against making payments or gifts of any size to subjects of any age.

Money won't buy a child's cooperation for the entire length of a study. Children will back out of studies simply because they're in a bad mood or don't like what happened to them during their last visit. Overly active toddlers literally have to be held down for blood draws.

Sometimes children, and their parents, will also underestimate the time consumed by follow-up visits and tests.

Choosing What Is Best for Your Child
The most important thing parents can do for their children is seek out an investigator they know and trust, rather than blindly responding to an advertisement, said Diane Murphy, M.D., associate director for pediatrics in the FDA's Center for Drug Evaluation and Research. "Parents need to know who they're getting involved with." Professional, well-recognized research centers, she added, are the safest bet.

Rights of the Mentally Ill

Federal regulations on the protection of human subjects do not yet specifically address clinical trials among people whose mental status is impaired. This vulnerable population includes people with psychiatric illnesses like schizophrenia, manic depression, neurological conditions like Alzheimer's disease and substance abusers. In the absence of regulatory guidance, the main concerns of the IRB are that subject selection is fair, risks are reasonable relative to potential benefit and that information about the trial is understandable to those capable of consenting or refusing to participate.

As a general rule, all adults regardless of their diagnosis or condition are presumed competent to consent unless there is evidence of serious mental disability that would impair reasoning or judgment. A legally responsible adult signs the consent form for subjects who are not competent. A "subject advocate" may participate in the consent process if there is question about the competency of an adult. Even subjects who are declared legally incompetent generally maintain their right to refuse participation in trials that involve no potentially beneficial diagnostic or therapeutic procedures.

As a result of greater IRB attention to the vulnerability of the mentally ill, volunteers in this population are less likely than in the past to be used as research subjects for drug and vaccine trials unrelated to their disorders or institutionalization.

Prisoners

Prisoners in federally funded trials were given their own set of regulatory protections in 1978. The chief concern was that they might, given limited choice as a prisoner, be at greater risk of being coerced into participating in a clinical trial. To guard against this, federal regulators have instructed IRBs to more carefully review all clinical trials using prisoners as research subjects. IRB duties include ensuring:

- That compensation isn't coercive. Better amenities and the opportunity to make money in prison may unduly impair a prisoner's ability to weigh the benefits and risks of a clinical trial
- The risks of participating would be acceptable to non-prisoner volunteers
- The selection of subjects within the prison system is fair and does not affect decisions regarding parole
- That adequate follow-up care is provided, if needed

The Department of Health and Human Services published an amendment to the Code of Federal Regulations on December 13, 2001. These regulations provide the following additional protections for prisoners:

- A majority of the IRB (excluding prison members) cannot have an association with the prison involved, apart from membership on the IRB
- At least one member of the IRB must be a prisoner or a prisoner representative

For the bulk of drug studies that are sponsored by pharmaceutical companies, prisoners have no specific regulatory protections due largely to the objection of prison advocacy groups. Still, the FDA recognizes prisoners as a "vulnerable population" in need of special IRB oversight. The types of clinical trials that prisoners volunteer for depend largely on the policy and available facilities of the particular prison where they reside.

The Elderly

A growing number of clinical trials are being conducted on treatments for illnesses that affect senior Americans. Older generations of Americans have typically held a more trusting view of health professionals. As a result, this population may be more vulnerable to being influenced to participate in clinical trials. Support networks are an extremely important part of the informed consent process for senior Americans interested in volunteering for clinical trials.

There are an estimated 785 drugs in development that have been designed to lengthen life as well as improve the quality of life for senior Americans. Approximately 260 investigational drugs target diseases that specifically affect the elderly. These drugs in development include:

- 44 investigational treatments for respiratory and lung disorders, the fourth leading cause of death among the elderly
- 23 drugs in development for diabetes, the sixth leading cause of death among people 65 and older
- 21 experimental treatments for Alzheimer's disease, which is expected to afflict as many as 14 million Americans by 2040 unless a cure or prevention is discovered
- 20 investigational drugs for depression, which affects 6% of the 65-and-older population.

Medicines in Development for Older Americans*			
Alzheimer's disease/dementias	21	Pain	13
Bladder/kidney disorders	14	Parkinson's disease	13
Depression	20	Prostate disease	5
Diabetes	23	Respirator/lung disorders	44
Eye disorders	23	Rheumatoid arthritis	22
Gastrointestinal disorders	19	Sepsis	8
Intermittent claudication	2	Sexual dysfunction	11
Osteoarthritis	3	Skin conditions	16
Osteoporosis	15	Other	15

* Some medicines are listed in more than one category

Source: PhRMA, 2001

Special Considerations for Pregnant Women

The Department of Health and Human Services (HHS) also published an amendment to the Code of Federal Regulations on December 13, 2001, to provide additional protections for pregnant women and their fetuses involved in clinical research. The amendment builds upon special protections for pregnant women and fetuses that have existed since 1975 and clarifies the role of the father's consent when research is conducted involving unborn children.

Although it is still relatively rare to find pregnant women in studies, this group—and more specifically, their unborn children—was the first to be given special protection by HSS in 1975. The protections, however, apply only to federally funded research. The protections limit the involvement of pregnant women to trials that pose no more than a minimal risk to the fetus or intend to meet the mother's health needs and put the fetus at risk only to the minimum extent necessary. A new regulatory change, put into effect at the end of 2001, says the father's informed consent is needed only if the research is solely to benefit the fetus. Previously, the father's consent was also needed if the research was likely to also benefit the mother or simply to provide important medical knowledge. Remember that HHS oversees government-sponsored clinical trials.

The FDA—at least for now—has no specific regulation on the matter. If the study drug is not designed specifically for pregnant women, the FDA expects pharmaceutical companies to first test the product in non-pregnant subjects. Researchers are advised not to play a role in decisions about the termination of a pregnancy or to offer inducements to end a pregnancy for purposes of a clinical trial. Study subjects who are pregnant are also expected to be given all information about the potential risk of fetal toxicity as gathered from animal studies or experience with similar types of drugs. If the effects of a study drug on a fetus are unknown, the mother must be told. It is also the reason the FDA is silent on the issue of paternal consent. FDA oversees industry-sponsored trials.

The FDA has a major drug labeling initiative under way that has stepped up the debate about how best to include pregnant women in clinical trials. Its Office of Women's Health recently provided funding for studies of two prescription medications (labetalol and atenolol) used by pregnant women to treat their high blood pressure. The goal is to identify the doses that will provide the greatest benefit and least risk for the mother and her baby. Such information is rarely available on any type of prescription drug taken during pregnancy. The research, the FDA says, "should demonstrate that this type of study can and should be done for medications widely used during pregnancy." Like most healthcare agencies and experts, however, it frowns on the involvement of pregnant women in early-phase studies of more general conditions affecting both pregnant and non-pregnant populations. That's because it puts the fetus at unknown—and unnecessary—risk.

CHAPTER SEVEN

What to Do When Things Go Wrong

Although there are cases where things have gone wrong during clinical trials, the majority of clinical trials are conducted safely and ethically. There are many professionals and procedures in place to ensure that your rights are protected and that the risk of participation is minimized. However, some violations still occur. The responsibilities of research center personnel, the institutional review board (IRB) and the study sponsor are mandated by federal guidelines. A review of these responsibilities shows a number of checks and balances designed to protect study volunteers:

Study Coordinator responsibilities include among other things:
- Managing daily study tasks
- Educating research center personnel about study requirements
- Submitting documents to the IRB
- Screening and enrolling study volunteers
- Collecting data and recording information on the study report forms
- Coordinating volunteer visits
- Following up and periodically touching base with study volunteers
- Storing, maintaining and dispensing investigational drugs
- Collecting and processing lab samples
- Maintaining volunteer and data confidentiality
- Communicating with the investigator, sponsor and study monitor

Investigator responsibilities include among other things:

- Instructing and supervising staff compliance with the study protocol
- Submitting protocol, amendments, consent forms and advertising material to the IRB
- Obtaining IRB approval
- Ensuring that volunteers meet eligibility criteria
- Adhering to study *randomization* and *blinding* requirements
- Maintaining patient case records and ensuring their completion
- Ensuring that data are complete and accurate
- Responding to data queries
- Documenting, conducting and delegating study tasks
- Notifying the IRB of serious adverse events (SAEs)
- Providing periodic progress reports to the IRB

IRB responsibilities include among other things:

- Ensuring that study risks to volunteers are minimized and reasonable in relation to the anticipated benefits
- Reviewing, approving/rejecting research studies and related activities
- Requiring modification of research activities
- Ensuring and documenting that volunteers have provided their informed consent
- Providing investigators and research center personnel with written documentation of approval, disapproval and modifications of research activities
- Ensuring that IRB committee membership complies with regulations
- Maintaining complete records of IRB activities (e.g., meeting minutes, correspondences with research center personnel and statements of significant new study findings communicated to volunteers during the study)

Sponsor responsibilities include among other things:

- Selecting qualified investigators and research centers
- Providing investigators and study staff with information to conduct the protocol
- Ensuring proper and effective study monitoring

- Ensuring that the study follows the protocol and plans in the Investigational New Drug (IND) application
- Providing prompt information about serious adverse events to the FDA and participating investigators
- Disclosing to the FDA the financial interests of participating investigators

Most offenses are minor, so they result in a warning letter from the FDA's Division of Scientific Investigations, which instructs them to take certain corrective actions. The FDA then monitors research investigators to make sure the proper corrective steps were implemented. Most of the 100 or so complaints the FDA investigates each year result from careless—though potentially dangerous—mistakes. Every last pill could not be accounted for, or a 72-year-old is enrolled in a study when the cut off age is 69. The opposite is also true—some investigations will not turn up even a single minor violation.

Fewer than 3% of unsolicited FDA audits uncover serious violations. However, in cases where inspections were solicited due to complaints filed against research centers, more than one-quarter of them received serious violations of good clinical practices (GCPs). These violations included falsification of records or the failure to report adverse events. When serious violations are cited, the FDA must suspend and even consider disqualifying the investigator from conducting future research. One or two investigators are actually disqualified each year and a few others "voluntarily" remove themselves from conducting clinical research. Sometimes, investigators instead consent to having restrictions placed on how they conduct future studies—to perform no more than two studies simultaneously, for example, or to participate in trials only as a subinvestigator.

Today, more than 50,000 clinical investigators are conducting at least one clinical trial every year. Since 1964, the FDA has disqualified 100 investigators for failing to comply with Good Clinical Practice guidelines. Another 29 have had restrictions placed on them by consent. Twenty have been prosecuted criminally. As a result of more "for-cause"—or solicited—inspections conducted annually by the FDA, the agency is finding more serious problems are being uncovered now than in the past. Given the large increase in the number of investigators and trials being conducted today, there are proportionately fewer violations than in the past.

The Office for Human Research Protections (OHRP) also uncovers a handful of serious violations from the more than 100 complaints it receives each year alleging misconduct by federally funded university-affiliated institutions. The percentage is small compared to the number of clinical trials conducted at these institutions. As many as 3,000 protocols are conducted annually at each of our nation's top 130 academic medical centers. Permanent suspension of studies or federal funding because of wrongdoing is rare. But when it does happen, it is quite serious.

What You Can Do

In situations where you feel that your safety and ethical treatment are in jeopardy, your best guide is the informed consent form. It is your bill of rights. If you feel, for example, that you have been subjected to unreasonable risk, that your concerns and wishes are not being respected or that you have witnessed unethical behavior, you need to contact the IRB immediately. A contact number for the IRB or patient advocate is provided with your informed consent form. The study staff can also provide this information for you at any time.

If you are not satisfied after talking with your IRB or patient advocate, or if it appears that the IRB and the study staff are unable to help, then you need to file a complaint directly with the FDA or OHRP.

To lodge a complaint with the FDA
For studies of biologics, including gene therapy and vaccine studies, you should contact the Division of Communication and Consumer Affairs in the Center for Biologics Evaluation and Research.
- Telephone (301) 827-2000
- Fax (301) 827-3843

For drug studies, the FDA contact is the Division of Scientific Investigations in the Office of Medical Policy at the Center for Drug Evaluation and Research.
- Telephone (301) 594-0020
- Fax (301) 594-1204

For medical device studies, the contact is the Division of Bioresearch Monitoring in the Office of Compliance at the Center for Devices and Radiological Health.

- Telephone (301) 594-4718
- Fax (301) 594-4731

To lodge a complaint with the Office of Human Research Protection

- Telephone (301) 496-7005
- Mailing Address
  Office for Human Research Protections
  Department of Health and Human Services
  The Tower Building
  1101 Wootton Parkway, Suite 200
  Rockville, MD 20852
- Email ohrp@osophs.dhhs.gov

You might also try the Office of Inspector General, Department of Health and Human Services (HHS).

- Telephone (202) 619-0257 or (877) 696-6775 (toll-free)
- Mailing Address
  The U.S. Department of Health and Human Services
  200 Independence Avenue, SW
  Washington, D.C. 20201

It usually does not make sense to file a complaint with the pharmaceutical company sponsoring the research, although you can try. Most pharmaceutical companies have limited resources established to handle direct contact with study volunteers. This is changing, however. A growing number of companies—particularly the largest ones—do offer toll-free hotlines that you can call to report an emergency. We have provided contact information for pharmaceutical and biotechnology companies in the appendix.

Self-help and various advocacy groups—health and medical associations—may be of some assistance in handling your reports and complaints. Associations that set national and local health policies may also be good contacts. These groups may be better equipped to help you locate and choose clinical trials than to help you deal with misconduct issues. Still, they can help you better understand your rights as a volunteer, and they may help you contact other more help-ful organizations and institutions. A list of some of these associations and groups are also included in the appendix.

It's impossible to test the safety of a drug in people with every conceivable combination of disease, drug interaction, age and genet-ic predisposition. Therefore, some general, and all long-term, side effects aren't discovered until after a drug has been on the market and used by millions.

Physicians, pharmacists and even patients themselves routinely report adverse events to the FDA through an ongoing drug-safety program known as *MedWatch*. A drug causing an adverse event in sufficient frequency, relative to how often it's prescribed, will usually have its label changed so that doctors are informed about the new information and about what, if anything, they can do to minimize the risk. Many safety-related labeling changes are made every year. Side effects are dangerous enough to take two or three prescription drugs off the market each year. There are a number of web sites that post MedWatch information online for you to refer to.

Although this may not address immediate concerns about safety and ethical treatment, you can play a more active role in the future by joining or participating in an IRB. This experience will help you increase your network of support. Motivated parents—especially those who have had a child in a clinical trial—make ideal IRB members.

Being involved on an IRB is no small task. Members often have to do a lot of reading and attend numerous meetings. It depends on the IRB. Some have a fixed number of members who look over, and comment on, every protocol. Others have a pool of members from which they draw, based on their area of interest and expertise.

CenterWatch estimates that there are approximately 3,000 IRBs operating within the United States that oversee government- and industry-funded clinical trials. Boards are established, trained and licensed differently from place to place. The OHRP offers general IRB training that focuses on research ethics (http://ohrp.osophs. dhhs.gov).

Steve Hirschfeld, M.D., Ph.D., medical officer with the FDA, said his hope is that people will start demanding quality in clinical trials as they do in most everything else—including their automobiles, food and regular medical care. Joining an IRB is a good starting point. Even people who are completely untrained in science and statistics can make substantial contributions to discussions about studies after only a few hours of training, he said.

A History of Specific Misconduct Examples

The incidence of misconduct and noncompliance is rare. When these acts are uncovered, the government and industry typically respond by modifying practices and adding new policies and procedures.

There are a lot of pressures placed on researchers today to enroll patients quickly, to conduct clinical trials faster, to review and approve study protocols in less time, and to compete against other research centers for new studies from industry and government study sponsors. Some research professionals are tempted, for example, by the potential to increase their salaries by doing more and larger clinical trials. Despite these pressures and temptations, history has shown that a very small number of investigators, coordinators and IRB personnel have been led astray. What follows are a few examples of their misconduct that have helped to shape new policies and legislation.

In 1999, California physician Robert Fiddes was disqualified as a clinical investigator and sent to prison for 15 months after he and two of his study coordinators conspired to falsify drug trial results by "inventing" patients and medical data. He also lost his medical license. The whistleblower was one of Dr. Fiddes' employees.

Similarly, a disgruntled employee tipped off the Medical College of Georgia in Augusta that Drs. Richard Borison and Bruce Diamond—a prominent psychiatrist and pharmacologist—were secretly conducting schizophrenia drug trials for eight years using university resources and pocketing the proceeds. They "coaxed" psychotic patients into trials with money and cigarettes, but gave scant attention to their care. Untrained staff took blood draws and adjusted doses of study drugs. The two were finally put behind bars in 1997, fined $125,000 a piece, and ordered to pay millions of dollars back to the college.

Jesse Gelsinger's Story

One of the largest concerns today relates to conflicts of interest. Investigators and universities that have an economic interest in the drug they're investigating tend to be less vigilant—consciously or unconsciously—about patient safety and ethical treatment. This is considered one of the many factors associated with the death of 18-year-old Jesse Gelsinger in a 1999 gene therapy experiment at the University of Pennsylvania. Jesse had a massive and fatal immune system reaction to a common-cold virus used to deliver a particular gene to his liver. (See Chapter Five, under "The Most Responsible Party" for more on financial conflicts of interest in research.)

Jesse had an inherited metabolic disorder that had landed him in a coma several times. But he was doing relatively well on medications before entering the trial. The university and principal investigator wanted to test a treatment for newborn babies, but they first needed adults to participate in a clinical trial focusing on how suitable the common-cold virus was for gene transport delivery. They also stood to profit if the drug worked. But the Gelsinger family was not informed about this conflict of interest—or all of the drug's dangers. Questions were raised later about whether Jesse fit the inclusion criteria and even whether federal regulators were notified of adverse events during earlier studies of the experimental intervention.

A subsequent investigation by the FDA revealed that established safety rules were not followed and that the study should have ended months earlier than it did. It ordered a halt to nine clinical research projects at the university's Institute of Human Gene Therapy. The family ultimately sued and won an out-of-court settlement. The university wrote a letter of apology to Jesse's family and was determined thereafter to make itself a model for human subject protection.

"Jesse just wanted to help," said his father, Paul. "There was nothing in it for him—no money and no treatment that was even applicable to him. His heart was totally in this, and it really impressed me. It was his chance to make a difference. When he died, I tried to adopt some of the heart he had and befriended the doctors. They were not bad men. They had simply become blind to the real purpose of what they were doing."

It was only when he became aware of lapses in the protocol that he sued. "Litigation was the only way to get their attention. The clinical trial should never have taken place," said Gelsinger. "It was too dangerous and of no benefit to those who participated."

Perhaps most disturbing, said Gelsinger, is that Jesse would probably still be alive today if a gene therapy information network had been set up. The FDA and National Institutes of Health (NIH) were discussing the idea back in 1995 but later dropped it. The reason, an FDA official confided in him, was because his supervisors "answered to industry." And industry fears that sharing information—including adverse events and deaths associated with certain types of trials—will cost them their competitive edge.

After examining close to 100 other gene therapy protocols, the FDA determined that gene therapy trials are no better or worse than standard drug trials in complying with federal research rules. "What happened in the Gelsinger case, and other serious cases we've had, is that the system was compromised in more than one area," commented David Lepay, the FDA's senior advisor for clinical science. Of greatest concern are uninformed IRBs, inadequate adverse event reporting and clinical investigators who double as study sponsors and thus conduct trials shy of a critical "control point." Education, and a special monitoring unit, may present at least a partial solution. Integrity in the doctor-patient relationship—something regulators can't control—also has to be there.

Another Case of Conflict of Interest

Allegations similar to those in the Gelsinger case have been reported at other universities and research centers since Jesse's death. These include an alleged breach of trust by the Fred Hutchinson Cancer Research Center, a top bone marrow transplant center in Seattle. The center's principal investigators—including a Nobel Prize winner—received consulting fees from the firm producing the drug for leukemia trials conducted there in the 1980s and 1990s. The center was given shares of stock in the company and rights to study drugs owned by the company for 20 years. Nearly all of the study's 82 participants have since died. A quarter of them would still be alive, family members believe, had they received an alternative therapy. But the doctors never fully informed them about the dangers of the experimental drug or other available treatments, they say. So they've filed a lawsuit against the center.

The "whistleblower," in this case, was a member of the research center's IRB. An independent review of patient protection practices, coordinated by the Hutchinson Center, suggested a host of changes be made. One major recommendation was that all individuals involved in human subject trials be prohibited from having a financial interest in for-profit corporations that may benefit from the result of such trials.

There is now growing concern among regulators, professionals and the public that financial conflict of interest—including stock ownership in the sponsoring drug company—are biasing the way studies are designed and conducted. There is also growing concern that conflicts of interest are biasing the way study findings are written up in prestigious medical journals. These kinds of influences are potentially harmful both to human research subjects and those who use the drugs once they're approved for sale. The U.S. General Accounting Office, in its November 2001 report on financial conflicts of interest in research, found that editors of major medical journals were concerned about the "competitive economic environment" in which some clinical research is conceived and conducted. In response, the International Committee of Medical Journal Editors has "revised and strengthened" the section of publication ethics in the reference that many medical journals use as the basis for their editorial policies. As part of the revised reporting requirements, authors will need to disclose details of their own and the sponsor's role in the study.

Another Recent Case Involving Misconduct

Participants in a clinical trial for a melanoma vaccine are suing the IRB at the University of Oklahoma Health Sciences Center for failure to adequately protect them. The lawsuit alleges that the IRB was negligent in its duties, including stopping the center from conducting the trial. The IRB is faulted for not reviewing the conduct of the trial, the informed consent documents that understated risks to subjects and the recruitment advertisements that falsely represented the vaccine as a "cure for cancer." When the trial closed prematurely in the spring of 2000, the IRB permitted researchers to tell participants that the reason was a shortage of the vaccine rather than safety violations discovered by the FDA. The university dismissed everyone involved in the alleged wrongdoing. The suspension has been lifted.

> ## Recent Legislation Now Requires Investigators to Disclose Potential Conflicts of Interest
>
> These include:
>
> ■ Stock in the sponsoring company
>
> ■ Proprietary interest in a particular drug or device (e.g., patent, trademark, copyright and license rights)
>
> ■ Payment arrangements that might benefit the investigator if a certain outcome occurs
>
> ■ Honoraria received by the sponsoring company
>
> ■ Gifts of equipment from the sponsoring company
>
> ■ Retainer and consulting fees for ongoing arrangements with the sponsor company

In a report issued in 1998, the inspector general of the U.S. Department of Health and Human Services concluded that many IRBs were operating over capacity. Following that report, OHRP has suspended research programs at a number of institutions. In 1999, it briefly shut down all 2,000 medical experiments at Duke University because of safety concerns—including inadequate informed consent procedures. In recent years, research has also been temporarily suspended at a number of university-affiliated sites because of human subject safety concerns. Violations have been made across several areas including informed consent noncompliance, poor record keeping, and poor reporting of serious adverse events.

One of the most recent suspensions was at Johns Hopkins University School of Medicine and its affiliated institutions following the death of Ellen Roche, a healthy 24-year-old woman, during an asthma experiment. She died of adult respiratory distress syndrome not long after being given an inhaled dosage of a non-marketed drug known as hexamethonium. The principal investigator said he could find no recent articles in the medical literature associating the drug with severe pulmonary disease, and no articles at all connecting it to pulmonary toxicity when delivered by inhalation. And researchers on the 1978 study attesting to the drug's safety failed to report that two of five volunteers in the study became sick.

An OHRP investigation found that Johns Hopkins' IRBs weren't providing adequate review of many new research programs and, when they did, the deliberations included board members with financial conflicts of interest. The OHRP briefly took away Johns Hopkins' Multiple Project Assurance—the permit needed to conduct federally funded research that holds institutions responsible for all trials involving human participants. Previously enrolled subjects were allowed to continue in a trial only if it was in their best interests. After four days, with a new plan in place to correct deficiencies, all research in which there was no more than a minimal risk to volunteers was allowed to resume.

Institutions Where Studies Have Been Temporarily Suspended

July 1998 through July 2001

- Rush-Presbyterian-St. Luke's Medical Center
- Friends Research Institute, Inc., West Coast Division
- Veterans Affairs Greater Los Angeles Health Care System
- Duke University Medical Center
- Virginia Commonwealth University
- University of Oklahoma, Tulsa Campus
- Johns Hopkins University School of Medicine and its affiliated institutions

Source: Office for Human Research Protections

Regulatory scrutiny of Johns Hopkins has changed the clinical trial process there in several potentially significant ways. Informed consent documents have been simplified and better cover key points. IRBs seek to be more ethnically diverse and have been tasked with more closely scrutinizing studies that don't involve the FDA. Investigators are also routinely reminded that changes in study protocols require IRB review and approval and that unanticipated problems involving risks to subjects must be promptly reported.

Reform is not always prompted by a complete suspension of research. An OHRP investigation, for example, led the University of Arkansas and Arkansas Children's Hospital to expand its IRB staff and require its investigators to be educated about their responsibilities to protect the safety of study volunteers. The move followed the death of a 3-year-old boy who had been placed in the wrong arm of a kidney cancer trial.

Other academic institutions and federal research agencies have undertaken similar reforms when OHRP has investigated alleged violations or suspended trials due to poor investigator compliance or IRB judgment.

Citizens for Responsible Care and Research advocates that 51% of IRB membership come from—and be selected by someone—outside research institutions. Gelsinger proposes that the NIH establish a user-fee program to fund the establishment of IRBs independent of institutional influence.

Unintended harm might sometimes occur from a drug long after it has been approved for sale on the open market. The incidence of these occurrences is extremely rare. Recently, the FDA shelved the popular cholesterol-lowering drug Baycol (cerivastatin) after linking it to 31 deaths in the United States from a rare muscle-destroying side effect. Volunteers involved in clinical trials for the popular diet pill "fen-phen" were informed years after the trials ended, and the drug had been prescribed to more than 7 million patients, that it was causing heart and lung problems in some patients who took it. By then, the drug had caused problems in 45,000 patients and approximately 300 deaths. People who took the drug and survived were compensated, but the damage to their health was permanent.

Many of these cases show what can happen when things go wrong. Every accident and death is significant, but the likelihood of their occurring is rare. Recent responses by regulatory agencies, sponsor companies and research centers suggest that measures are being taken to help prevent these accidents from happening again. For example, during 2000 and 2001, institutional and independent IRBs have been implementing initiatives designed to improve IRB effectiveness. These initiatives involve increasing IRB headcount, creating toll-free numbers for volunteers, providing more training and education and improving standard operating procedures.

Some suggested steps that you can take to better protect yourself

- Ask who wrote the study protocol and what qualified that person to do so.
- Call the IRB to learn about how much time was spent reviewing the study protocol and what specific areas, if any, gave members cause for discussion or concern.

- Find out if there is or has been professional debate about the risks associated with the study drug. If so, ask for referrals to medical publications where these risks are discussed.
- Request that the study staff speak to you in plain English (or Spanish, French, sign language, etc.)—or find someone who can.
- Quiz the researcher and study coordinator about how many adverse events and deaths have been reported during trials of this study drug—whether or not they were actually attributed to the drug. If they don't know, call the IRB. If the IRB doesn't know, call the pharmaceutical company.
- Ask the researchers if they would advise you to enroll in the trial if you were a member of their family.
- Gather as much information as you can from published reports and news coverage about your study medication.
- If possible, go to another research center conducting the same clinical trial. Go through the same set of questions and see if you get the same answers. Seek explanations for inconsistencies.
- Share everything you learned with your family doctor and other friends and family within your support network before enrolling.

The danger of sharing these examples of misconduct is that they can increase your fears and anxieties about participating in clinical trials. But, the danger of not sharing these examples is more serious. They illustrate the worst cases and the responses they prompted from the government, the public, academic institutions and from industry. This chapter is intended to help you avoid these worst case situations.

As in all things, knowledge is power. Whereas reading this chapter, or this book, is no guarantee that you will be protected from all the potential risks associated with a clinical trial, reading it does give you the knowledge and the power to recognize when your rights and your health are at risk and to take steps to protect yourself from these risks.

CHAPTER EIGHT

Finding Clinical Trials

With 6,000 protocols comprising approximately 80,000 government- and industry-sponsored clinical trials conducted in the United States each year, there is a good chance that you will find trials for new treatments targeting your illness. There is also a good chance that some clinical trials may find you—through notices in your doctor's office to radio, television and newspaper advertisements.

Only 10 years ago, it was very difficult for patients to actively identify clinical trials. The vast majority of clinical trials were done in academic medical centers—many of them within major metropolitan areas. Unless your physician was close in proximity and affiliated with an academic medical center, it is unlikely that you would have found a clinical trial opportunity.

Today, there are numerous resources in print and online for professionals and patients to use. And with more clinical trials being conducted by independent, community-based physicians, there is a far greater chance that your own primary and specialty care physicians and nurses will be able to assist you in identifying clinical trials that you may be right for. Your family and friends may be able to assist you in conducting a broad search, and then narrowing down your options to a few targeted opportunities.

Remember that when you begin your search, your goal is to be as thorough and comprehensive as possible. Every piece of information that you collect and every individual you speak with may assist you in tracking down a clinical trial that could hold some potential for you. Once you have isolated a few clinical trials whose posted inclusion and exclusion criteria you meet, then you—and your support network—can begin to scrutinize whether any of these trials might be a good match for you.

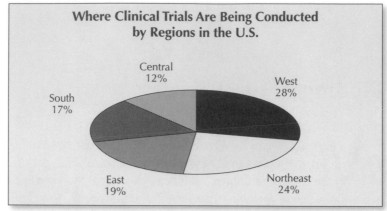

Source: CenterWatch, 2001

Search Strategies for Finding Trials

Today, two out of three patients refer themselves to clinical trials. There are essentially two ways to find them. One is to search for the trials themselves. The other, perhaps easier, approach is to search for investigational drugs and then determine where they are being tested. A few health web sites allow you to conduct both types of searches at the same time.

Regardless of your approach, there are numerous people, organizations and publications available to assist you. But you have to know whom to ask and where to look. Here are a few good bets:

Health professionals. Primary and specialty care physicians and nurses, in particular, may have access to some specialized (and expensive) medical journals and online databases where clinical trials, and study drugs, are routinely discussed topics. These professionals are also worth consulting after you've found some initial sources of information. Not all medical publications and web sites provide accurate information. Health professionals can generally help you narrow down your list. They're also invaluable when it comes to translating medical jargon into everyday language and to finding sources that may assist in extending your search.

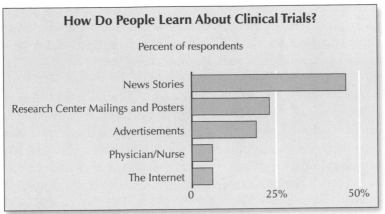

How Do People Learn About Clinical Trials?

Percent of respondents

Source: Harris Interactive/BBK Healthcare Survey of 5,348 People, 2001

Libraries. Public libraries, college and university libraries, pharmacy libraries and hospital medical libraries are all terrific sources of information on trials and investigational drugs. Many libraries subscribe to the "Gale Group's Health & Wellness Resource Center" database, which has journal articles on study drugs and how they're faring in clinical trials. University libraries often subscribe to *Dialog*, a leading provider of online health information. The libraries of hospitals and universities with an affiliated medical center are both particularly good sources of print editions of medical journals that carry news of drugs under development and the latest study results. Hospital libraries tend also to be good places to find trial-listing pamphlets for big research centers like the Mayo Clinic and Johns Hopkins.

But medical libraries aren't always accessible to the public. If they are, they may be open at odd hours and staffed by volunteers rather than a trained medical librarian. The ability to order full-text medical articles from services like MEDLINE (for about $8 to $10) may be limited to staff physicians. But for anyone without a home computer, public libraries generally provide free access to all sorts of helpful online databases, medical journals, major newspapers and web sites (discussed below). Those that have a research librarian on staff will even do the search for you, but there may be a fee.

Online databases. Some great databases, such as those offered by The Dialog Corporation and The Gale Group, are available only by subscription and are out of the price range of most home computer users. But there are many others available, for free, over the public access Internet. These include databases offered by CenterWatch, the National Library of Medicine, pharmaceutical companies and professional societies. All are discussed in more detail below.

Web sites. The web has become an extremely valuable way to find information about clinical trials. Pharmaceutical companies, professional associations, non-profit organizations and research institutes all provide varying levels of online information about clinical trials and investigational drugs. Many general health web sites also periodically run articles about drugs in development, though the content is of mixed quality and reliability. (See "Most Popular Health Web Sites," below.) There are more than a dozen web sites that focus on listing clinical trials.

One of the best ways to look for information online is to do a keyword search. Simply enter a search term, like "clinical trial," to single out documents and materials that contain these specific words. Putting them in quotation marks turns up only entries where two words are found together in a phrase. Try several different forms, and combination, of words—such as "clinical trials," "clinical research," "experimental drug," and "study drugs"—because each search may turn up considerably different results. If you find an article that seems to provide what you're looking for, cross-reference the researchers listed or drugs used to find other relevant articles. You can also search for drugs and trials by typing in the name of a particular disease, like "mesothelioma" (an incurable cancer).

Research centers. Plan to contact local clinical research centers with expertise in your medical condition. Some of these centers may be advertising for trials that they are currently recruiting for. Research centers that are not actively recruiting for their own trials may know about those going on at other locations near you. Some centers, however, may not be comfortable referring you to their competitors.

You can identify research centers in a variety of ways. Your physician or nurse, and even friends and family, may know of reputable centers. The phone book may also contain listings. Many research centers have their own web sites and, they may be linked to academic health centers if they are an affiliate. The CenterWatch web site (www.centerwatch.com) has an online list of more than 750 research centers that you can search. You may find several centers conducting trials near you for your specific medical condition that you can contact directly by phone or email.

Drug experts. Once you learn the name of a specific investigational drug (or its number, if it's very new), you might try calling the pharmaceutical company that manufactures it for more information—or an outside pharmacologist with some expertise in the therapeutic area it targets. Some pharmaceutical companies offer toll-free information lines for patients. When perusing through medical journals and newspaper clips about an investigational drug, you should jot down the names of scientists who authored the papers or offered commentary on the drug's prospects and limitations.

Consider tapping into your support network to help cover all the bases. It also wouldn't be a bad idea to cultivate a relationship with someone in the media with access to a newswire service. Announcements about new clinical trials, and recent trial results, are routinely posted. Only a fraction of those announcements make it into the editorial section of most local newspapers.

Trial Listings on the Web

One of the top information sources on the Internet is the CenterWatch Clinical Trials Listing Service (www.centerwatch.com), which each year provides an online listing of more than 42,000 clinical trials—industry- and government-sponsored trials—that can be searched by location or disease category. The CenterWatch Patient Notification Service offers patients, their family and friends an opportunity to receive a free and confidential email message every time a new trial is listed on the CenterWatch web site. Patients can sign up for notification at www.centerwatch.com. Several thousand patients are notified each week of new trials listed. CenterWatch also has databases of drugs in clinical trials and clinical trial results. Many professional societies and associations that list trials on their web site draw their information from the CenterWatch databases. In 2002, an estimated 8 million patients and their advocates will refer to CenterWatch clinical trials information on the Internet. The CenterWatch web site has been listing clinical trials since 1995, making it the oldest and largest source for information on industry-sponsored clinical trials.

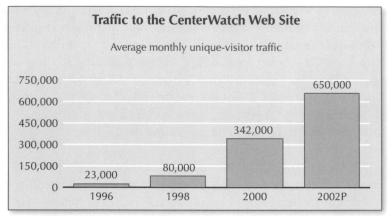

Traffic to the CenterWatch Web Site

Average monthly unique-visitor traffic

Source: CenterWatch

The National Institutes of Health lists many thousands of government-funded studies through the National Library of Medicine at (www.clinicaltrials.gov). Other web sites offering listings of clinical trials include AmericasDoctor (www.americasdoctor.com), Veritas Medicine (www.veritasmedicine.com), Acurian (www.acurian.com), Clinical Trial Directory (www.clinicaltrialdirectory.com), DrugDev 123 (www.drugdev123.com), Drug Study Central (www.drugstudy-central.com), and Pharmaceutical Research Plus (www.clinicaltrials.com). Many web sites tend to list government-funded clinical research studies, some of which are studies that look at tissue samples, treatments already on the market and behavioral programs, so they are not all clinical trials. And some web sites—including Acurian, Veritas Medicine and EmergingMed.com (www.emergingmed.com)—also provide matching services where they can actively recruit you for their clients' trials. This service may be particularly helpful for patients suffering from severe illnesses for which they do not have time to conduct a search on their own.

Web sites, including Acurian and Veritas Medicine, usually offer online registration for the purpose of pre-screening study subjects for trials and "matching" them with an appropriate clinical trial. Typically, these web sites receive a fee of $300 to more than $1,000 for matching you with a clinical trial sponsored by one of their client companies. It remains to be seen how receptive people are to this approach and how these web sites plan to deal with privacy issues. At this time, the vast majority of people conducting searches on the Internet are not comfortable divulging personal medical information online.

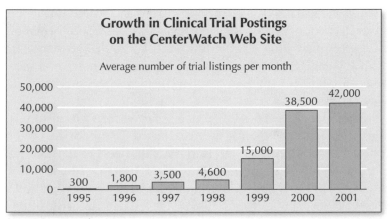

Growth in Clinical Trial Postings on the CenterWatch Web Site

Average number of trial listings per month

Source: CenterWatch, 2001

When considering the use of a matching service, remember that these companies receive incentives to enroll you in specific trials, not to provide you with a comprehensive list of trials. As a result, they may match you with a trial that isn't as good an option as others outside of their listings.

A number of health information sites, including WebMD (www.webmd.com) and TrialsCentral (www.trialscentral.org), offer general information and links for patients seeking clinical trials. Patient support groups also share information about clinical trials over the Internet.

For cancer-related trials, one of the best listings is at PDQ® (Physicians Data Query), accessible from the National Cancer Institute's (NCI's) web site (www.cancer.gov/cancer_information). You can also go to www.cancer.gov/clinical_trials. The same information, along with personal assistance in searching for an appropriate trial, is available by calling the NCI's Cancer Information Service at (800) 422-6237. The HopeLink Clinical Trial Service (www.hopelink. com) is networked with more than 20 organizations that offer cancer studies. Recently, HopeLink teamed up with Angel Flight America to offer free, private flights to patients who pre-screen for a clinical trial through their listing service and later wish to participate in the trial. The intent is to make the geographic limitations of getting into trials less of a problem.

If you are seeking studies specific to HIV and AIDS, you might want to start your search with the AIDS Clinical Trials Information Service, accessible by the web (www.actis.org) or by dialing (800) 874-2572. ACRC, a non-profit organization addressing the needs of under-served communities, also has a few gene therapy trials listed at its site (www.acrc.org).

Studies of investigational treatments and vaccines for infectious, immunologic and allergic diseases conducted or supported by the National Institute of Allergy and Infectious Diseases (a branch of the NIH) can be found at the NIAID Clinical Trials Database (www. niaid.nih.gov). The NIH's Office of Rare Diseases also has links from its site to many different clinical trials databases (visit http:// rarediseases.info.nih.gov). Some specialty medical groups and non-profit associations also list trials seeking enrollees on their web site, as do some of the sites sponsored by self-help groups and pharmaceutical companies. We have provided a list of health association web addresses in the appendix.

URAC is a Washington, D.C.-based health accreditation organization, also known as the American Accreditation Healthcare Commission, which measures general health web sites against rigorous standards for quality of information and ethical accountability. Of the 13 health web sites that have received URAC's seal of approval, five contain helpful information about clinical trials and investigational treatments. URAC-accredited web sites with clinical trials information include InteliHealth (www.intelihealth.com); Laurus

Health (VHA) (www.laurushealth.com); Veritas Medicine (www.veritasmedicine.com); WebMD (www.webmd.com); and WellMed (www.wellmed.com). It is important to note that in order to be accredited, a web site must pay several thousand dollars in commissions or fees to URAC. As a result, this list is somewhat biased.

Amgen, a biotechnology company, has devoted an entire section of its web site (www.amgen.com) to clinical trials for medical conditions ranging from recurrent cancer to juvenile rheumatoid arthritis. A brief description of the study's purpose is preceded by a comprehensive explanation of the disease condition. Contact information is provided to places where the trials are taking place. Visitors can also email Amgen with questions about the trials directly from the web site.

Abbott Laboratories (www.abbott.com) web site also has an excellent clinical trials section that provides information on research as well as a state-by-state listing of trials for 15 different medical conditions.

A list of hundreds of other biotechnology and pharmaceutical companies is provided in the appendix. These companies can be excellent sources of information on developing drugs.

The Endocrine Society has partnered with CenterWatch to offer the Endocrine Clinical Trials Network, which offers information on drugs in clinical trials as well as the trials themselves. The same information can be found at the Hormone Foundation site (www.hormone.org). You can log on to the American Gastroenterological Association site (www.gastro.org) for links to information on 4,000 trials pulled from NIH and FDA databases. Or you can go to the American Liver Foundation's site (www.liverfoundation.org) for information and links to most major clinical trial listing services. The National Alliance for the Mentally Ill (www.nami.org) lists clinical trials that have been reviewed by the group's research department.

The FDA and the National Institute on Aging jointly run the Alzheimer's Disease Clinical Trials Database (www.alzheimers.org/trials/index.html). It's accessible from the Alzheimer's Association web site (www.alz.org), which also separately lists trials that are currently recruiting volunteers. The government sponsors most of these studies. The American Health Assistance Foundation (www.ahaf.org), which funds Alzheimer's research, has linked itself to all the major clinical trial listing services. It also publishes drug development news on Alzheimer's disease, glaucoma, macular degeneration, heart disease and stroke.

Many major research centers, such as the Diabetes Research Institute in Hollywood, Fla. (www.drinet.org) and the City of Hope in Duarte, Calif. (a comprehensive cancer center, at www.cityofhope.org), also post information about the trials that they are conducting on their web site.

The Black Health Network (www.blackhealthnetwork.com) and the Association of Black Cardiologists (ABC) (www.abcardio.org) both contain valuable clinical trials information, but ABC's web site has no clinical trials listings. ABC's web site has an excellent online brochure called "The African-American Guide to Clinical Trials," which covers how participants are protected, how clinical trials work, what to expect and how to decide whether or not to participate.

Drug Information

If you are starting your search by first identifying investigational drugs, you will find no shortage of information online. Major newspapers are all available online. The science and technology sections of *The New York Times*, *The Wall Street Journal* and the *Los Angeles Times* are particularly reputable sources of information on drugs.

There are also many web sites to visit. The Pharmaceutical Research and Manufacturers of America has a great web site (www.newmedicines.org) that discusses new drugs under development and the companies that are developing them.

The American Society for Pharmacology and Experimental Therapeutics (www.aspet.org), though designed for clinical investigators, provides links to dozens of pharmacology-related web sites. The most useful links include the American Association of Pharmaceutical Scientists, Bio, BioMedNet, Drug Discovery Online Newsletter and HMS Beagle. The site also offers a link to a directory of pharmacology departments worldwide (including names and emails), where you can try to get your drug questions answered directly.

The American Heart Association (www.americanheart.org) has a wealth of information on research under way on treatments for cardiovascular disease and stroke, as well as the full text of several useful online journals. The American Diabetes Association (www.diabetes.org) offers a free online publication, *Diabetes E-News*, which contains stories on drugs in clinical trials. The American Society on Aging (www.asaging.org) sometimes runs helpful articles on developing drugs for conditions like osteoporosis. Anyone willing to pay $20 annually to become a member of Children of Aging Parents, www.caps4caregivers.org or (800) 227-7294, will get a newsletter that occasionally announces clinical trials of interest to its readers. BreastLink (www.breastlink.org) features lots of helpful drug development news, as well as a list of upcoming breast cancer conferences. Imaginis (www.imaginis.com) provides access to a number of general and breast cancer-related medical journals and offers a free breast health newsletter with information on newly published medical studies. Check with the health associations for your specific medical condition to see if they publish information on new medical treatments either online or in print form.

Associations and advocacy group web sites are also valuable resources. The Arthritis Foundation (www.arthritis.org) reports on the latest important research advances in rheumatology, including chronic fatigue syndrome, back pain and osteoporosis. It also provides information on lupus researchers that they are funding.

The National Foundation for Infectious Diseases (www.nfid.org) makes online announcements of annual conferences on vaccine research and provides access to vaccine research abstracts. Medscape (www.medscape.com) is a free and authoritative site for news in virtually every therapeutic area. You should go to the medical professional section and scroll down and click on "pharmacotherapy." Once there, you can find your way to the journal room, where you'll have access to the content of *Clinical Drug Investigation*, which publishes information about drugs in all phases of drug discovery and development.

Doctors pay hundreds of dollars every year for access to a database of medical journals. But many of them—including the venerable *New England Journal of Medicine (NEJM)* and *Drug Topics*, which covers new drugs in the pipeline and who's making them—are available at no cost online. The list of free medical journals online continues to grow. These online versions include, in many cases, the full text of articles—not just abstracts. They can be accessed on the web at www.freemedicaljournals.com.

The National Library of Medicine (www.nlm.nih.gov/nlmhome. html) offers some of the largest and best-known databases. These include MEDLINE, which provides citations and abstracts from over 4,600 biomedical journals worldwide, and MEDLINEplus, an easier-to-use version that also offers access to top consumer health libraries and organizations. AIDS and HIV information is best sought through the Library's Specialized Information Services. BioMedNet (www. bmn.com) offers free access to journal abstracts, as well as next-day news from major scientific conferences and a database of reviewed biomedical web sites used by clinical investigators. Articles appearing in top-notch medical journals can also be viewed from News-Directory.com (www.newsdirectory.com) under both the subjects of "medical" and "pharmacy." These include some articles appearing in *Applied Clinical Trials*—otherwise distributed primarily at industry trade shows.

One of the most comprehensive sites is MedBioWorld (www.sci-encekomm.at). It is the largest resource for medical and bioscience journals, associations and databases. The available publications include abstracts and even some full-text articles appearing in the *Journal of the American Medical Association (JAMA)*. There are several dozen pharmacology databases alone, including New Medicines in Development, the CenterWatch clinical trial listings and other clinical trial listings. In fact, there are links to many general and specialty trial listing services. You can also do a search for medical conferences.

Offline Resources

CenterWatch's directory of clinical trials is now available in print form through select public and specialty medical libraries. It is published four times a year. If you are having difficulty conducting your search online, you may want to use this reference. Many newsletters also list trials, especially those focused on cancer and AIDS. Newsletter publishers include government agencies, universities and even some health maintenance organizations.

CenterWatch publishes a series of illness-specific reports called *New Medical Therapies*. These reports are updated at least once a year and provide an overview of ongoing clinical research activity by disease, including a summary of different treatments under development, results of completed trials and listings of trials currently being conducted. The *CenterWatch Monthly* and *CenterWatch Weekly* newsletters also list drugs about to enter new clinical trials. Many of these publications can be found at pharmaceutical company and institution libraries. You can also contact local research centers to review their copies of these newsletters. The CenterWatch newsletters and reports are described in detail at the online bookstore at (www.centerwatch.com).

Finding a trial is sometimes just a matter of asking around. Some people learn about trials through friends or relatives who work at a research site or know someone who does. If there are research centers in your area, you can also call the sites to see what kinds of trials are currently under way. Your family physicians may alert you to upcoming trials, although some doctors are reluctant to make referrals to studies where they do not control care and treatment. Self-help and support groups also tend to be very good about alerting members to the latest studies and how to contact sponsor companies and research centers.

Medical libraries tend to be good places to look for information on studies and research results to date. The science reference section of most university libraries is likely to have *The Merck Index*, an encyclopedia of drugs and biologicals—including the most important ones in phase II and III clinical trials. The print version provides information on chemical, common and generic names; associated companies; literature references; toxicity data; and statements about each drug's scientific significance. *The Merck Index* has limited value because it is updated infrequently. As a result, unless you're looking at a recently published edition, the information may be out of date.

College campuses are often worth scouting out for news about clinical studies happening there or at a nearby research hospital. The hospital can also provide a great deal of useful information. But you can't necessarily count on the colleges for much up-to-date information on ailments that are uncommon among student-age populations.

A surprising number of patients attend scientific meetings and professional medical conferences where the latest research is being discussed. The fees are sometimes steep—$300 to $500—but you may walk away with a wealth of information from hallway conversations with physicians and leading scientists. The conferences aren't all held in large cities. Most major health associations and medical societies list the calendars of conferences and upcoming events in their newsletters and web sites. A list of association web sites is included in the appendix. Contact these associations to learn about their conferences and meetings.

Most non-profit associations, like the Alzheimer's Association and the American Heart Association, put out annual reports filled with news about promising new drugs in the development pipeline. They're always happy to put interested patients and their caregivers on the mailing list. Online versions of the reports, while often available, may be abbreviated or tough to read using slow computers.

Some libraries still carry print editions of major newspapers, such as *The New York Times*, that regularly carry news (and often many ads about) drugs under study. Engel Publishing Partners (West Trenton, N.J.) puts out a magazine called *R & D Directions* that offers write-ups on drugs that pharmaceutical companies are developing. F-D-C (Chevy Chase, Md.), a division of Elsevier-Sciences, also publishes several valuable magazines and directories of drugs under development. F-D-C's book, *The NDA Pipeline*, contains profiles of drugs, their research phase and manufacturer by major disease categories.

These magazines and directories are very expensive. However, you may be able to access them through medical and pharmaceutical company libraries.

It might also be a good idea for you to ask your cardiologist or primary care doctor to take a peek at the front of the *PDR Monthly Subscribing Guide* (by Thomson Healthcare, publishers of the *Physicians' Desk Reference*). A special section entitled "In the Pipeline" is now devoted to new drugs in later-stage clinical trials. This may be another good point for you to begin your search.

How Research Finds You

Studies aren't hard to find, even for those people not actively looking to participate. Studies are regularly advertised in newspapers and on the radio and TV. They're posted on bulletin boards in community centers and physician waiting rooms. Call centers now routinely contact homes soliciting volunteers. Trials are also detailed in direct-mail brochures, discussed at patient support group meetings and health fairs, and personally offered as treatment options by thousands of investigators across all 50 states.

Major medical centers and doctors doing research part time generally look to patients in their practice for studies. These centers use direct mail, flyers in their offices and even receptionists who quickly schedule patients who happen to call in with a relevant complaint. Some centers look for potential subjects at free screening programs and health fairs. Other research centers rely heavily on referrals from related clinics or offices, or informal word of mouth. Research centers that are dedicated to conducting clinical trials are more apt to employ mass media approaches to reaching the patient community. If they're large enough, some centers may have several people on staff who are on the phone night and day trying to solicit patients for studies.

Pharmaceutical companies will sometimes hire a patient recruitment company to develop national advertising campaigns to reach health consumers directly, particularly for large clinical trials.

Breaking the Ice

There is no set way that discussions with a study site begin. After learning about a clinical trial, most people telephone the research center directly. But you may prefer to contact a center by email, or to show up at the center in person. None of these approaches is inappropriate. It's a matter of preference.

Regardless of your approach, you should plan to deal directly with the study coordinator at the research center. In most centers, coordinators handle most patient recruitment responsibilities, along with the daily research study activities. It pays to get to know the study coordinator early and by name.

Once you've identified several clinical trials, and made initial inquiries into whether those trials are appropriate, you and your support network are now ready to carefully learn about and evaluate the best clinical trial opportunities for you.

AFTERWORD

Throughout the United States, a growing number of people want to learn about clinical trials for a wide variety of medical conditions. In 2002, for example, an estimated 10 million to 12 million people will contact research centers for information about clinical trials and the thousands of medical treatments that have yet to receive approval from the Food and Drug Administration.

Like these people, you or a loved one may be interested in volunteering for a clinical trial because you want to help researchers understand how to treat diseases in the future. You may be looking for better medical treatment yet you don't have health insurance. You may be looking to receive free medical care. You may not be happy with your current treatment and would like to try a new therapy that is only accessible through a clinical trial.

Patients and their advocates, health professionals—even the general public—are far more aware today of the importance of knowing about investigational drugs and therapies when considering their treatment options. Every year, millions of people participate in industry- and government-sponsored trials with the promise of excellent quality care and, often, with the hope of a better treatment alternative than that which is currently available to them. In some cases, clinical trials may offer access to treatments that can dramatically improve and extend the lives of people suffering from serious and chronic illnesses. And in some instances, clinical trials have offered life-saving alternatives to people facing severe and terminal diseases.

Although there is promise and hope, there are numerous risks in clinical research studies. The clinical research process is highly regulated, it is managed by very experienced professionals and it has many built-in safeguards to help ensure a safe and positive volunteer experience. But, even the most well-run clinical trials are never completely free of risk.

Informed Consent™*: A Consumer's Guide to the Risks and Benefits of Participating in Clinical Trials* was written to provide the facts and information that you need to know before choosing whether or not to participate in a clinical study. We hope that you have found this book useful and that you, your family and friends will refer to it often for insight and guidance into the clinical trial process, your rights as a volunteer and the many ways that your rights are protected.

Choosing to be a volunteer in a clinical trial takes a great deal of courage and conviction. It also takes a lot of time and effort to gather the facts and information thoroughly and to weigh your many options thoughtfully. But the decision to participate in a clinical trial is not one that you should make alone. It is a team effort. In order to make a truly informed decision, you need to involve your family and friends, your physician and nurse, the clinical investigator and study staff.

We welcome your feedback and comments. Please send us an email at **cw.informedconsent@centerwatch.com** with your thoughts and ideas. Tell us what questions of yours were not well answered and what was missing. Tell us what you liked and disliked about the book, and how we can make future editions better. You can also visit our web site—www.centerwatch.com—to learn more about the many publications and services that we have developed for patients and their advocates and research and health professionals.

The discovery of life-saving and life-enhancing new treatments requires a partnership that is based on communication and trust between researchers, health professionals, and patients. Your responsibility as a volunteer is essential to the progress of all clinical research programs. And your role in this partnership begins with your informed consent.

—Ken Getz & Deborah Borfitz

Glossary of Terms

Adverse Drug Reaction (ADR)
An unintended reaction to a drug taken at normal doses. In clinical trials, an ADR would include any injuries due to overdosing, abuse/dependence and unintended interactions with other medical treatments.

Adverse Event (AE)
A negative experience encountered by a volunteer during the course of a clinical trial, that is associated with the drug. An AE can include previously undetected symptoms, or the exacerbation of a pre-existing condition. When an AE has been determined to be related to the investigational drug, it is considered an Adverse Drug Reaction.

Biologic
A virus, therapeutic serum, toxin, antitoxin, vaccine, blood, blood component or derivative, allergenic product, or analogous product applicable to the prevention, treatment or cure of human diseases or injuries.

Biotechnology
Any technique that uses living organisms, or substances from organisms, biological systems, or processes to make or modify a product or process, to change plants or animals, or to develop micro-organisms for specific uses.

Blinding

The process through which one or more parties involved in a clinical trial are unaware of the treatment assignments. In a single-blinded study, usually the volunteers are unaware of the treatment assignments. In a double-blinded study, both volunteers and the investigator are unaware of the treatment assignments. Also, in a double-blinded study, the monitors and sometimes the data analysts are unaware. "Blinded" studies are conducted to prevent the unintentional biases that can affect subject data when treatment assignments are known.

Case Report Form (CRF)

A record of pertinent information collected on each volunteer during a clinical trial, as outlined in the study protocol.

Clinical Investigation

A systematic study designed to evaluate a product (drug, device, or biologic) using human subjects, in the treatment, prevention, or diagnosis of a disease or condition, as determined by the product's benefits relative to its risks. Clinical investigations can only be conducted with the approval of the Food and Drug Administration (FDA).

Clinical Trial

Any investigation in human subjects intended to determine the clinical pharmacological, pharmacokinetic, and/or other pharmacodynamic effects of an investigational agent, and/or to identify any adverse reactions to an investigational agent to assess the agent's safety and efficacy.

Control Group

The comparison group of subjects who are not treated with the investigational agent. The volunteers in this group may receive no therapy, a different therapy, or a placebo.

Data Management
The process of handling the data gathered during a clinical trial. May also refer to the department responsible for managing data entry and database generation and/or maintenance.

Declaration of Helsinki
A series of guidelines adopted by the 18th World Medical Assembly in Helsinki, Finland in 1964. Address ethical issues for physicians conducting biomedical research involving human subjects. Recommendations include the procedures required to ensure subject safety in clinical trials, including informed consent and Ethics Committee reviews.

Demographic Data
Refers to the characteristics of study participants, including sex, age, family medical history, and other characteristics relevant to the study in which they are enrolled.

Device
An instrument, apparatus, implement, machine, contrivance, implant, in vitro reagent, or other similar or related article, including any component, part or accessory, which is intended for use in the diagnosis, cure, treatment or prevention of disease. A device does not achieve its intended purpose through chemical action in the body and is not dependent upon being metabolized to achieve its purpose.

Double-Blind
The design of a study in which neither the investigator nor the volunteer knows which medication (or placebo) the volunteer is receiving.

Drug
As defined by the Food, Drug and Cosmetic Act, drugs are "articles (other than food) intended for the use in the diagnosis, cure, mitigation, treatment, or prevention of disease in man or other animals, or to affect the structure or any function of the body of man or other animals."

Drug Product
A final dosage form (e.g. table, capsule, or solution) that contains the active drug ingredient usually combined with inactive ingredients.

Effective Dose
The dose of an investigational agent that produces the outcome considered "effective," as defined in the study protocol. This could mean a cure of the disease in question or simply the mitigation of symptoms.

Efficacy
A product's ability to produce beneficial effects on the duration or course of a disease. Efficacy is measured by evaluating the clinical and statistical results of clinical tests.

Ethical Review Board
An independent group of both medical and non-medical professionals who are responsible for verifying the integrity of a study and ensuring the safety, integrity, and human rights of the study participants.

Exclusion Criteria
Refers to the characteristics that would prevent a subject from participating in a clinical trial, as outlined in the study protocol.

Food and Drug Administration (FDA)
A US government agency responsible for ensuring compliance with the Food, Drug, and Cosmetics Act of 1938. All drugs sold in the U.S. must receive marketing approval from the FDA.

Formulation
The mixture of chemicals and/or biological substances and excipients used to prepare dosage forms. An excipient is a substance that is basically inert. It is used in a prescription to help give a drug its proper form.

Generic Drug
A medicinal product with the same active ingredient, but not necessarily the same inactive ingredients as a brand-name drug. A generic drug may only be marketed after the original drug's patent has expired.

Good Clinical Practice (GCP)
The FDA has established regulations and guidelines that specify the responsibilities of sponsors, investigators, monitors, and IRBs involved in clinical drug testing. These regulations are meant to protect the safety, rights and welfare of the patients in addition to ensuring the accuracy of the collected study data.

Human Subject
A human subject as an individual who voluntarily is or becomes a participant in research, either as a recipient of the test article or as a control. A subject may be either a healthy human or a patient.

Inclusion Criteria
A list of criteria that must be met in order to participate in a clinical trial.

In Vitro Testing
Non-clinical testing conducted in an artificial environment such as a test tube or culture medium.

In Vivo Testing
Testing conducted in living animal and human systems.

Informed Consent
The voluntary verification of a patient's willingness to participate in a clinical trial, along with documentation. This verification is requested only after complete, objective information has been provided about the trial, including an explanation of the study's objectives, potential benefits, and risks and inconveniences, alternative therapies available, and of the volunteer's rights and responsibilities in accordance with the current revision of the Declaration of Helsinki.

Institutional Review Board (IRB)
An independent group of professionals designated to review and approve the clinical protocol, informed consent forms, study advertisements, and patient brochures, to ensure that the study is safe and effective for human participation. It is also the IRB's responsibility to ensure that the study adheres to the FDA's regulations.

Investigational New Drug Application (IND)
The petition through which a drug sponsor requests the FDA to allow human testing of its drug product.

Investigator
A medical professional, usually a physician but may also be a nurse, pharmacist or other health care professional, under whose direction an investigational drug is administered or dispensed. A principal investigator is responsible for the overall conduct of the clinical trial at his or her site.

Longitudinal Study
A study conducted over a long period of time.

MedWatch Program
An FDA program designed to monitor adverse events (AE) from drugs marketed in the U.S. Through the MedWatch program, health professionals may report AEs voluntarily to the FDA. Drug manufacturers are required to report all AEs brought to their attention.

New Drug Application (NDA)
The compilation of all nonclinical, clinical, pharmacological, pharmacokinetic and stability information required about a drug by the FDA in order to approve the drug for marketing in the U.S.

Nuremberg Code
As a result of the medical experimentation conducted by Nazis during World War II, the U.S. Military Tribunal in Nuremberg in 1947 set forth a code of medical ethics for researchers conducting clinical trials. The code is designed to protect the safety and integrity of study participants.

Off Label
The unauthorized use of a drug for a purpose other than that approved of by the FDA.

Open-Label Study

A study in which all parties, (patient, physician and study coordinator) are informed of the drug and dose being administered. In an open-label study, none of the participants are given placebos. These are usually conducted with Phase I & II studies.

Orphan Drug

A designation of the FDA to indicate a therapy developed to treat a rare disease (one which afflicts a U.S. population of less than 200,000 people). Because there are few financial incentives for drug companies to develop therapies for diseases that afflict so few people, the U.S. government offers additional incentives to drug companies (i.e. tax advantages and extended marketing exclusivity) that develop these drugs.

Over-the-Counter (OTC)

Drugs available for purchase without a physician's prescription.

Pharmacoeconomics

The study of cost-benefit ratios of drugs with other therapies or with similar drugs. Pharmacoeconomic studies compare various treatment options in terms of their cost, both financial and quality-of-life. Also referred to as "outcomes research".

Phase I Study

The first of four phases of clinical trials, Phase I studies are designed to establish the effects of a new drug in humans. These studies are usually conducted on small populations of healthy people to specifically determine a drug's toxicity, absorption, distribution and metabolism.

Phase II Study

After the successful completion of phase I trials, a drug is then tested for safety and efficacy in a slightly larger population of individuals who are afflicted with the disease or condition for which the drug was developed.

Phase III Study
The third and last pre-approval round of testing of a drug is conducted on large populations of afflicted patients. Phase III studies usually test the new drug in comparison with the standard therapy currently being used for the disease in question. The results of these trials usually provide the information that is included in the package insert and labeling.

Phase IV Study
After a drug has been approved by the FDA, phase IV studies are conducted to compare the drug to a competitor, explore additional patient populations, or to further study any adverse events.

Pivotal Study
Usually a phase III study which presents the data that the FDA uses to decide whether or not to approve a drug. A pivotal study will generally be well-controlled, randomized, of adequate size, and whenever possible, double-blind.

Placebo
An inactive substance designed to resemble the drug being tested. It is used as a control to rule out any psychological effects testing may present. Most well-designed studies include a control group of volunteers which is unwittingly taking a placebo.

Pre-Clinical Testing
Before a drug may be tested on humans, pre-clinical studies must be conducted either in vitro but usually in vivo on animals to determine that the drug is safe.

Protocol
A detailed plan that sets forth the objectives, study design, and methodology for a clinical trial. A study protocol must be approved by an IRB before investigational drugs may be administered to humans.

Quality Assurance
Systems and procedures designed to ensure that a study is being performed in compliance with Good Clinical Practice (GCP) guidelines and that the data being generated is accurate.

Randomization
Study participants are usually assigned to groups in such a way that each participant has an equal chance of being assigned to each treatment (or control) group. Since randomization ensures that no specific criteria are used to assign any patients to a particular group, all the groups will be equally comparable.

Regulatory Affairs
In clinical trials, the department or function that is responsible for ensuring compliance with government regulations and interacts with the regulatory agencies. Each drug sponsor has a regulatory affairs department that manages the entire drug approval process.

Serious Adverse Event (SAE)
Any adverse event (AE) that is fatal, life-threatening, permanently disabling, or which results in hospitalization, initial or prolonged.

Sponsor
Person or entity who initiates and takes responsibility for a clinical study. This is often a pharmaceutical company, but can also be a medical device manufacturer, government agency, academic institution, private organization, or even an individual researcher.

Standard Operating Procedure (SOP)
Official, detailed, written instructions for the management of clinical trials. SOPs ensure that all the functions and activities of a clinical trial are carried out in a consistent and efficient manner.

Standard Treatment
The currently accepted treatment or intervention considered to be effective in the treatment of a specific disease or condition.

Study Coordinator
The individual who assists the principal investigator and who runs the clinical trial. This person may also be called clinical research coordinator, research nurse, or protocol nurse.

Treatment IND
A method through which the FDA allows seriously ill patients with no acceptable therapeutic alternative to access promising investigational drugs still in clinical development. The drug must show "sufficient evidence of safety and effectiveness." In recent decades many AIDs patients have been able to access unapproved therapies through this program.

A History of Regulations Affecting Patient Protection in Clinical Research

1938

Federal Food, Drug, and Cosmetic Act

New law requires pharmaceutical companies to submit to the U.S. Food and Drug Administration (FDA) evidence of drug safety, in the form of a new drug application (NDA), before marketing a drug. The catalyst is 107 human deaths attributed to a liquid preparation of the first sulfa drug used to treat certain infectious bacteria, including pneumonia and strep throat.

1946

AMA Code of Ethics

Responding to concerns about research abuses, the American Medical Association adopts its first code of research ethics for physicians.

1947

Nuremberg Code

In reaction to atrocities committed by German scientists during World War II, the Nuremberg Military Tribunal writes a set of ten principles for research involving human participants, including an absolute requirement for informed consent. Primary responsibility for the ethical conduct of research placed on investigators.

1961

First Investigator investigation
FDA starts a file of clinical investigators "who have contributed incredible reports to NDAs." The first to be investigated is a general practitioner who had undertaken clinical trials on adults, infants, and children for 25 different drug companies. It was discovered that he mostly fabricated study results from his kitchen table. In subsequent years, the FDA investigated researchers who neglected any number of their responsibilities, including seeing study subjects and reporting adverse events.

1962

Kefauver-Harris Amendments to the Food, Drug and Cosmetic Act
Changes in federal regulations are triggered by a thalidomide trial that caused women who took the experimental drug during their first trimester of pregnancy to give birth to deformed babies. The amendment requires drug manufacturers to prove effectiveness before marketing any new product and researchers to obtain informed consent of study subjects and report adverse events. FDA placed in supervisory position. With the Act's passage, the number of new drug approvals fell dramatically.

1963

Investigational Drug Regulations
New regulations establish the Investigational New Drug (IND) application, detailed plans pharmaceutical companies must submit to the FDA before starting human testing of their drug products. Companies must now prove efficacy as well as safety before a drug will be approved for marketing. They also must submit to the FDA-proposed study protocols, the names and qualifications of investigators who are to conduct those studies and the identity of research sites to be used.

Certification of informed consent
FDA regulations enacted this year also require clinical investigators to certify to sponsors of drug research that informed consent would be obtained in accordance with the 1962 amendments.

1964

Declaration of Helsinki
World Medical Association issues 32-point statement of ethical principles defining the rules for "therapeutic" and "non-therapeutic" research. Repeats many of the requirements in the Nuremberg Code but allows certain patients to be enrolled in therapeutic research without consent. Also allows legal guardians to grant permission to enroll subjects in research.

1966

HHS policy of independent review
The U.S. Department of Health and Human Services (HHS) requires independent review of research it funds by a committee of the investigator's "institutional associates." Review is to include, among other things, appropriateness of the methods used to secure informed consent.

FDA consent requirements
FDA requires consent in all non-therapeutic drug studies and in all but exceptional cases of therapeutic application of an experimental drug.

Beecher article
Henry Beecher publishes an article outlining 22 examples of "unethical or questionably ethical studies" appearing in mainstream medical journals, including the ingestion of the hepatitis virus into retarded children at Willowbrook State school in New York.

AMA ethical guidelines
Ethical guidelines for clinical investigation are adopted by the AMA.

1967

Division of Scientific Investigations
A new division of the FDA is created to do inspections of the work of clinical investigators, using the previously established suspect list, prison-based testing operations and requests by IND and NDA reviewers.

Changes to FDA consent regulations
FDA permits oral informed consent in certain situations and clarifies the information that needs to be given to subjects, including whether they might receive a placebo.

1971

Institutional Review Boards (IRBs)
FDA regulations require studies involving experimental drugs and biologics performed on institutionalized human subjects to receive review and approval by an institutional review board (IRB).

1972

Office for Protection from Research Risks (OPRR)
OPRR, housed within the National Institutes of Health (NIH), was established to protect participants in research conducted or sponsored by HHS. This is the same year details emerged about the Public Health Service's (PHS's) natural history study of syphilis in poor, black males in Alabama who were misled into believing they were receiving treatment. The FDA also reiterates that a drug study's sponsor must play a more active role in monitoring trials and in making sure that researchers are competent and understand their obligations.

1974

HHS human subjects protection regulations
Researchers are required to get voluntary informed consent from all persons taking part in studies done or federally funded by HHS.

National Research Act
The National Research Act, an amendment to the Public Health Services Act, establishes the National Commission for the Protection of Human Subjects in Biomedical and Behavioral Research (the National Commission), charged with identifying basic principles of research conduct and suggesting ways to ensure those principles are followed. IRBs were established as one subject protection method for federally funded research. The motivation is mistakes made in the PHS syphilis study.

1975

Helsinki Accords
The United States and 34 other nations sign the Declaration of Helsinki and recommendations guiding the moral treatment of patients in biomedical research. Responsibility for trial conduct is put on the shoulders of physician investigators.

Special protections for pregnant women
Special protections pertaining to federally funded research involving fetuses, pregnant women and human in vitro fertilization is adopted by HHS. IRBs are directed to give adequate consideration to the manner in which potential subjects are selected and informed consent is handled. Research involving pregnant women is limited to trials that intend to meet the mother's health needs and put the fetus at no more risk than necessary to meet those needs.

Acceptance of foreign studies
The FDA accepts non-U.S. clinical studies as primary evidence for U.S. marketing approval of drugs for a major health gain, uncommon disease or a strikingly favorable ratio of benefit to risk.

1976

GAO report/Expanded bioresearch monitoring

Using data from an earlier FDA survey, the General Accounting Office (GAO) concludes that human test subjects and the public are not being adequately protected. The FDA is infused with funding to expand bioresearch monitoring and come up with regulations and compliance programs.

1977

Bioresearch Monitoring Program

FDA expands on-site reviews of IRBs to include clinical investigators, research sponsors, study monitors and non-clinical (animal) laboratories. The intent is less about noncompliance than ensuring the quality of data submitted to the FDA and protection of human subjects of research.

Inclusion of women

FDA guidelines forbid the inclusion of women of childbearing potential in phase I and early phase II studies, excepting those with a life-threatening disease.

1978

Special protections for prisoners

HHS gives additional protections to prisoners involved in research. Federally funded studies involving inmates now require the approval of the OPRR and must have a prisoner or prison representative sit on the IRB. Research cannot provide special advantages to prisoners, subject them to risks greater than would be accepted by nonprisoner volunteers or involve unfair selection of study subjects. While the FDA has no similar set of regulations to this day, it routinely refers researchers to these protections.

1979

Belmont Report
Ethical Principles and Guidelines for the Protection of Human Subjects of Research published in the Federal Register. Written by the National Commission, the report outlines the ethical principles of respect for persons, beneficence and justice upon which current regulations on human subject protection are based.

1981

Federal Policy for the Protection of Human Subjects in Research
Regulations of both the HHS and the FDA are revised to reflect principles contained in the Belmont Report. They ensure broad backgrounds, and community attitudes, are represented on IRBs. Specific elements of informed consent are also spelled out.

President's Commission
The President's Commission for the Study of Ethical Problems in Medicine and Biomedical and Behavioral Research is established. One of its reports recommends a uniform federal regulatory system.

1982

CIOMS Guidelines
The Council for International Organizations of Medical Sciences publishes the first version of its International Ethical Guidelines for Biomedical Research Involving Human Subjects, aimed at researchers conducting studies in developing countries. The guidelines allow for cultural differences in ethical standards.

Consent agreement process
The FDA develops a "consent agreement" process for some investigators who might otherwise be disqualified via legal channels from conducting research. Investigators generally agree to do no further studies of drugs within FDA jurisdiction or agree to some specific restric-

tion on their use of investigational drugs, such as conducting no more phase III studies.

1983

Special protections for children
HHS gives additional protections for children involved as subjects in federally funded research.

1985

NDA regulations revised
With a rewrite of NDA regulations, the FDA begins accepting foreign clinical trial data as the sole basis for drug approval—sometimes with and sometimes without the need for an on-site inspection of the research site.

1987

IND rewrite
Contract research organizations (CROs) recognized as a regulated entity and can be transferred responsibility for certain parts of a study delegated to them. Trial sponsors are also required to identify studies they have audited or reviewed when submitting an NDA.

1988

Guidelines for the monitoring of clinical investigators
FDA requires sponsors to conduct quality assurance audits of the work of clinical investigators.

1990

International Conference on Harmonization (ICH)
Government agencies and pharmaceutical trade organizations from Europe, Japan and the United States create guidelines for clinical drug trials that cross national borders.

1991

Common Rule
The common rule is agreement by 15 federal departments and agencies to adopt a common set of human subject protections. It includes required review of research by an IRB, informed consent of subjects and assurances of compliance by research institutions receiving federal support. The Common Rule has since been adopted by three additional federal agencies.

1993

Advisory Committee on Human Radiation Experiments (ACHRE)
National press coverage about Cold War-era radiation experiments leads President Clinton to establish ACHRE to investigate reports of federally funded human research involving radioactive materials conducted between 1944 and 1972. The Committee urges that federal oversight of human subject protections focus on outcomes and performance, punishment be in proportion to violation and protections broaden to include research that is not federally funded.

NIH Revitalization Act
A controversial provision in the NIH Revitalization Act requires all NIH-funded studies to include representative samples of subpopulations, including women and members of diverse racial and ethnic groups, unless their exclusion is justified.

New FDA guidelines on inclusion of women
FDA sets guidelines calling for a "reasonable" number of women to be included in all new clinical trials, reversing its 1977 policy.

1995

National Bioethics Advisory Commission
On the advice of ACHRE, President Clinton establishes think tank group composed of physicians, theologians, ethicists, scientists, lawyers, psychologists and members of the public. Their charge is to make recommendations to government regarding ethical issues surrounding research on humans. The Commission is funded and led by HHS.

NDA regulations amended
The FDA amended the Code of Federal Regulation, requiring NDAs to include analysis of efficacy and safety data by gender, age and racial subgroups.

1997

Food and Drug Administration Modernization Act
This new law gives pharmaceutical companies a huge financial incentive to conduct pediatric studies of drugs already FDA-approved for use in adults. In return for testing the efficacy and safety of drugs in children, companies are granted an extra six months of patent protection on those drugs. This Pediatric Exclusivity Provision is scheduled to expire on January 1, 2002, although federal legislators have the option of extending it. The FDA Modernization Act also expedited the development and review of applications for approval of products that treat a serious or life-threatening condition and have the potential to address an unmet medical need.

1998

FDA Financial Disclosure Regulations
FDA requires study sponsors to reveal any financial link between themselves and clinical investigators that may bias the design, conduct, or reporting of clinical studies.

Sex-related data presentation
FDA requires that safety and efficacy data be presented separately for men and women in NDA summaries. Also requires tabulation of the number of study participants by sex in investigational new drug reports.

1999

Office for Human Research Protections (OHRP)
OPRR was renamed OHRP and elevated to department status within HHS to convey the importance of the function—and to avoid the appearance of a conflict of interest (since NIH also funds studies). It assumes responsibility for protection of human research subjects at institutions receiving federal funds, as well as implementing the 18-agency Common Rule.

2000

FDA Pediatric Rule
FDA's Pediatric Rule is finalized, requiring pediatric studies on any new drug that will be, or could be, used by children. (In March 2002, the FDA announced plans to suspend the Pediatric Rule for two years. During that time period, the FDA hopes to evaluate whether the incentive provision of the FDA Modernization Act is enough to entice pharmaceutical and biotechnology companies to adequately test investigational treatments for children on a voluntary basis.)

New research-suspending authority

FDA gives itself the authority to stop proposed research for life-threatening conditions if men or women are excluded because of their reproductive potential.

Medicare coverage of clinical trials

Health Care Financing Administration (now the Centers for Medicare and Medicaid Services) adopts new policy for Medicare to cover routine costs of qualifying clinical trials, as well as reasonable and necessary items and services used to diagnose and complications arising from participation in trials. Federally funded trials and trials under an investigational new drug application reviewed by the FDA automatically qualify. The policy also applies to enrollees in both the traditional Medicare and Medicare+Choice programs.

2001

Clinical Investigation of Medicinal
Products in the Pediatric Population

FDA establishes new rule, mandated by the Children's Health Act of 2000, that sets the standards for determining whether proposed pediatric clinical trials can be safely and ethically conducted. It is the FDA's first specific protections for children. The rule seeks, among other things, to assure children assent to participate in clinical trials (when possible) and that their parents or guardians give fully informed consent to that participation. It adopts the principles, with some modifications, of HHS protections from 1983.

Public disclosure rule

FDA establishes new rule making information on all new and ongoing clinical trials involving gene therapy or xenotransplantation publicly available. Much of the gene therapy information to be disclosed is already publicly discussed in open meetings of the Recombinant DNA Advisory Committee of the NIH.

Office of Good Clinical Practice (OGCP)
OGCP was opened by he FDA in order to establish consistency in policy. This office is broadly responsible for ensuring FDA's protective role in clinical research, from trial design through trial conduct, trial analyses, trial oversight, data integrity and data quality. One of OGCP's highest priorities will be to bring about GCP compliance globally.

2002

Best Phamaceuticals for Children Act
Best Pharmaceuticals for Children Act is designed to ensure that many more drugs already on the market will continue to be carefully studied in children. The new law not only gives pharmaceutical companies longer patent protection in exchange for conducting pediatric studies; it requires them to share what they learn as a result of those studies, good or bad. If they refuse to do a study that is requested by the FDA, a third party can do it as permitted by a fundraising organization for the NIH. A competitive bidding process for $200 million in funding will be set up through the new NIH office to encourage pediatric clinical trials of older drugs whose patent has expired, meaning that generic versions of the drug are allowed to be produced.

World Medical Association Declaration of Helsinki

Ethical Principles for Medical
Research Involving Human Subjects

A. Introduction

1. The World Medical Association has developed the Declaration of Helsinki as a statement of ethical principles to provide guidance to physicians and other participants in medical research involving human subjects. Medical research involving human subjects includes research on identifiable human material or identifiable data.

2. It is the duty of the physician to promote and safeguard the health of the people. The physician's knowledge and conscience are dedicated to the fulfillment of this duty.

3. The Declaration of Geneva of the World Medical Association binds the physician with the words, "The health of my patient will be my first consideration," and the International Code of Medical Ethics declares that, "A physician shall act only in the patient's interest when providing medical care which might have the effect of weakening the physical and mental condition of the patient."

4. Medical progress is based on research which ultimately must rest in part on experimentation involving human subjects.

5. In medical research on human subjects, considerations related to the well-being of the human subject should take precedence over the interests of science and society.

6. The primary purpose of medical research involving human subjects is to improve prophylactic, diagnostic and therapeutic procedures and the understanding of the aetiology and pathogenesis of disease. Even the best proven prophylactic, diagnostic and therapeutic methods must continuously be challenged through research for their effectiveness, efficiency, accessibility and quality.
7. In current medical practice and in medical research, most prophylactic, diagnostic and therapeutic procedures involve risks and burdens.
8. Medical research is subject to ethical standards that promote respect for all human beings and protect their health and rights. Some research populations are vulnerable and need special protection. The particular needs of the economically and medically disadvantaged must be recognized. Special attention is also required for those who cannot give or refuse consent for themselves, for those who may be subject to giving consent under duress, for those who will not benefit personally from the research and for those for whom the research is combined with care.
9. Research Investigators should be aware of the ethical, legal and regulatory requirements for research on human subjects in their own countries as well as applicable international requirements. No national ethical, legal or regulatory requirement should be allowed to reduce or eliminate any of the protections for human subjects set forth in this Declaration.

B. Basic Principles for All Medical Research

10. It is the duty of the physician in medical research to protect the life, health, privacy and dignity of the human subject.
11. Medical research involving human subjects must conform to generally accepted scientific principles, be based on a thorough knowledge of the scientific literature, other relevant sources of information and on adequate laboratory and, where appropriate, animal experimentation.
12. Appropriate caution must be exercised in the conduct of research which may affect the environment, and the welfare of animals used for research must be respected.
13. The design and performance of each experimental procedure involving human subjects should be clearly formulated in an

experimental protocol. This protocol should be submitted for consideration, comment, guidance and, where appropriate, approval to a specially appointed ethical review committee, which must be independent of the investigator, the sponsor or any other kind of undue influence. This independent committee should be in conformity with the laws and regulations of the country in which the research experiment is performed. The committee has the right to monitor ongoing trials. The researcher has the obligation to provide monitoring information to the committee, especially any serious adverse events. The researcher should also submit to the committee, for review, information regarding funding, sponsors, institutional affiliations, other potential conflicts of interest and incentives for subjects.

14. The research protocol should always contain a statement of the ethical considerations involved and should indicate that there is compliance with the principles enunciated in this Declaration.

15. Medical research involving human subjects should be conducted only by scientifically qualified persons and under the supervision of a clinically competent medical person. The responsibility for the human subject must always rest with a medically qualified person and never rest on the subject of the research, even though the subject has given consent.

16. Every medical research project involving human subjects should be preceded by careful assessment of predictable risks and burdens in comparison with foreseeable benefits to the subject or to others. This does not preclude the participation of healthy volunteers in medical research. The design of all studies should be publicly available.

17. Physicians should abstain from engaging in research projects involving human subjects unless they are confident that the risks involved have been adequately assessed and can be satisfactorily managed. Physicians should cease any investigation if the risks are found to outweigh the potential benefits or if there is conclusive proof of positive and beneficial results.

18. Medical research involving human subjects should only be conducted if the importance of the objective outweighs the inherent risks and burdens to the subject. This is especially important when the human subjects are healthy volunteers.

19. Medical research is only justified if there is a reasonable likelihood that the populations in which the research is carried out stand to benefit from the results of the research.

20. The subjects must be volunteers and informed participants in the research project.

21. The right of research subjects to safeguard their integrity must always be respected. Every precaution should be taken to respect the privacy of the subject, the confidentiality of the patient's information and to minimize the impact of the study on the subject's physical and mental integrity and on the personality of the subject.

22. In any research on human beings, each potential subject must be adequately informed of the aims, methods, sources of funding, any possible conflicts of interest, institutional affiliations of the researcher, the anticipated benefits and potential risks of the study and the discomfort it may entail. The subject should be informed of the right to abstain from participation in the study or to withdraw consent to participate at any time without reprisal. After ensuring that the subject has understood the information, the physician should then obtain the subject's freely given informed consent, preferably in writing. If the consent cannot be obtained in writing, the non-written consent must be formally documented and witnessed.

23. When obtaining informed consent for the research project the physician should be particularly cautious if the subject is in a dependent relationship with the physician or may consent under duress. In that case the informed consent should be obtained by a well-informed physician who is not engaged in the investigation and who is completely independent of this relationship.

24. For a research subject who is legally incompetent, physically or mentally incapable of giving consent or is a legally incompetent minor, the investigator must obtain informed consent from the legally authorized representative in accordance with applicable law. These groups should not be included in research unless the research is necessary to promote the health of the population represented and this research cannot instead be performed on legally competent persons.

25. When a subject deemed legally incompetent, such as a minor child, is able to give assent to decisions about participation in

research, the investigator must obtain that assent in addition to the consent of the legally authorized representative.

26. Research on individuals from whom it is not possible to obtain consent, including proxy or advance consent, should be done only if the physical/mental condition that prevents obtaining informed consent is a necessary characteristic of the research population. The specific reasons for involving research subjects with a condition that renders them unable to give informed consent should be stated in the experimental protocol for consideration and approval of the review committee. The protocol should state that consent to remain in the research should be obtained as soon as possible from the individual or a legally authorized surrogate.

27. Both authors and publishers have ethical obligations. In publication of the results of research, the investigators are obliged to preserve the accuracy of the results. Negative as well as positive results should be published or otherwise publicly available. Sources of funding, institutional affiliations and any possible conflicts of interest should be declared in the publication. Reports of experimentation not in accordance with the principles laid down in this Declaration should not be accepted for publication.

C. Additional Principles for Medical Research Combined with Medical Care

28. The physician may combine medical research with medical care, only to the extent that the research is justified by its potential prophylactic, diagnostic or therapeutic value. When medical research is combined with medical care, additional standards apply to protect the patients who are research subjects.

29. The benefits, risks, burdens and effectiveness of a new method should be tested against those of the best current prophylactic, diagnostic, and therapeutic methods. This does not exclude the use of placebo, or no treatment, in studies where no proven prophylactic, diagnostic or therapeutic method exists.

30. At the conclusion of the study, every patient entered into the study should be assured of access to the best proven prophylactic, diagnostic and therapeutic methods identified by the study.

31. The physician should fully inform the patient which aspects of the care are related to the research. The refusal of a patient to par-

ticipate in a study must never interfere with the patient-physician relationship.

32. In the treatment of a patient, where proven prophylactic, diagnostic and therapeutic methods do not exist or have been ineffective, the physician, with informed consent from the patient, must be free to use unproven or new prophylactic, diagnostic and therapeutic measures, if in the physician's judgment it offers hope of saving life, re-establishing health or alleviating suffering. Where possible, these measures should be made the object of research, designed to evaluate their safety and efficacy. In all cases, new information should be recorded and, where appropriate, published. The other relevant guidelines of this Declaration should be followed.

The Belmont Report

Ethical Principles & Guidelines for
Research Involving Human Subjects

Scientific research has produced substantial social benefits. It has also posed some troubling ethical questions. Public attention was drawn to these questions by reported abuses of human subjects in biomedical experiments, especially during the Second World War. During the Nuremberg War Crime Trials, the Nuremberg Code was drafted as a set of standards for judging physicians and scientists who had conducted biomedical experiments on concentration camp prisoners. This code became the prototype of many later codes[1] intended to assure that research involving human subjects would be carried out in an ethical manner.

The codes consist of rules, some general, others specific, that guide the investigators or the reviewers of research in their work. Such rules often are inadequate to cover complex situations; at times they come into conflict, and they are frequently difficult to interpret or apply. Broader ethical principles will provide a basis on which specific rules may be formulated, criticized and interpreted.

Three principles, or general prescriptive judgments, that are relevant to research involving human subjects are identified in this statement. Other principles may also be relevant. These three are comprehensive, however, and are stated at a level of generalization that should assist scientists, subjects, reviewers and interested citizens to understand the ethical issues inherent in research involving human subjects. These principles cannot always be applied so as to resolve beyond dispute particular ethical problems. The objective is to provide an analytical framework that will guide the resolution of ethical problems arising from research involving human subjects.

This statement consists of a distinction between research and practice, a discussion of the three basic ethical principles, and remarks about the application of these principles.

A. Boundaries Between Practice and Research

It is important to distinguish between biomedical and behavioral research, on the one hand, and the practice of accepted therapy on the other, in order to know what activities ought to undergo review for the protection of human subjects of research. The distinction between research and practice is blurred partly because both often occur together (as in research designed to evaluate a therapy) and partly because notable departures from standard practice are often called "experimental" when "research" are not carefully defined.

For the most part, the term "practice" refers to interventions that are designed solely to enhance the well-being of an individual patient or client and that have a reasonable expectation of success. The purpose of medical or behavioral practice is to provide diagnosis, preventive treatment or therapy to particular individuals.[2] By contrast, the term "research' designates an activity designed to test an hypothesis, permit conclusions to be drawn, and thereby to develop or contribute to generalizable knowledge (expressed, for example, in theories, principles, and statements of relationships). Research is usually described in a formal protocol that sets forth an objective and a set of procedures designed to reach that objective.

When a clinician departs in a significant way from standard or accepted practice, the innovation does not, in and of itself, constitute research. The fact that a procedure is "experimental," in the sense of new, untested or different, does not automatically place it in the category of research. Radically new procedures of this description should, however, be made the object of formal research at an early stage in order to determine whether they are safe and effective. Thus, it is the responsibility of medical practice committees, for example, to insist that a major innovation be incorporated into a formal research project.[3]

Research and practice may be carried on together when research is designed to evaluate the safety and efficacy of a therapy. This need not cause any confusion regarding whether or not the activity requires review; the general rule is that if there is any element of research in an activity, that activity should undergo review for the protection of human subjects.

B. Basic Ethical Principles

The expression "basic ethical principles" refers to those general judgments that serve as a basic justification for the many particular ethical prescriptions and evaluations of human actions. Three basic principles, among those generally accepted in our cultural tradition, are particularly relevant to the ethics of research involving human subjects: the principles of respect of persons, beneficence and justice.

1. Respect for Persons—Respect for persons incorporates at least two ethical convictions: first, that individuals should be treated as autonomous agents, and second, that persons with diminished autonomy are entitled to protection. The principle of respect for persons thus divides into two separate moral requirements: the requirement to acknowledge autonomy and the requirement to protect those with diminished autonomy.

An autonomous person is an individual capable of deliberation about personal goals and of acting under the direction of such deliberation. To respect autonomy is to give weight to autonomous persons' considered opinions and choices while refraining from obstructing their actions unless they are clearly detrimental to others. To show lack of respect for an autonomous agent is to repudiate that person's considered judgments, to deny an individual the freedom to act on those considered judgments, or to withhold information necessary to make a considered judgment, when there are no compelling reasons to do so.

However, not every human being is capable of self-determination. The capacity for self-determination matures during an individual's life, and some individuals lose this capacity wholly or in part because of illness, mental disability, or circumstances that severely restrict liberty. Respect for the immature and the incapacitated may require protecting them as they mature or while they are incapacitated.

Some persons are in need of extensive protection, even to the point of excluding them from activities which may harm them; other persons require little protection beyond making sure they undertake activities freely and with awareness of possible adverse consequence. The extent of protection afforded should depend upon the risk of harm and the likelihood of benefit. The judgment that any individual lacks autonomy should be periodically re-evaluated and will vary in different situations.

In most cases of research involving human subjects, respect for persons demands that subjects enter into the research voluntarily and with adequate information. In some situations, however, application of the principle is not obvious. The involvement of prisoners as subjects of research provides an instructive example. On the one hand, it would seem that the principle of respect for persons requires that prisoners not be deprived of the opportunity to volunteer for research. On the other hand, under prison conditions they may be subtly coerced or unduly influenced to engage in research activities for which they would not otherwise volunteer. Respect for persons would then dictate that prisoners be protected. Whether to allow prisoners to "volunteer" or to "protect" them presents a dilemma. Respecting persons, in most hard cases, is often a matter of balancing competing claims urged by the principle of respect itself.

2. **Beneficence**—Persons are treated in an ethical manner not only by respecting their decisions and protecting them from harm, but also by making efforts to secure their well-being. Such treatment falls under the principle of beneficence. The term "beneficence" is often understood to cover acts of kindness or charity that go beyond strict obligation. In this document, beneficence is understood in a stronger sense, as an obligation. Two general rules have been formulated as complementary expressions of beneficent actions in this sense: (1) do not harm and (2) maximize possible benefits and minimize possible harms.

The Hippocratic maxim "do no harm" has long been a fundamental principle of medical ethics. Claude Bernard extended it to the realm of research, saying that one should not injure one person regardless of the benefits that might come to others. However, even avoiding harm requires learning what is harmful; and, in the process of obtaining this information, persons may be exposed to risk of harm. Further, the Hippocratic Oath requires physicians to benefit their patients "according to their best judgment." Learning what will in fact benefit may require exposing persons to risk. The problem posed by these imperatives is to decide when it is justifiable to seek certain benefits despite the risks involved, and when the benefits should be foregone because of the risks.

The obligations of beneficence affect both individual investigators and society at large, because they extend both to particular research projects and to the entire enterprise of research. In the case of particular projects, investigators and members of their institutions are obliged to give forethought to the maximization of benefits and the reduction of risk that might occur from the research investigation. In the case of scientific research in general, members of the larger society are obliged to recognize the longer term benefits and risks that may result from the improvement of knowledge and from the development of novel medical, psychotherapeutic, and social procedures.

The principle of beneficence often occupies a well-defined justifying role in many areas of research involving human subjects. An example is found in research involving children. Effective ways of treating childhood diseases and fostering healthy development are benefits that serve to justify research involving children—even when individual research subjects are not direct beneficiaries. Research also makes it possible to avoid the harm that may result from the application of previously accepted routine practices that on closer investigation turn out to be dangerous. But the role of the principle of beneficence is not always so unambiguous. A difficult ethical problem remains, for example, about research that presents more than minimal risk without immediate prospect of direct benefit to the children involved. Some have argued that such research is inadmissible, while others have pointed out that this limit would rule out much research promising great benefit to children in the future. Here again, as with all hard cases, the different claims covered by the principle of beneficence may come into conflict and force difficult choices.

3.   **Justice**—Who ought to receive the benefits of research and bear its burdens? This is a question of justice, in the sense of "fairness in distribution" or "what is deserved." An injustice occurs when some benefit to which a person is entitled is denied without good reason

or when some burden is imposed unduly. Another way of conceiving the principle of justice is that equals ought to be treated equally. However, this statement requires explication. Who is equal and who is unequal? What considerations justify departure from equal distribution? Almost all commentators allow that distinctions based on experience, age, deprivation, competence, merit and position do sometimes constitute criteria justifying differential treatment for certain purposes. It is necessary, then, to explain in what respects people should be treated equally. There are several widely accepted formulations of just ways to distribute burdens and benefits. Each formulation mentions some relevant property on the basis of which burdens and benefits should be distributed. These formulations are (1) to each person an equal share, (2) to each person according to individual need, (3) to each person according to individual effort, (4) to each person according to societal contribution, and (5) to each person according to merit.

Questions of justice have long been associated with social practices such as punishment, taxation and political representation. Until recently these questions have not generally been associated with scientific research. However, they are foreshadowed even in the earliest reflections on the ethics of research involving human subjects. For example, during the 19th and early 20th centuries the burdens of serving as research subjects fell largely upon poor ward patients, while the benefits of improved medical care flowed primarily to private patients. Subsequently, the exploitation of unwilling prisoners as research subjects in Nazi concentration camps was condemned as a particularly flagrant injustice. In this country, in the 1940's, the Tuskegee syphilis study used disadvantaged, rural black men to study the untreated course of a disease that is by no means confined to that population. These subjects were deprived of demonstrably effective treatment in order not to interrupt the project, long after such treatment became generally available.

Against this historical background, it can be seen how conceptions of justice are relevant to research involving human subjects. For example, the selection of research subjects needs to be scrutinized in order to determine whether some classes (e.g., welfare patients, particular racial and ethnic minorities, or persons confined to institutions) are being systematically selected simply because of their easy availability, their compromised position, or their manipulability, rather than for reasons directly related to the problem being studied. Finally, whenever research supported by public funds leads to the development of therapeutic devices and procedures, justice demands both that these not provide advantages only to those who can afford them and that such research should not unduly involve persons from groups unlikely to be among the beneficiaries of subsequent applications of the research.

C. Applications

Applications of the general principles to the conduct of research leads to consideration of the following requirements: informed consent, risk/benefit assessment, and the selection of subjects of research.

1. Informed Consent—Respect for persons requires that subjects, to the degree that they are capable, be given the opportunity to choose what shall or shall not happen to them. This opportunity is provided when adequate standards for informed consent are satisfied.

While the importance of informed consent is unquestioned, controversy prevails over the nature and possibility of an informed consent. Nonetheless, there is widespread agreement that the consent process can be analyzed as containing three elements: information, comprehension and voluntariness.

Information. Most codes of research establish specific items for disclosure intended to assure that subjects are given sufficient information. These items generally include: the research procedure, their purposes, risks and anticipated benefits, alternative procedures (where therapy is involved), and a statement offering the subject the opportunity to ask questions and to withdraw at any time from the research. Additional items have been proposed, including how subjects are selected, the person responsible for the research, etc.

However, a simple listing of items does not answer the question of what the standard should be for judging how much and what sort of information should be provided. One standard frequently invoked in medical practice, namely the information commonly provided by practitioners in the field or in the locale, is inadequate since research takes place precisely when a common understanding does not exist. Another standard, currently popular in malpractice law, requires the practitioner to reveal the information that reasonable persons would wish to know in order to make a decision regarding their care. This, too, seems insufficient since the research subject, being in essence a volunteer, may wish to know considerably more about risks gratuitously undertaken than do patients who deliver themselves into the hand of a clinician for needed care. It may be that a standard of "the reasonable volunteer" should be proposed: the extent and nature of information should be such that persons, knowing that the procedure is neither necessary for their care nor perhaps fully understood, can decide whether they wish to participate in the furthering of knowledge. Even when some direct benefit to them is anticipated, the subjects should understand clearly the range of risk and the voluntary nature of participation.

A special problem of consent arises where informing subjects of some pertinent aspect of the research is likely to impair the validity of the research. In many cases, it is sufficient to indicate to subjects that they are being invited to participate in research of which some features will not be revealed until the research is concluded. In all cases of research involving incomplete disclosure, such research is justified only if it is clear that (1) incomplete disclosure is truly necessary to accomplish the goals of the research, (2) there are no undisclosed risks to subjects that are more than minimal, and (3) there is an adequate plan for debriefing subjects, when appropriate, and for dissemination of research results to them. Information about risks should never be withheld for the purpose of eliciting the cooperation of subjects, and truthful answers should always be given to direct questions about the research. Care should be taken to distinguish cases in which disclosure would destroy or invalidate the research from cases in which disclosure would simply inconvenience the investigator.

Comprehension. The manner and context in which information is conveyed is as important as the information itself. For example, presenting information in a disorganized and rapid fashion, allowing too little time for consideration or curtailing opportunities for questioning, all may adversely affect a subject's ability to make an informed choice.

Because the subject's ability to understand is a function of intelligence, rationality, maturity and language, it is necessary to adapt the presentation of the information to the subject's capacities.

Investigators are responsible for ascertaining that the subject has comprehended the information. While there is always an obligation to ascertain that the information about risk to subjects is complete and adequately comprehended, when the risks are more serious, that obligation increases. On occasion, it may be suitable to give some oral or written tests of comprehension.

Special provision may need to be made when comprehension is severely limited—for example, by conditions of immaturity or mental disability. Each class of subjects that one might consider as incompetent (e.g., infants and young children, mentally disabled patients, the terminally ill and the comatose) should be considered on its own terms. Even for these persons, however, respect requires giving them the opportunity to choose to the extent they are able, whether or not to participate in research. The objections of these subjects to involvement should be honored, unless the research entails providing them a therapy unavailable elsewhere. Respect for persons also requires seeking the permission of other parties in order to protect the subjects from harm. Such persons are thus respected both by acknowledging their own wishes and by the use of third parties to protect them from harm.

The third parties chosen should be those who are most likely to understand the incompetent subject's situation and to act in that person's best interest. The person authorized to act on behalf of the subject should be given an opportunity to observe the research as it proceeds in order to be able to withdraw the subject from the research, if such action appears in the subject's best interest.

Voluntariness. An agreement to participate in research constitutes a valid consent only if voluntarily given. This element of informed consent requires conditions free of coercion and undue influence. Coercion occurs when an overt threat of harm is intentionally presented by one person to another in order to obtain compliance. Undue influence, by contrast, occurs through an offer of an excessive, unwarranted, inappropriate or improper reward or other overture in order to obtain compliance. Also, inducements that would ordinarily be acceptable may become undue influences if the subject is especially vulnerable.

Unjustifiable pressures usually occur when persons in positions of authority or commanding influence—especially where possible sanctions are involved—urge a course of action for a subject. A continuum of such influencing factors exists, however, and it is impossible to state precisely where justifiable persuasion ends and undue influence begins. But undue influence would include actions such as manipulating a person's choice through the controlling influence of a close relative and threatening to withdraw health services to which an individual would otherwise be entitled.

2. Assessment of Risks and Benefits.—The assessment of risks and benefits requires a careful arrayal of relevant data, including, in some cases, alternative ways of obtaining the benefits sought in the research. Thus, the assessment presents both an opportunity and a responsibility to gather systematic and comprehensive information about proposed research. For the investigator, it is a means to examine whether the proposed research is properly designed. For a review committee, it is a method for determining whether the risks that will be presented to subjects are justified. For prospective subjects, the assessment will assist the determination whether or not to participate.

The Nature and Scope of Risks and Benefits. The requirement that research be justified on the basis of a favorable risk/benefit assessment bears a close relation to the principle of beneficence, just as the moral requirement that informed consent be obtained is derived primarily from the principle of respect for persons. The term "risk" refers to a possibility that harm may occur. However, when expressions such as "small risk" or "high risk" are used, they usually refer (often ambiguously) both to the chance (probability) of experiencing a harm and the severity (magnitude) of the envisioned harm.

The term "benefit" is used in the research context to refer to something of positive value related to health or welfare. Unlike, "risk," "benefit" is not a term that expresses probabilities. Risk is properly contrasted to probability of benefits, and benefits are properly contrasted with harms rather than risks of harm. Accordingly, so-called risk/benefit assessments are concerned with the probabilities and magnitudes of possible harm and anticipated benefits. Many kinds of possible harms and benefits need to be taken into account. There are, for example, risks of psychological harm, physical harm, legal harm, social harm and economic harm and the corresponding benefits.

While the most likely types of harms to research subjects are those of psychological or physical pain or injury, other possible kinds should not be overlooked.

Risks and benefits of research may affect the individual subjects, the families of the individual subjects, and society at large (or special groups of subjects in society). Previous codes and Federal regulations have required that risks to subjects be outweighed by the sum of both the anticipated benefit to the subject, if any, and the anticipated benefit to society in the form of knowledge to be gained from the research. In balancing these different elements, the risks and benefits affecting the immediate research subject will normally carry special weight. On the other hand, interests other than those of the subject may on some occasions be sufficient by themselves to justify the risks involved in the research, so long as the subjects' rights have been protected. Beneficence thus requires that we protect against risk of harm to subjects and also that we be concerned about the loss of the substantial benefits that might be gained from research.

The Systematic Assessment of Risks and Benefits. It is commonly said that benefits and risks must be "balanced" and shown to be "in a favorable ratio." The metaphorical character of these terms draws attention to the difficulty of making precise judgments. Only on rare occasions will quantitative techniques be available for the scrutiny of research protocols. However, the idea of systematic, nonarbitrary analysis of risks and benefits should be emulated insofar as possible. This ideal requires those making decisions about the justifiability of research to be thorough in the accumulation and assessment of information about all aspects of the research, and to consider alternatives systematically. This procedure renders the assessment of research more rigorous and precise, while making communication between review board members and investigators less subject to misinterpretation, misinformation and conflicting judgments. Thus, there should first be a determination of the validity of the presuppositions of the research; then the nature, probability and magnitude of risk should be distinguished with as much clarity as possible. The method of ascertaining risks should be explicit, especially where there is no alternative to the use of such vague categories as small or slight risk. It should also be determined whether an investigator's estimates of the probability of harm or benefits are reasonable, as judged by known facts or other available studies.

Finally, assessment of the justifiability of research should reflect at least the following considerations: (i) Brutal or inhumane treatment of human subjects is never morally justified. (ii) Risks should be reduced to those necessary to achieve the research objective. It should be determined whether it is in fact necessary to use human subjects at all. Risk can perhaps never be entirely eliminated, but it can often be reduced by careful attention to alternative procedures. (iii) When research involves significant risk of serious impairment, review committees should be extraordinarily insistent on the justification of the risk (looking usually to the likelihood of benefit to the subject—or, in some rare cases, to the manifest voluntariness of the participation). (iv) When vulnerable populations are involved in research, the appropriateness of involving them should itself be demonstrated. A number of variables go into such judgments, including the nature and degree of risk, the condition of the particular population involved, and the nature and level of the anticipated benefits. (v) Relevant risks and benefits must be thoroughly arrayed in documents and procedures used in the informed consent process.

3. Selection of Subjects—Just as the principle of respect for persons finds expression in the requirements for consent, and the principle of beneficence in risk/benefit assessment, the principle of justice gives rise to moral requirements that there be fair procedures and outcomes in the selection of research subjects.

Justice is relevant to the selection of subjects of research at two levels: the social and the individual. Individual justice in the selection of subjects would require that researchers exhibit fairness: thus, they should not offer potentially beneficial research only to some patients who are in their favor or select only "undesirable" persons for risky research. Social justice requires that distinction be drawn between classes of subjects that ought, and ought not, to participate in any particular kind of research, based on the ability of members of that class to bear burdens and on the appropriateness of placing further burdens on already burdened persons. Thus, it can be considered a matter of social justice that there is an order of preference in the selection of classes of subjects (e.g., adults before children) and that some classes of potential subjects (e.g., the institutionalized mentally infirm or prisoners) may be involved as research subjects, if at all, only on certain conditions.

Injustice may appear in the selection of subjects, even if individual subjects are selected fairly by investigators and treated fairly in the course of research. Thus injustice arises from social, racial, sexual and cultural biases institutionalized in society. Thus, even if individual researchers are treating their research subjects fairly, and even if IRBs are taking care to assure that subjects are selected fairly within a particular institution, unjust social patterns may nevertheless appear in the overall distribution of the burdens and benefits of research. Although individual institutions or investigators may not be able to resolve a problem that is pervasive in their social setting, they can consider distributive justice in selecting research subjects.

Some populations, especially institutionalized ones, are already burdened in many ways by their infirmities and environments. When research is proposed that involves risks and does not include a therapeutic component, other less burdened classes of persons should be called upon first to accept these risks of research, except where the research is directly related to the specific conditions of the class involved. Also, even though public funds for research may often flow in the same directions as public funds for health care, it seems unfair that populations dependent on public health care constitute a pool of preferred research subjects if more advantaged populations are likely to be the recipients of the benefits.

One special instance of injustice results from the involvement of vulnerable subjects. Certain groups, such as racial minorities, the economically disadvantaged, the very sick, and the institutionalized may continually be sought as research subjects, owing to their ready availability in settings where research is conducted. Given their dependent status and their frequently compromised capacity for free consent, they should be protected against the danger of being involved in research solely for administrative convenience, or because they are easy to manipulate as a result of their illness or socioeconomic condition.

---

[1] Since 1945, various codes for the proper and responsible conduct of human experimentation in medical research have been adopted by different organizations. The best known of these

codes are the Nuremberg Code of 1947, the Helsinki Declaration of 1964 (revised in 1975), and the 1971 Guidelines (codified into Federal Regulations in 1974) issued by the U.S. Department of Health, Education, and Welfare Codes for the conduct of social and behavioral research have also been adopted, the best known being that of the American Psychological Association, published in 1973.

[2] Although practice usually involves interventions designed solely to enhance the well-being of a particular individual, interventions are sometimes applied to one individual for the enhancement of the well-being of another (e.g., blood donation, skin grafts, organ transplants) or an intervention may have the dual purpose of enhancing the well-being of a particular individual, and, at the same time, providing some benefit to others (e.g., vaccination, which protects both the person who is vaccinated and society generally). The fact that some forms of practice have elements other than immediate benefit to the individual receiving an intervention, however, should not confuse the general distinction between research and practice. Even when a procedure applied in practice may benefit some other person, it remains an intervention designed to enhance the well-being of a particular individual or groups of individuals; thus, it is practice and need not be reviewed as research.

[3] Because the problems related to social experimentation may differ substantially from those of biomedical and behavioral research, the Commission specifically declines to make any policy determination regarding such research at this time. Rather, the Commission believes that the problem ought to be addressed by one of its successor bodies.

45 CFR 46 Federal Policy for the Protection of Human Subjects

Federal Regulations for Government-Funded Trials

A. Basic HHS Policies for Protection of Human subject Research

Sec. 46.101 To what does this policy apply?

a. Except as provided in paragraph (b) of this section, this policy applies to all research involving human subjects conducted, supported or otherwise subject to regulation by any federal department or agency which takes appropriate administrative action to make the policy applicable to such research. This includes research conducted by federal civilian employees or military personnel, except that each department or agency head may adopt such procedural modifications as may be appropriate from an administrative standpoint. It also includes research conducted, supported, or otherwise subject to regulation by the federal government outside the United States.

    1. Research that is conducted or supported by a federal department or agency, whether or not it is regulated as defined in Sec. 46.102(e), must comply with all sections of this policy.

    2. Research that is neither conducted nor supported by a federal department or agency but is subject to regulation as defined in Sec. 46.102(e) must be reviewed and approved, in compliance with Sec. 46.101, Sec. 46.102, and Sec. 46.107 through Sec. 46.117 of this policy, by an institutional review board (IRB) that operates in accordance with the pertinent requirements of this policy.

b. Unless otherwise required by department or agency heads, research activities in which the only involvement of human subjects will be in one or more of the following categories are exempt from this policy:

1. Research conducted in established or commonly accepted educational settings, involving normal educational practices, such as **i.** research on regular and special education instructional strategies, or **ii.** research on the effectiveness of or the comparison among instructional techniques, curricula, or classroom management methods.

2. Research involving the use of educational tests (cognitive, diagnostic, aptitude, achievement), survey procedures, interview procedures or observation of public behavior, unless: **i.** Information obtained is recorded in such a manner that human subjects can be identified, directly or through identifiers linked to the subjects; and **ii.** any disclosure of the human subjects' responses outside the research could reasonably place the subjects at risk of criminal or civil liability or be damaging to the subjects' financial standing, employability, or reputation.

3. Research involving the use of educational tests (cognitive, diagnostic, aptitude, achievement), survey procedures, interview procedures, or observation of public behavior that is not exempt under paragraph (b)(2) of this section, if: **i.** The human subjects are elected or appointed public officials or candidates for public office; or **ii.** federal statute(s) require(s) without exception that the confidentiality of the personally identifiable information will be maintained throughout the research and thereafter.

4. Research, involving the collection or study of existing data, documents, records, pathological specimens, or diagnostic specimens, if these sources are publicly available or if the information is recorded by the investigator in such a manner that subjects cannot be identified, directly or through identifiers linked to the subjects.

5. Research and demonstration projects which are conducted by or subject to the approval of department or agency heads, and which are designed to study, evaluate, or otherwise examine: **i.** Public benefit or service programs; **ii.** procedures for obtaining benefits or services under those programs; **iii.** possible changes

in or alternatives to those programs or procedures; or **iv.** possible changes in methods or levels of payment for benefits or services under those programs.

6. Taste and food quality evaluation and consumer acceptance studies, **i.** if wholesome foods without additives are consumed or **ii.** if a food is consumed that contains a food ingredient at or below the level and for a use found to be safe, or agricultural chemical or environmental contaminant at or below the level found to be safe, by the Food and Drug Administration or approved by the Environmental Protection Agency or the Food Safety and Inspection Service of the U.S. Department of Agriculture.

c. Department or agency heads retain final judgment as to whether a particular activity is covered by this policy.

d. Department or agency heads may require that specific research activities or classes of research activities conducted, supported, or otherwise subject to regulation by the department or agency but not otherwise covered by this policy, comply with some or all of the requirements of this policy.

e. Compliance with this policy requires compliance with pertinent federal laws or regulations which provide additional protections for human subjects.

f. This policy does not affect any state or local laws or regulations which may otherwise be applicable and which provide additional protections for human subjects.

g. This policy does not affect any foreign laws or regulations which may otherwise be applicable and which provide additional protections to human subjects of research.

h. When research covered by this policy takes place in foreign countries, procedures normally followed in the foreign countries to protect human subjects may differ from those set forth in this policy. [An example is a foreign institution which complies with guidelines consistent with the World Medical Assembly Declaration (Declaration of Helsinki amended 1989) issued either by sovereign states or by an organization whose function for the protection of human research subjects is internationally recognized.] In these circumstances, if a department or agency head determines that the procedures prescribed by the institution afford protections that are at least equivalent to those provided in this policy, the department or agency head may approve the substitution of the foreign procedures in lieu of the procedural requirements provided in this policy. Except when otherwise required by statute, Executive Order, or the department or agency head, notices of these actions as they occur will be published in the FEDERAL REGISTER or will be otherwise published as provided in department or agency procedures.

i. Unless otherwise required by law, department or agency heads may waive the applicability of some or all of the provisions of this policy to specific research activities or classes of research activities otherwise covered by this policy. Except when otherwise required by statute or Executive Order, the department or agency head shall forward advance notices of these actions to the Office for Protection from Research Risks, Department of Health and Human Services (HHS), and shall also publish them in the FEDERAL REGISTER or in such other manner as provided in department or agency procedures.[1]

---

[1] Institutions with HHS-approved assurances on file will abide by provisions of title 45 CFR part 46 subparts A-D. Some of the other Departments and Agencies have incorporated all provisions of title 45 CFR part 46 into their policies and procedures as well. However, the exemptions at 45 CFR 46.101(b) do not apply to research involving prisoners, fetuses, pregnant women, or human in vitro fertilization, subparts B and C. The exemption at 45 CFR 46.101(b)(2), for research involving survey or interview procedures or observation of public behavior, does not apply to research with children, subpart D, except for research involving observations of public behavior when the investigator(s) do not participate in the activities being observed.

Sec. 46.102 Definitions.

a. *Department or agency head* means the head of any federal department or agency and any other officer or employee of any department or agency to whom authority has been delegated.

b. *Institution* means any public or private entity or agency (including federal, state, and other agencies).

c. *Legally authorized representative* means an individual or judicial or other body authorized under applicable law to consent on behalf of a prospective subject to the subject's participation in the procedure(s) involved in the research.

d. *Research* means a systematic investigation, including research development, testing and evaluation, designed to develop or contribute to generalizable knowledge. Activities which meet this definition constitute research for purposes of this policy, whether or not they are conducted or supported under a program which is considered research for other purposes. For example, some demonstration and service programs may include research activities.

e. *Research subject to regulation*, and similar terms are intended to encompass those research activities for which a federal department or agency has specific responsibility for regulating as a research activity, (for example, Investigational New Drug requirements administered by the Food and Drug Administration). It does not include research activities which are incidentally regulated by a federal department or agency solely as part of the department's or agency's broader responsibility to regulate certain types of activities whether research or non-research in nature (for example, Wage and Hour requirements administered by the Department of Labor).

f. *Human subject* means a living individual about whom an investigator (whether professional or student) conducting research obtains

    1. Data through intervention or interaction with the individual, or

    2. Identifiable private information.

Intervention includes both physical procedures by which data are gathered (for example, venipuncture) and manipulations of the subject or the subject's environment that are performed for research purposes. *Interaction* includes communication or interpersonal contact between investigator and subject. *Private information* includes information about behavior that occurs in a context in which an individual can reasonably expect that no observation or recording is taking place, and information which has been provided for specific purposes by an individual and which the individual can reasonably expect will not be made public (for example, a medical record). Private information must be individually identifiable (i.e., the identity of the subject is or may readily be ascertained by the investigator or associated with the information) in order for obtaining the information to constitute research involving human subjects.

g. *IRB* means an institutional review board established in accord with and for the purposes expressed in this policy.

h. *IRB approval* means the determination of the IRB that the research has been reviewed and may be conducted at an institution within the constraints set forth by the IRB and by other institutional and federal requirements.

i. *Minimal risk* means that the probability and magnitude of harm or discomfort anticipated in the research are not greater in and of themselves than those ordinarily encountered in daily life or during the performance of routine physical or psychological examinations or tests.

j. *Certification* means the official notification by the institution to the supporting department or agency, in accordance with the requirements of this policy, that a research project or activity involving human subjects has been reviewed and approved by an IRB in accordance with an approved assurance.

Sec. 46.103 Assuring compliance with this policy—research conducted or supported by any Federal Department or Agency.

a. Each institution engaged in research which is covered by this policy and which is conducted or supported by a federal department or agency shall provide written assurance satisfactory to the department or agency head that it will comply with the requirements set forth in this policy. In lieu of requiring submission of an assurance, individual department or agency heads shall accept the existence of a current assurance, appropriate for the research in question, on file with the Office for Protection from Research Risks, HHS, and approved for federalwide use by that office. When the existence of an HHS-approved assurance is accepted in lieu of requiring submission of an assurance, reports (except certification) required by this policy to be made to department and agency heads shall also be made to the Office for Protection from Research Risks, HHS.

b. Departments and agencies will conduct or support research covered by this policy only if the institution has an assurance approved as provided in this section, and only if the institution has certified to the department or agency head that the research has been reviewed and approved by an IRB provided for in the assurance, and will be subject to continuing review by the IRB. Assurances applicable to federally supported or conducted research shall at a minimum include:

    1. A statement of principles governing the institution in the discharge of its responsibilities for protecting the rights and welfare of human subjects of research conducted at or sponsored by the institution, regardless of whether the research is subject to federal regulation. This may include an appropriate existing code, declaration, or statement of ethical principles, or a statement formulated by the institution itself. This requirement does not preempt provisions of this policy applicable to department- or agency-supported or regulated research and need not be applicable to any research exempted or waived under Sec. 46.101 (b) or (i).

2. Designation of one or more IRBs established in accordance with the requirements of this policy, and for which provisions are made for meeting space and sufficient staff to support the IRB's review and recordkeeping duties.

3. A list of IRB members identified by name; earned degrees; representative capacity; indications of experience such as board certifications, licenses, etc., sufficient to describe each member's chief anticipated contributions to IRB deliberations; and any employment or other relationship between each member and the institution; for example: full-time employee, part-time employee, member of governing panel or board, stockholder, paid or unpaid consultant. Changes in IRB membership shall be reported to the department or agency head, unless in accord with Sec. 46.103(a) of this policy, the existence of an HHS-approved assurance is accepted. In this case, change in IRB membership shall be reported to the Office for Protection from Research Risks, HHS.

4. Written procedures which the IRB will follow **i.** for conducting its initial and continuing review of research and for reporting its findings and actions to the investigator and the institution; **ii.** for determining which projects require review more often than annually and which projects need verification from sources other than the investigators that no material changes have occurred since previous IRB review; and **iii.** for ensuring prompt reporting to the IRB of proposed changes in a research activity, and for ensuring that such changes in approved research, during the period for which IRB approval has already been given, may not be initiated without IRB review and approval except when necessary to eliminate apparent immediate hazards to the subject.

5. Written procedures for ensuring prompt reporting to the IRB, appropriate institutional officials, and the department or

agency head of **i.** any unanticipated problems involving risks to subjects or others or any serious or continuing noncompliance with this policy or the requirements or determinations of the IRB and **ii.** any suspension or termination of IRB approval.

c. The assurance shall be executed by an individual authorized to act for the institution and to assume on behalf of the institution the obligations imposed by this policy and shall be filed in such form and manner as the department or agency head prescribes.

d. The department or agency head will evaluate all assurances submitted in accordance with this policy through such officers and employees of the department or agency and such experts or consultants engaged for this purpose as the department or agency head determines to be appropriate. The department or agency head's evaluation will take into consideration the adequacy of the proposed IRB in light of the anticipated scope of the institution's research activities and the types of subject populations likely to be involved, the appropriateness of the proposed initial and continuing review procedures in light of the probable risks, and the size and complexity of the institution.

e. On the basis of this evaluation, the department or agency head may approve or disapprove the assurance, or enter into negotiations to develop an approvable one. The department or agency head may limit the period during which any particular approved assurance or class of approved assurances shall remain effective or otherwise condition or restrict approval.

f. Certification is required when the research is supported by a federal department or agency and not otherwise exempted or waived under Sec. 46.101 (b) or (i). An institution with an approved assurance shall certify that each application or proposal for research covered by the assurance and by Sec. 46.103 of this Policy has been reviewed and approved by the IRB. Such certification must be submitted with the application or proposal or by such later date as may be prescribed by the department or agency to which the application or proposal is submitted. Under no condition shall research covered by Sec. 46.103 of the Policy be supported prior to receipt of the certification that the research has been reviewed and approved by the IRB. Institutions without an approved assurance covering the research shall certify within 30 days after receipt of a request for such a certification from the department or agency, that the application or proposal has been approved by the IRB. If the certification is not submitted within these time limits, the application or proposal may be returned to the institution.

Secs. 46.104—46.106 [Reserved]

Sec. 46.107 IRB membership.

a. Each IRB shall have at least five members, with varying backgrounds to promote complete and adequate review of research activities commonly conducted by the institution. The IRB shall be sufficiently qualified through the experience and expertise of its members, and the diversity of the members, including consideration of race, gender, and cultural backgrounds and sensitivity to such issues as community attitudes, to promote respect for its advice and counsel in safeguarding the rights and welfare of human subjects. In addition to possessing the professional competence necessary to review specific research activities, the IRB shall be able to ascertain the acceptability of proposed research in terms of institutional commitments and regulations, applicable law, and standards of professional conduct and practice. The IRB shall therefore include persons knowledgeable in these areas. If an IRB regularly reviews research that involves a vulnerable category of subjects, such as children, prisoners, pregnant women, or handicapped or mentally disabled persons, consideration shall be given to the inclusion of one or more individuals who are knowledgeable about and experienced in working with these subjects.
b. Every nondiscriminatory effort will be made to ensure that no IRB consists entirely of men or entirely of women, including the institution's consideration of qualified persons of both sexes, so long as no selection is made to the IRB on the basis of gender. No IRB may consist entirely of members of one profession.
c. Each IRB shall include at least one member whose primary concerns are in scientific areas and at least one member whose primary concerns are in nonscientific areas.
d. Each IRB shall include at least one member who is not otherwise affiliated with the institution and who is not part of the immediate family of a person who is affiliated with the institution.
e. No IRB may have a member participate in the IRB's initial or continuing review of any project in which the member has a conflicting interest, except to provide information requested by the IRB.

f. An IRB may, in its discretion, invite individuals with competence in special areas to assist in the review of issues which require expertise beyond or in addition to that available on the IRB. These individuals may not vote with the IRB.

Sec. 46.108 IRB functions and operations.

In order to fulfill the requirements of this policy each IRB shall:

a. Follow written procedures in the same detail as described in Sec. 46.103(b)(4) and, to the extent required by, Sec. 46.103(b)(5).

b. Except when an expedited review procedure is used (see Sec. 46.110), review proposed research at convened meetings at which a majority of the members of the IRB are present, including at least one member whose primary concerns are in nonscientific areas. In order for the research to be approved, it shall receive the approval of a majority of those members present at the meeting.

Sec. 46.109 IRB review of research.

a. An IRB shall review and have authority to approve, require modifications in (to secure approval), or disapprove all research activities covered by this policy.

b. An IRB shall require that information given to subjects as part of informed consent is in accordance with Sec. 46.116. The IRB may require that information, in addition to that specifically mentioned in Sec. 46.116, be given to the subjects when in the IRB's judgment the information would meaningfully add to the protection of the rights and welfare of subjects.

c. An IRB shall require documentation of informed consent or may waive documentation in accordance with Sec. 46.117.

d. An IRB shall notify investigators and the institution in writing of its decision to approve or disapprove the proposed research activity, or of modifications required to secure IRB approval of the research activity. If the IRB decides to disapprove a research activity, it shall include in its written notification a statement of the reasons for its decision and give the investigator an opportunity to respond in person or in writing.

e. An IRB shall conduct continuing review of research covered by this policy at intervals appropriate to the degree of risk, but not less than once per year, and shall have authority to observe or have a third party observe the consent process and the research.

Sec. 46.110 Expedited review procedures for certain kinds of research involving no more than minimal risk, and for minor changes in approved research.

a. The Secretary, HHS, has established, and published as a Notice in the FEDERAL REGISTER, a list of categories of research that may be reviewed by the IRB through an expedited review procedure. The list will be amended, as appropriate after consultation with other departments and agencies, through periodic republication by the Secretary, HHS, in the FEDERAL REGISTER. A copy of the list is available from the Office for Protection from Research Risks, National Institutes of Health, HHS, Bethesda, Maryland 20892.

b. An IRB may use the expedited review procedure to review either or both of the following:

   1. Some or all of the research appearing on the list and found by the reviewer(s) to involve no more than minimal risk,

   2. Minor changes in previously approved research during the period (of one year or less) for which approval is authorized.

Under an expedited review procedure, the review may be carried out by the IRB chairperson or by one or more experienced reviewers designated by the chairperson from among members of the IRB. In reviewing the research, the reviewers may exercise all of the authorities of the IRB except that the reviewers may not disapprove the research. A research activity may be disapproved only after review in accordance with the non-expedited procedure set forth in Sec. 46.108(b).

c. Each IRB which uses an expedited review procedure shall adopt a method for keeping all members advised of research proposals which have been approved under the procedure.

d. The department or agency head may restrict, suspend, terminate, or choose not to authorize an institution's or IRB's use of the expedited review procedure.

Sec. 46.111 Criteria for IRB approval of research.

a. In order to approve research covered by this policy the IRB shall determine that all of the following requirements are satisfied:

   1. Risks to subjects are minimized: **i.** By using procedures which are consistent with sound research design and which do not unnecessarily expose subjects to risk, and **ii.** whenever appropriate, by using procedures already being performed on the subjects for diagnostic or treatment purposes.

2. Risks to subjects are reasonable in relation to anticipated benefits, if any, to subjects, and the importance of the knowledge that may reasonably be expected to result. In evaluating risks and benefits, the IRB should consider only those risks and benefits that may result from the research (as distinguished from risks and benefits of therapies subjects would receive even if not participating in the research). The IRB should not consider possible long-range effects of applying knowledge gained in the research (for example, the possible effects of the research on public policy) as among those research risks falling within the purview of its responsibility.

3. Selection of subjects is equitable. In making this assessment the IRB should take into account the purposes of the research and the setting in which the research will be conducted and should be particularly cognizant of the special problems of research involving vulnerable populations, such as children, prisoners, pregnant women, mentally disabled persons, or economically or educationally disadvantaged persons.

4. Informed consent will be sought from each prospective subject or the subject's legally authorized representative, in accordance with, and to the extent required by Sec. 46.116.

5. Informed consent will be appropriately documented, in accordance with, and to the extent required by Sec. 46.117.

6. When appropriate, the research plan makes adequate provision for monitoring the data collected to ensure the safety of subjects.

7. When appropriate, there are adequate provisions to protect the privacy of subjects and to maintain the confidentiality of data.

b. When some or all of the subjects are likely to be vulnerable to coercion or undue influence, such as children, prisoners, pregnant women, mentally disabled persons, or economically or educationally disadvantaged persons, additional safeguards have been included in the study to protect the rights and welfare of these subjects.

Sec. 46.112 Review by institution.

Research covered by this policy that has been approved by an IRB may be subject to further appropriate review and approval or disapproval by officials of the institution. However, those officials may not approve the research if it has not been approved by an IRB.

Sec. 46.113 Suspension or termination of IRB approval of research.

An IRB shall have authority to suspend or terminate approval of research that is not being conducted in accordance with the IRB's requirements or that has been associated with unexpected serious harm to subjects. Any suspension or termination of approval shall include a statement of the reasons for the IRB's action and shall be reported promptly to the investigator, appropriate institutional officials, and the department or agency head.

Sec. 46.114 Cooperative research.

Cooperative research projects are those projects covered by this policy which involve more than one institution. In the conduct of cooperative research projects, each institution is responsible for safeguarding the rights and welfare of human subjects and for complying with this policy. With the approval of the department or agency head, an institution participating in a cooperative project may enter into a joint review arrangement, rely upon the review of another qualified IRB, or make similar arrangements for avoiding duplication of effort.

Sec. 46.115 IRB records.

a.   An institution, or when appropriate an IRB, shall prepare and maintain adequate documentation of IRB activities, including the following:

1.   Copies of all research proposals reviewed, scientific evaluations, if any, that accompany the proposals, approved sample consent documents, progress reports submitted by investigators, and reports of injuries to subjects.

2.   Minutes of IRB meetings which shall be in sufficient detail to show attendance at the meetings; actions taken by the IRB; the vote on these actions including the number of members voting for, against, and abstaining; the basis for requiring changes in or disapproving research; and a written summary of the discussion of controverted issues and their resolution.

3.   Records of continuing review activities.

4. Copies of all correspondence between the IRB and the investigators.

5. A list of IRB members in the same detail as described is Sec. 46.103(b)(3).

6. Written procedures for the IRB in the same detail as described in Sec. 46.103(b)(4) and Sec. 46.103(b)(5).

7. Statements of significant new findings provided to subjects, as required by Sec. 46.116(b)(5).

b. The records required by this policy shall be retained for at least 3 years, and records relating to research which is conducted shall be retained for at least 3 years after completion of the research. All records shall be accessible for inspection and copying by authorized representatives of the department or agency at reasonable times and in a reasonable manner.

Sec. 46.116 General requirements for informed consent.

Except as provided elsewhere in this policy, no investigator may involve a human being as a subject in research covered by this policy unless the investigator has obtained the legally effective informed consent of the subject or the subject's legally authorized representative. An investigator shall seek such consent only under circumstances that provide the prospective subject or the representative sufficient opportunity to consider whether or not to participate and that minimize the possibility of coercion or undue influence. The information that is given to the subject or the representative shall be in language understandable to the subject or the representative. No informed consent, whether oral or written, may include any exculpatory language through which the subject or the representative is made to waive or appear to waive any of the subject's legal rights, or releases or appears to release the investigator, the sponsor, the institution or its agents from liability for negligence.

a. Basic elements of informed consent. Except as provided in paragraph (c) or (d) of this section, in seeking informed consent the following information shall be provided to each subject:

1. A statement that the study involves research, an explanation of the purposes of the research and the expected duration of the subject's participation, a description of the procedures to be followed, and identification of any procedures which are experimental;

2. A description of any reasonably foreseeable risks or discomforts to the subject;

3. A description of any benefits to the subject or to others which may reasonably be expected from the research;

4. A disclosure of appropriate alternative procedures or courses of treatment, if any, that might be advantageous to the subject;

5. A statement describing the extent, if any, to which confidentiality of records identifying the subject will be maintained;

6. For research involving more than minimal risk, an explanation as to whether any compensation and an explanation as to whether any medical treatments are available if injury occurs and, if so, what they consist of, or where further information may be obtained;

7. An explanation of whom to contact for answers to pertinent questions about the research and research subjects' rights, and whom to contact in the event of a research-related injury to the subject; and

8. A statement that participation is voluntary, refusal to participate will involve no penalty or loss of benefits to which the subject is otherwise entitled, and the subject may discontinue participation at any time without penalty or loss of benefits to which the subject is otherwise entitled.

b. Additional elements of informed consent. When appropriate, one or more of the following elements of information shall also be provided to each subject:

1. A statement that the particular treatment or procedure may involve risks to the subject (or to the embryo or fetus, if the subject is or may become pregnant) which are currently unforeseeable;

2. Anticipated circumstances under which the subject's participation may be terminated by the investigator without regard to the subject's consent;

3. Any additional costs to the subject that may result from participation in the research;

4. The consequences of a subject's decision to withdraw from the research and procedures for orderly termination of participation by the subject;

5. A statement that significant new findings developed during the course of the research which may relate to the subject's willingness to continue participation will be provided to the subject; and

6. The approximate number of subjects involved in the study.

c. An IRB may approve a consent procedure which does not include, or which alters, some or all of the elements of informed consent set forth above, or waive the requirement to obtain informed consent provided the IRB finds and documents that:

1. The research or demonstration project is to be conducted by or subject to the approval of state or local government officials and is designed to study, evaluate, or otherwise examine: **i.** Public benefit of service programs; **ii.** procedures for obtaining benefits or services under those programs; **iii.** possible changes in or alternatives to those programs or procedures; or **iv.** possible changes in methods or levels of payment for benefits or services under those programs; and

2. The research could not practicably be carried out without the waiver or alteration.

d. An IRB may approve a consent procedure which does not include, or which alters, some or all of the elements of informed consent set forth in this section, or waive the requirements to obtain informed consent provided the IRB finds and documents that:

1. The research involves no more than minimal risk to the subjects;

2. The waiver or alteration will not adversely affect the rights and welfare of the subjects;

3. The research could not practicably be carried out without the waiver or alteration; and

4. Whenever appropriate, the subjects will be provided with additional pertinent information after participation.

e. The informed consent requirements in this policy are not intended to preempt any applicable federal, state, or local laws which require additional information to be disclosed in order for informed consent to be legally effective.

f. Nothing in this policy is intended to limit the authority of a physician to provide emergency medical care, to the extent the physician is permitted to do so under applicable federal, state, or local law.

Sec. 46.117 Documentation of informed consent.

a. Except as provided in paragraph (c) of this section, informed consent shall be documented by the use of a written consent form approved by the IRB and signed by the subject or the subject's legally authorized representative. A copy shall be given to the person signing the form.

b. Except as provided in paragraph (c) of this section, the consent form may be either of the following:

1. A written consent document that embodies the elements of informed consent required by Sec. 46.116. This form may be read to the subject or the subject's legally authorized representative, but in any event, the investigator shall give either the subject or the representative adequate opportunity to read it before it is signed; or

2. A short form written consent document stating that the elements of informed consent required by Sec. 46.116 have been presented orally to the subject or the subject's legally authorized representative. When this method is used, there shall be a witness to the oral presentation. Also, the IRB shall approve a written summary of what is to be said to the subject or the representative. Only the short form itself is to be signed by the subject or the representative. However, the witness shall sign both the short form and a copy of the summary, and the person actually obtaining consent shall sign a copy of the summary. A copy of the summary shall be given to the subject or the representative, in addition to a copy of the short form.

c. An IRB may waive the requirement for the investigator to obtain a signed consent form for some or all subjects if it finds either:

1. That the only record linking the subject and the research would be the consent document and the principal risk would be potential harm resulting from a breach of confidentiality. Each subject will be asked whether the subject wants documentation linking the subject with the research, and the subject's wishes will govern; or

2. That the research presents no more than minimal risk of harm to subjects and involves no procedures for which written consent is normally required outside of the research context.

In cases in which the documentation requirement is waived, the IRB may require the investigator to provide subjects with a written statement regarding the research.

Sec. 46.118 Applications and proposals lacking definite plans for involvement of human subjects.

Certain types of applications for grants, cooperative agreements, or contracts are submitted to departments or agencies with the knowledge that subjects may be involved within the period of support, but definite plans would not normally be set forth in the application or proposal. These include activities such as institutional type grants when selection of specific projects is the institution's responsibility; research training grants in which the activities involving subjects remain to be selected; and projects in which human subjects' involvement will depend upon completion of instruments, prior animal studies, or purification of compounds. These applications need not be reviewed by an IRB before an award may be made. However, except for research exempted or waived under Sec. 46.101 (b) or (i), no human subjects may be involved in any project supported by these awards until the project has been reviewed and approved by the IRB, as provided in this policy, and certification submitted, by the institution, to the department or agency.

Sec. 46.119 Research undertaken without the intention of involving human subjects.

In the event research is undertaken without the intention of involving human subjects, but it is later proposed to involve human subjects in the research, the research shall first be reviewed and approved by an IRB, as provided in this policy, a certification submitted, by the institution, to the department or agency, and final approval given to the proposed change by the department or agency.

Sec. 46.120 Evaluation and disposition of applications and proposals for research to be conducted or supported by a Federal Department or Agency.

a.   The department or agency head will evaluate all applications and proposals involving human subjects submitted to the department or agency through such officers and employees of the department or agency and such experts and consultants as the department or agency

head determines to be appropriate. This evaluation will take into consideration the risks to the subjects, the adequacy of protection against these risks, the potential benefits of the research to the subjects and others, and the importance of the knowledge gained or to be gained.
b. On the basis of this evaluation, the department or agency head may approve or disapprove the application or proposal, or enter into negotiations to develop an approvable one.

Sec. 46.121 [Reserved]

Sec. 46.122 Use of Federal funds.
Federal funds administered by a department or agency may not be expended for research involving human subjects unless the requirements of this policy have been satisfied.

Sec. 46.123 Early termination of research support: Evaluation of applications and proposals.
a. The department or agency head may require that department or agency support for any project be terminated or suspended in the manner prescribed in applicable program requirements, when the department or agency head finds an institution has materially failed to comply with the terms of this policy.
b. In making decisions about supporting or approving applications or proposals covered by this policy the department or agency head may take into account, in addition to all other eligibility requirements and program criteria, factors such as whether the applicant has been subject to a termination or suspension under paragarph (a) of this section and whether the applicant or the person or persons who would direct or has have directed the scientific and technical aspects of an activity has have, in the judgment of the department or agency head, materially failed to discharge responsibility for the protection of the rights and welfare of human subjects (whether or not the research was subject to federal regulation).

Sec. 46.124 Conditions.
With respect to any research project or any class of research projects the department or agency head may impose additional conditions prior to or at the time of approval when in the judgment of the

department or agency head additional conditions are necessary for the protection of human subjects.

B. Additional Protections Pertaining to Research, Development and Related Activities Involving Fetuses, Pregnant Women and Human In-Vitro Fertilization

Sec. 46.201 Applicability.
a. The regulations in this subpart are applicable to all Department of Health and Human Services grants and contracts supporting research, development, and related activities involving: 1. The fetus, 2. pregnant women, and 3. human in vitro fertilization.
b. Nothing in this subpart shall be construed as indicating that compliance with the procedures set forth herein will in any way render inapplicable pertinent State or local laws bearing upon activities covered by this subpart.
c. The requirements of this subpart are in addition to those imposed under the other subparts of this part.

Sec. 46.202 Purpose.
It is the purpose of this subpart to provide additional safeguards in reviewing activities to which this subpart is applicable to assure that they conform to appropriate ethical standards and relate to important societal needs.

Sec. 46.203 Definitions.
As used in this subpart:
a. Secretary means the Secretary of Health and Human Services and any other officer or employee of the Department of Health and Human Services to whom authority has been delegated.
b. Pregnancy encompasses the period of time from confirmation of implantation (through any of the presumptive signs of pregnancy, such as missed menses, or by a medically acceptable pregnancy test), until expulsion or extraction of the fetus.
c. Fetus means the product of conception from the time of implantation (as evidenced by any of the presumptive signs of pregnancy, such as missed menses, or a medically acceptable pregnancy test),

until a determination is made, following expulsion or extraction of the fetus, that it is viable.

d. Viable as it pertains to the fetus means being able, after either spontaneous or induced delivery, to survive (given the benefit of available medical therapy) to the point of independently maintaining heart beat and respiration. The Secretary may from time to time, taking into account medical advances, publish in the FEDERAL REGISTER guidelines to assist in determining whether a fetus is viable for purposes of this subpart. If a fetus is viable after delivery, it is a premature infant.

e. Nonviable fetus means a fetus ex utero which, although living, is not viable.

f. Dead fetus means a fetus ex utero which exhibits neither heartbeat, spontaneous respiratory activity, spontaneous movement of voluntary muscles, nor pulsation of the umbilical cord (if still attached).

g. In vitro fertilization means any fertilization of human ova which occurs outside the body of a female, either through admixture of donor human sperm and ova or by any other means.

Sec. 46.204 Ethical Advisory Boards.

a. One or more Ethical Advisory Boards shall be established by the Secretary. Members of these board(s) shall be so selected that the board(s) will be competent to deal with medical, legal, social, ethical, and related issues and may include, for example, research scientists, physicians, psychologists, sociologists, educators, lawyers, and ethicists, as well as representatives of the general public. No board member may be a regular, full-time employee of the Department of Health and Human Services.

b. At the request of the Secretary, the Ethical Advisory Board shall render advice consistent with the policies and requirements of this part as to ethical issues, involving activities covered by this subpart, raised by individual applications or proposals. In addition, upon request by the Secretary, the Board shall render advice as to classes of applications or proposals and general policies, guidelines, and procedures.

c. A Board may establish, with the approval of the Secretary, classes of applications or proposals which: **1.** Must be submitted to the Board, or **2.** need not be submitted to the Board. Where the Board so establishes a class of applications or proposals which must be submitted, no application or proposal within the class may be funded by the Department or any component thereof until the application or proposal has been reviewed by the Board and the Board has rendered advice as to its acceptability from an ethical standpoint.

Sec. 46.205 Additional duties of the Institutional Review Boards in connection with activities involving fetuses, pregnant women, or human in vitro fertilization.

a. In addition to the responsibilities prescribed for Institutional Review Boards under Subpart A of this part, the applicant's or offeror's Board shall, with respect to activities covered by this subpart, carry out the following additional duties:

1. Determine that all aspects of the activity meet the requirements of this subpart;

2. Determine that adequate consideration has been given to the manner in which potential subjects will be selected, and adequate provision has been made by the applicant or offeror for monitoring the actual informed consent process (e.g., through such mechanisms, when appropriate, as participation by the Institutional Review Board or subject advocates in: i. Overseeing the actual process by which individual consents required by this subpart are secured either by approving induction of each individual into the activity or verifying, perhaps through sampling, that approved procedures for induction of individuals into the activity are being followed, and ii. monitoring the progress of the activity and intervening as necessary through such steps as visits to the activity site and continuing evaluation to determine if any unanticipated risks have arisen);

3. Carry out such other responsibilities as may be assigned by the Secretary.

b. No award may be issued until the applicant or offeror has certified to the Secretary that the Institutional Review Board has made the determinations required under paragraph (a) of this section and the Secretary has approved these determinations, as provided in Sec. 46.120 of Subpart A of this part.

c. Applicants or offerors seeking support for activities covered by this subpart must provide for the designation of an Institutional

Review Board, subject to approval by the Secretary, where no such Board has been established under Subpart A of this part.

Sec. 46.206 General limitations.
a. No activity to which this subpart is applicable may be undertaken unless:

> **1.** Appropriate studies on animals and nonpregnant individuals have been completed;
>
> **2.** Except where the purpose of the activity is to meet the health needs of the mother or the particular fetus, the risk to the fetus is minimal and, in all cases, is the least possible risk for achieving the objectives of the activity.
>
> **3.** Individuals engaged in the activity will have no part in: **i.** Any decisions as to the timing, method, and procedures used to terminate the pregnancy, and **ii.** determining the viability of the fetus at the termination of the pregnancy; and
>
> **4.** No procedural changes which may cause greater than minimal risk to the fetus or the pregnant woman will be introduced into the procedure for terminating the pregnancy solely in the interest of the activity.

b. No inducements, monetary or otherwise, may be offered to terminate pregnancy for purposes of the activity.

Sec. 46.207 Activities directed toward pregnant women as subjects.
a. No pregnant woman may be involved as a subject in an activity covered by this subpart unless: **1.** The purpose of the activity is to meet the health needs of the mother and the fetus will be placed at risk only to the minimum extent necessary to meet such needs, or **2.** the risk to the fetus is minimal.

b. An activity permitted under paragraph (a) of this section may be conducted only if the mother and father are legally competent and have given their informed consent after having been fully informed regarding possible impact on the fetus, except that the father's informed consent need not be secured if: **1.** The purpose of the activity is to meet the health needs of the mother; **2.** his identity or whereabouts cannot reasonably be ascertained; **3.** he is not reasonably available; or **4.** the pregnancy resulted from rape.

Sec. 46.208 Activities directed toward fetuses in utero as subjects.

a. No fetus in utero may be involved as a subject in any activity covered by this subpart unless: 1. The purpose of the activity is to meet the health needs of the particular fetus and the fetus will be placed at risk only to the minimum extent necessary to meet such needs, or 2. the risk to the fetus imposed by the research is minimal and the purpose of the activity is the development of important biomedical knowledge which cannot be obtained by other means.

b. An activity permitted under paragraph (a) of this section may be conducted only if the mother and father are legally competent and have given their informed consent, except that the father's consent need not be secured if: 1. His identity or whereabouts cannot reasonably be ascertained, 2. he is not reasonably available, or 3. the pregnancy resulted from rape.

Sec. 46.209 Activities directed toward fetuses ex utero, including nonviable fetuses, as subjects.

a. Until it has been ascertained whether or not a fetus ex utero is viable, a fetus ex utero may not be involved as a subject in an activity covered by this subpart unless:

    1. There will be no added risk to the fetus resulting from the activity, and the purpose of the activity is the development of important biomedical knowledge which cannot be obtained by other means, or

    2. The purpose of the activity is to enhance the possibility of survival of the particular fetus to the point of viability.

b. No nonviable fetus may be involved as a subject in an activity covered by this subpart unless:

    1. Vital functions of the fetus will not be artificially maintained,

    2. Experimental activities which of themselves would terminate the heartbeat or respiration of the fetus will not be employed, and

    3. The purpose of the activity is the development of important biomedical knowledge which cannot be obtained by other means.

c. In the event the fetus ex utero is found to be viable, it may be included as a subject in the activity only to the extent permitted by and in accordance with the requirements of other subparts of this part.

d. An activity permitted under paragraph (a) or (b) of this section may be conducted only if the mother and father are legally competent and have given their informed consent, except that the father's informed consent need not be secured if: **1.** His identity or whereabouts cannot reasonably be ascertained, **2.** he is not reasonably available, or **3.** the pregnancy resulted from rape.

Sec. 46.210 Activities involving the dead fetus, fetal material, or the placenta.

Activities involving the dead fetus, mascerated fetal material, or cells, tissue, or organs excised from a dead fetus shall be conducted only in accordance with any applicable State or local laws regarding such activities.

Sec. 46.211 Modification or waiver of specific requirements.

Upon the request of an applicant or offeror (with the approval of its Institutional Review Board), the Secretary may modify or waive specific requirements of this subpart, with the approval of the Ethical Advisory Board after such opportunity for public comment as the Ethical Advisory Board considers appropriate in the particular instance. In making such decisions, the Secretary will consider whether the risks to the subject are so outweighed by the sum of the benefit to the subject and the importance of the knowledge to be gained as to warrant such modification or waiver and that such benefits cannot be gained except through a modification or waiver. Any such modifications or waivers will be published as notices in the FEDERAL REGISTER.

C. Additional Protections Pertaining to Biomedical and Behavioral Research Involving Prisoners as Subjects

Sec. 46.301 Applicability.

a. The regulations in this subpart are applicable to all biomedical and behavioral research conducted or supported by the Department of Health and Human Services involving prisoners as subjects.

b. Nothing in this subpart shall be construed as indicating that compliance with the procedures set forth herein will authorize research involving prisoners as subjects, to the extent such research is limited or barred by applicable State or local law.

c. The requirements of this subpart are in addition to those imposed under the other subparts of this part.

Sec. 46.302 Purpose.

Inasmuch as prisoners may be under constraints because of their incarceration which could affect their ability to make a truly voluntary and uncoerced decision whether or not to participate as subjects in research, it is the purpose of this subpart to provide additional safeguards for the protection of prisoners involved in activities to which this subpart is applicable.

Sec. 46.303 Definitions.

As used in this subpart:

a. Secretary means the Secretary of Health and Human Services and any other officer or employee of the Department of Health and Human Services to whom authority has been delegated.

b. DHHS means the Department of Health and Human Services.

c. Prisoner means any individual involuntarily confined or detained in a penal institution. The term is intended to encompass individuals sentenced to such an institution under a criminal or civil statute, individuals detained in other facilities by virtue of statutes or commitment procedures which provide alternatives to criminal prosecution or incarceration in a penal institution, and individuals detained pending arraignment, trial, or sentencing.

d. Minimal risk is the probability and magnitude of physical or psychological harm that is normally encountered in the daily lives, or in the routine medical, dental, or psychological examination of healthy persons.

Sec. 46.304 Composition of Institutional Review Boards where prisoners are involved.

In addition to satisfying the requirements in Sec. 46.107 of this part, an Institutional Review Board, carrying out responsibilities under this part with respect to research covered by this subpart, shall also meet the following specific requirements:

a. A majority of the Board (exclusive of prisoner members) shall have no association with the prison(s) involved, apart from their membership on the Board.

b. At least one member of the Board shall be a prisoner, or a prisoner representative with appropriate background and experience to serve in that capacity, except that where a particular research project is reviewed by more than one Board only one Board need satisfy this requirement.

Sec. 46.305 Additional duties of the Institutional Review Boards where prisoners are involved.

a. In addition to all other responsibilities prescribed for Institutional Review Boards under this part, the Board shall review research covered by this subpart and approve such research only if it finds that:

1. The research under review represents one of the categories of research permissible under Sec. 46.306(a)(2);

2. Any possible advantages accruing to the prisoner through his or her participation in the research, when compared to the general living conditions, medical care, quality of food, amenities and opportunity for earnings in the prison, are not of such a magnitude that his or her ability to weigh the risks of the research against the value of such advantages in the limited choice environment of the prison is impaired;

3. The risks involved in the research are commensurate with risks that would be accepted by nonprisoner volunteers;

4. Procedures for the selection of subjects within the prison are fair to all prisoners and immune from arbitrary intervention by prison authorities or prisoners. Unless the principal investigator provides to the Board justification in writing for following some other procedures, control subjects must be selected randomly from the group of available prisoners who meet the characteristics needed for that particular research project;

5. The information is presented in language which is understandable to the subject population;

6. Adequate assurance exists that parole boards will not take into account a prisoner's participation in the research in making decisions regarding parole, and each prisoner is clearly informed in advance that participation in the research will have no effect

on his or her parole; and

7. Where the Board finds there may be a need for follow-up examination or care of participants after the end of their participation, adequate provision has been made for such examination or care, taking into account the varying lengths of individual prisoners' sentences, and for informing participants of this fact.

b. The Board shall carry out such other duties as may be assigned by the Secretary.

c. The institution shall certify to the Secretary, in such form and manner as the Secretary may require, that the duties of the Board under this section have been fulfilled.

Sec. 46.306 Permitted research involving prisoners.

a. Biomedical or behavioral research conducted or supported by DHHS may involve prisoners as subjects only if:

1. The institution responsible for the conduct of the research has certified to the Secretary that the Institutional Review Board has approved the research under Sec. 46.305 of this subpart; and

2. In the judgment of the Secretary the proposed research involves solely the following: i. Study of the possible causes, effects, and processes of incarceration, and of criminal behavior, provided that the study presents no more than minimal risk and no more than inconvenience to the subjects; ii. Study of prisons as institutional structures or of prisoners as incarcerated persons, provided that the study presents no more than minimal risk and no more than inconvenience to the subjects; iii. Research on conditions particularly affecting prisoners as a class (for example, vaccine trials and other research on hepatitis which is much more prevalent in prisons than elsewhere; and research on social and psychological problems such as alcoholism, drug addiction and sexual assaults) provided that the study may proceed only after the Secretary has consulted with appropriate experts including experts in penology medicine and ethics, and published notice, in the FEDERAL REGISTER, of his intent to approve such research; or iv. Research on practices, both innovative and accepted, which have the intent and reasonable probability of improving the health or well-being of the subject. In cases in which those studies require the assignment of prisoners in a

manner consistent with protocols approved by the IRB to control groups which may not benefit from the research, the study may proceed only after the Secretary has consulted with appropriate experts, including experts in penology medicine and ethics, and published notice, in the FEDERAL REGISTER, of his intent to approve such research.

b. Except as provided in paragraph (a) of this section, biomedical or behavioral research conducted or supported by DHHS shall not involve prisoners as subjects.

D. Additional Protections for Children Involved as Subjects in Research

Sec. 46.401 To what do these regulations apply?

a. This subpart applies to all research involving children as subjects, conducted or supported by the Department of Health and Human Services.

1. This includes research conducted by Department employees, except that each head of an Operating Division of the Department may adopt such nonsubstantive, procedural modifications as may be appropriate from an administrative standpoint.

2. It also includes research conducted or supported by the Department of Health and Human Services outside the United States, but in appropriate circumstances, the Secretary may, under paragraph (e) of Sec. 46.101 of Subpart A, waive the applicability of some or all of the requirements of these regulations for research of this type.

b. Exemptions at Sec. 46.101(b)(1) and (b)(3) through (b)(6) are applicable to this subpart. The exemption at Sec. 46.101(b)(2) regarding educational tests is also applicable to this subpart. However, the exemption at Sec. 46.101(b)(2) for research involving survey or interview procedures or observations of public behavior does not apply to research covered by this subpart, except for research involving observation of public behavior when the investigator(s) do not participate in the activities being observed.

c. The exceptions, additions, and provisions for waiver as they appear in paragraphs (c) through (i) of Sec. 46.101 of Subpart A are applicable to this subpart.

Sec. 46.402 Definitions.
The definitions in Sec. 46.102 of Subpart A shall be applicable to this subpart as well. In addition, as used in this subpart:

a. Children are persons who have not attained the legal age for consent to treatments or procedures involved in the research, under the applicable law of the jurisdiction in which the research will be conducted.

b. Assent means a child's affirmative agreement to participate in research. Mere failure to object should not, absent affirmative agreement, be construed as assent.

c. Permission means the agreement of parent(s) or guardian to the participation of their child or ward in research.

d. Parent means a child's biological or adoptive parent.

e. Guardian means an individual who is authorized under applicable State or local law to consent on behalf of a child to general medical care.

Sec. 46.403 IRB duties.
In addition to other responsibilities assigned to IRBs under this part, each IRB shall review research covered by this subpart and approve only research which satisfies the conditions of all applicable sections of this subpart.

Sec. 46.404 Research not involving greater than minimal risk.
HHS will conduct or fund research in which the IRB finds that no greater than minimal risk to children is presented, only if the IRB finds that adequate provisions are made for soliciting the assent of the children and the permission of their parents or guardians, as set forth in Sec. 46.408.

Sec. 46.405 Research involving greater than minimal risk but presenting the prospect of direct benefit to the individual subjects.
HHS will conduct or fund research in which the IRB finds that more than minimal risk to children is presented by an intervention or procedure that holds out the prospect of direct benefit for the individual

subject, or by a monitoring procedure that is likely to contribute to the subject's well-being, only if the IRB finds that:

a. The risk is justified by the anticipated benefit to the subjects;

b. The relation of the anticipated benefit to the risk is at least as favorable to the subjects as that presented by available alternative approaches; and

c. Adequate provisions are made for soliciting the assent of the children and permission of their parents or guardians, as set forth in Sec. 46.408.

Sec. 46.406 Research involving greater than minimal risk and no prospect of direct benefit to individual subjects, but likely to yield generalizable knowledge about the subject's disorder or condition.

HHS will conduct or fund research in which the IRB finds that more than minimal risk to children is presented by an intervention or procedure that does not hold out the prospect of direct benefit for the individual subject, or by a monitoring procedure which is not likely to contribute to the well-being of the subject, only if the IRB finds that:

a. The risk represents a minor increase over minimal risk;

b. The intervention or procedure presents experiences to subjects that are reasonably commensurate with those inherent in their actual or expected medical, dental, psychological, social, or educational situations;

c. The intervention or procedure is likely to yield generalizable knowledge about the subjects' disorder or condition which is of vital importance for the understanding or amelioration of the subjects' disorder or condition; and

d. Adequate provisions are made for soliciting assent of the children and permission of their parents or guardians, as set forth in Sec. 46.408.

Sec. 46.407 Research not otherwise approvable which presents an opportunity to understand, prevent, or alleviate a serious problem affecting the health or welfare of children.

HHS will conduct or fund research that the IRB does not believe meets the requirements of Sec. 46.404, Sec. 46.405, or Sec. 46.406 only if:

a. The IRB finds that the research presents a reasonable opportunity to further the understanding, prevention, or alleviation of a serious problem affecting the health or welfare of children; and

b. The Secretary, after consultation with a panel of experts in pertinent disciplines (for example: science, medicine, education, ethics, law) and following opportunity for public review and comment, has determined either:

    1. That the research in fact satisfies the conditions of Sec. 46.404, Sec. 46.405, or Sec. 46.406, as applicable, or

    2. The following: **i.** The research presents a reasonable opportunity to further the understanding, prevention, or alleviation of a serious problem affecting the health or welfare of children; **ii.** The research will be conducted in accordance with sound ethical principles; **iii.** Adequate provisions are made for soliciting the assent of children and the permission of their parents or guardians, as set forth in Sec. 46.408.

Sec. 46.408 Requirements for permission by parents or guardians and for assent by children.

a. In addition to the determinations required under other applicable sections of this subpart, the IRB shall determine that adequate provisions are made for soliciting the assent of the children, when in the judgment of the IRB the children are capable of providing assent. In determining whether children are capable of assenting, the IRB shall take into account the ages, maturity, and psychological state of the children involved. This judgment may be made for all children to be involved in research under a particular protocol, or for each child, as the IRB deems appropriate. If the IRB determines that the capability of some or all of the children is so limited that they cannot reasonably be consulted or that the intervention or procedure involved in the research holds out a prospect of direct benefit that is important to the health or well-being of the children and is available only in the context of the research, the assent of the children is not a necessary condition for proceeding with the research. Even where the IRB determines that the subjects are capable of assenting, the IRB may still waive the assent requirement under circumstances in which consent may be waived in accord with Sec. 46.116 of Subpart A.

b. In addition to the determinations required under other applicable sections of this subpart, the IRB shall determine, in accordance with and to the extent that consent is required by Sec. 46.116 of Subpart A, that adequate provisions are made for soliciting the permission of each child's parents or guardian. Where parental permission is to be obtained, the IRB may find that the permission of one parent is sufficient for research to be conducted under Sec. 46.404 or Sec. 46.405. Where research is covered by Secs. 46.406 and 46.407 and permission is to be obtained from parents, both parents must give their permission unless one parent is deceased, unknown, incompetent, or not reasonably available, or when only one parent has legal responsibility for the care and custody of the child.

c.   In addition to the provisions for waiver contained in Sec. 46.116 of Subpart A, if the IRB determines that a research protocol is designed for conditions or for a subject population for which parental or guardian permission is not a reasonable requirement to protect the subjects (for example, neglected or abused children), it may waive the consent requirements in Subpart A of this part and paragraph (b) of this section, provided an appropriate mechanism for protecting the children who will participate as subjects in the research is substituted, and provided further that the waiver is not inconsistent with Federal, state or local law. The choice of an appropriate mechanism would depend upon the nature and purpose of the activities described in the protocol, the risk and anticipated benefit to the research subjects, and their age, maturity, status, and condition.

d.   Permission by parents or guardians shall be documented in accordance with and to the extent required by Sec. 46.117 of Subpart A.

e.   When the IRB determines that assent is required, it shall also determine whether and how assent must be documented.

Sec. 46.409 Wards.

a.   Children who are wards of the state or any other agency, institution, or entity can be included in research approved under Sec. 46.406 or Sec. 46.407 only if such research is:

1.   Related to their status as wards; or

2.   Conducted in schools, camps, hospitals, institutions, or similar settings in which the majority of children involved as subjects are not wards.

b.   If the research is approved under paragraph (a) of this section, the IRB shall require appointment of an advocate for each child who is a ward, in addition to any other individual acting on behalf of the child as guardian or in loco parentis. One individual may serve as advocate for more than one child. The advocate shall be an individual who has the background and experience to act in, and agrees to act in, the best interests of the child for the duration of the child's participation in the research and who is not associated in any way (except in the role as advocate or member of the IRB) with the research, the investigator(s), or the guardian organization.

21 CFR 50 Protection of Human Subjects

Federal Regulations for Industry-Sponsored Trials

A. General Provisions

Sec. 50.1 Scope.
a. This part applies to all clinical investigations regulated by the Food and Drug Administration under sections 505(i), 507(d), and 520(g) of the Federal Food, Drug, and Cosmetic Act, as well as clinical investigations that support applications for research or marketing permits for products regulated by the Food and Drug Administration, including food and color additives, drugs for human use, medical devices for human use, biological products for human use, and electronic products. Additional specific obligations and commitments of, and standards of conduct for, persons who sponsor or monitor clinical investigations involving particular test articles may also be found in other parts (e.g., parts 312 and 812). Compliance with these parts is intended to protect the rights and safety of subjects involved in investigations filed with the Food and Drug Administration pursuant to sections 406, 409, 502, 503, 505, 506, 507, 510, 513-516, 518-520, 721, and 801 of the Federal Food, Drug, and Cosmetic Act and sections 351 and 354-360F of the Public Health Service Act.
b. References in this part to regulatory sections of the Code of Federal Regulations are to chapter I of title 21, unless otherwise noted.

Sec. 50.3 Definitions.

As used in this part:

a. Act means the Federal Food, Drug, and Cosmetic Act, as amended (secs. 201–902, 52 Stat. 1040 et seq. as amended (21 U.S.C. 321–392)).

b. Application for research or marketing permit includes:

1. A color additive petition, described in part 71.

2. A food additive petition, described in parts 171 and 571.

3. Data and information about a substance submitted as part of the procedures for establishing that the substance is generally recognized as safe for use that results or may reasonably be expected to result, directly or indirectly, in its becoming a component or otherwise affecting the characteristics of any food, described in Secs. 170.30 and 570.30.

4. Data and information about a food additive submitted as part of the procedures for food additives permitted to be used on an interim basis pending additional study, described in Sec. 180.1.

5. Data and information about a substance submitted as part of the procedures for establishing a tolerance for unavoidable contaminants in food and food-packaging materials, described in section 406 of the act.

6. An investigational new drug application, described in part 312 of this chapter.

7. A new drug application, described in part 314.

8. Data and information about the bioavailability or bioequivalence of drugs for human use submitted as part of the procedures for issuing, amending, or repealing a bioequivalence requirement, described in part 320.

9. Data and information about an over-the-counter drug for human use submitted as part of the procedures for classifying these drugs as generally recognized as safe and effective and not misbranded, described in part 330.

10. Data and information about a prescription drug for human use submitted as part of the procedures for classifying these drugs as generally recognized as safe and effective and not misbranded, described in this chapter.

11. Data and information about an antibiotic drug submitted as part of the procedures for issuing, amending, or repealing regulations for these drugs, described in Sec. 314.300 of this chapter.

12. An application for a biological product license, described in part 601.

13. Data and information about a biological product submitted as part of the procedures for determining that licensed biological products are safe and effective and not misbranded, described in part 601.

14. Data and information about an in vitro diagnostic product submitted as part of the procedures for establishing, amending, or repealing a standard for these products, described in part 809.

15. An Application for an Investigational Device Exemption, described in part 812.

16. Data and information about a medical device submitted as part of the procedures for classifying these devices, described in section 513.

17. Data and information about a medical device submitted as part of the procedures for establishing, amending, or repealing a standard for these devices, described in section 514.

18. An application for premarket approval of a medical device, described in section 515.

19. A product development protocol for a medical device, described in section 515.

20. Data and information about an electronic product submitted as part of the procedures for establishing, amending, or repealing a standard for these products, described in section 358 of the Public Health Service Act.

21. Data and information about an electronic product submitted as part of the procedures for obtaining a variance from any electronic product performance standard, as described in Sec. 1010.4.

22. Data and information about an electronic product submitted as part of the procedures for granting, amending, or extending an exemption from a radiation safety performance standard, as described in Sec. 1010.5.

c. Clinical investigation means any experiment that involves a test article and one or more human subjects and that either is subject to requirements for prior submission to the Food and Drug Administration under section 505(i), 507(d), or 520(g) of the act, or is not subject to requirements for prior submission to the Food and

Drug Administration under these sections of the act, but the results of which are intended to be submitted later to, or held for inspection by, the Food and Drug Administration as part of an application for a research or marketing permit. The term does not include experiments that are subject to the provisions of part 58 of this chapter, regarding nonclinical laboratory studies.

d.   Investigator means an individual who actually conducts a clinical investigation, i.e., under whose immediate direction the test article is administered or dispensed to, or used involving, a subject, or, in the event of an investigation conducted by a team of individuals, is the responsible leader of that team.

e.   Sponsor means a person who initiates a clinical investigation, but who does not actually conduct the investigation, i.e., the test article is administered or dispensed to or used involving, a subject under the immediate direction of another individual. A person other than an individual (e.g., corporation or agency) that uses one or more of its own employees to conduct a clinical investigation it has initiated is considered to be a sponsor (not a sponsor-investigator), and the employees are considered to be investigators.

f.   Sponsor-investigator means an individual who both initiates and actually conducts, alone or with others, a clinical investigation, i.e., under whose immediate direction the test article is administered or dispensed to, or used involving, a subject. The term does not include any person other than an individual, e.g., corporation or agency.

g.   Human subject means an individual who is or becomes a participant in research, either as a recipient of the test article or as a control. A subject may be either a healthy human or a patient.

h.   Institution means any public or private entity or agency (including Federal, State, and other agencies). The word facility as used in section 520(g) of the act is deemed to be synonymous with the term institution for purposes of this part.

i.   Institutional review board (IRB) means any board, committee, or other group formally designated by an institution to review biomedical research involving humans as subjects, to approve the initiation of and conduct periodic review of such research. The term has the same meaning as the phrase institutional review committee as used in section 520(g) of the act.

j. Test article means any drug (including a biological product for human use), medical device for human use, human food additive, color additive, electronic product, or any other article subject to regulation under the act or under sections 351 and 354-360F of the Public Health Service Act (42 U.S.C. 262 and 263b-263n).

k. Minimal risk means that the probability and magnitude of harm or discomfort anticipated in the research are not greater in and of themselves than those ordinarily encountered in daily life or during the performance of routine physical or psychological examinations or tests.

l. Legally authorized representative means an individual or judicial or other body authorized under applicable law to consent on behalf of a prospective subject to the subject's particpation in the procedure(s) involved in the research.

m. Family member means any one of the following legally competent persons: Spouse; parents; children (including adopted children); brothers, sisters, and spouses of brothers and sisters; and any individual related by blood or affinity whose close association with the subject is the equivalent of a family relationship.

B. Informed Consent of Human Subjects

Sec. 50.20 General requirements for informed consent.

Except as provided in Sec. 50.23, no investigator may involve a human being as a subject in research covered by these regulations unless the investigator has obtained the legally effective informed consent of the subject or the subject's legally authorized representative. An investigator shall seek such consent only under circumstances that provide the prospective subject or the representative sufficient opportunity to consider whether or not to participate and that minimize the possibility of coercion or undue influence. The information that is given to the subject or the representative shall be in language understandable to the subject or the representative. No informed consent, whether oral or written, may include any exculpatory language through which the subject or the representative is made to waive or appear to waive any of the subject's legal rights, or releases or appears to release the investigator, the sponsor, the institution, or its agents from liability for negligence.

Sec. 50.23 Exception from general requirements.

a. The obtaining of informed consent shall be deemed feasible unless, before use of the test article (except as provided in paragraph (b) of this section), both the investigator and a physician who is not otherwise participating in the clinical investigation certify in writing all of the following:

 1. The human subject is confronted by a life-threatening situation necessitating the use of the test article.

 2. Informed consent cannot be obtained from the subject because of an inability to communicate with, or obtain legally effective consent from, the subject.

 3. Time is not sufficient to obtain consent from the subject's legal representative.

 4. There is available no alternative method of approved or generally recognized therapy that provides an equal or greater likelihood of saving the life of the subject.

b. If immediate use of the test article is, in the investigator's opinion, required to preserve the life of the subject, and time is not sufficient to obtain the independent determination required in paragraph (a) of this section in advance of using the test article, the determinations of the clinical investigator shall be made and, within 5 working days after the use of the article, be reviewed and evaluated in writing by a physician who is not participating in the clinical investigation.

c. The documentation required in paragraph (a) or (b) of this section shall be submitted to the IRB within 5 working days after the use of the test article.

d. 1. The Commissioner may also determine that obtaining informed consent is not feasible when the Assistant Secretary of Defense (Health Affairs) requests such a determination in connection with the use of an investigational drug (including an antibiotic or biological product) in a specific protocol under an investigational new drug application (IND) sponsored by the Department of Defense (DOD). DOD's request for a determination that obtaining informed consent from military personnel is not feasible must be limited to a specific military operation involving combat or the immediate threat of combat. The request must also include a written justification supporting the conclusions of the physician(s) responsible for the medical care of the military personnel involved and the investigator(s) identified in the IND that a military combat exigency exists because of special military combat (actual or threatened) circumstances in which, in order to facilitate the accomplishment of the military mission, preservation of the health of the individual and the safety of other personnel require that a particular treatment be provided to a specified group of military personnel, without regard to what might be any individual's personal preference for no treatment or for some alternative treatment. The written request must also include a statement that a duly constituted institutional review board has reviewed and approved the use of the investigational drug without informed consent. The Commissioner may find that informed consent is not feasible only when withholding treatment would be contrary to the best interests of military personnel and there is no available satisfactory alternative therapy.

2.   In reaching a determination under paragraph (d)(1) of this section that obtaining informed consent is not feasible and withholding treatment would be contrary to the best interests of military personnel, the Commissioner will review the request submitted under paragraph (d)(1) of this section and take into account all pertinent factors, including, but not limited to: i. The extent and strength of the evidence of the safety and effectiveness of the investigational drug for the intended use; ii. The context in which the drug will be administered, e.g., whether it is intended for use in a battlefield or hospital setting or whether it will be self-administered or will be administered by a health professional; iii. The nature of the disease or condition for which the preventive or therapeutic treatment is intended; and iv. The nature of the information to be provided to the recipients of the drug concerning the potential benefits and risks of taking or not taking the drug.

3.   The Commissioner may request a recommendation from appropriate experts before reaching a determination on a request submitted under paragraph (d)(1) of this section.

4.   A determination by the Commissioner that obtaining informed consent is not feasible and withholding treatment would be contrary to the best interests of military personnel will

expire at the end of 1 year, unless renewed at DOD's request, or when DOD informs the Commissioner that the specific military operation creating the need for the use of the investigational drug has ended, whichever is earlier. The Commissioner may also revoke this determination based on changed circumstances.

Sec. 50.24 Exception from informed consent requirements for emergency research.

a. The IRB responsible for the review, approval, and continuing review of the clinical investigation described in this section may approve that investigation without requiring that informed consent of all research subjects be obtained if the IRB (with the concurrence of a licensed physician who is a member of or consultant to the IRB and who is not otherwise participating in the clinical investigation) finds and documents each of the following:

1. The human subjects are in a life-threatening situation, available treatments are unproven or unsatisfactory, and the collection of valid scientific evidence, which may include evidence obtained through randomized placebo-controlled investigations, is necessary to determine the safety and effectiveness of particular interventions.

2. Obtaining informed consent is not feasible because: **i.** The subjects will not be able to give their informed consent as a result of their medical condition; **ii.** The intervention under investigation must be administered before consent from the subjects' legally authorized representatives is feasible; and **iii.** There is no reasonable way to identify prospectively the individuals likely to become eligible for participation in the clinical investigation.

3. Participation in the research holds out the prospect of direct benefit to the subjects because: **i.** Subjects are facing a life-threatening situation that necessitates intervention; **ii.** Appropriate animal and other preclinical studies have been conducted, and the information derived from those studies and related evidence support the potential for the intervention to provide a direct benefit to the individual subjects; and **iii.** Risks associated with the investigation are reasonable in relation to what is known about the medical condition of the potential class of subjects, the risks and benefits of standard therapy, if any, and what is known

about the risks and benefits of the proposed intervention or activity.

4. The clinical investigation could not practicably be carried out without the waiver.

5. The proposed investigational plan defines the length of the potential therapeutic window based on scientific evidence, and the investigator has committed to attempting to contact a legally authorized representative for each subject within that window of time and, if feasible, to asking the legally authorized representative contacted for consent within that window rather than proceeding without consent. The investigator will summarize efforts made to contact legally authorized representatives and make this information available to the IRB at the time of continuing review.

6. The IRB has reviewed and approved informed consent procedures and an informed consent document consistent with Sec. 50.25. These procedures and the informed consent document are to be used with subjects or their legally authorized representatives in situations where use of such procedures and documents is feasible. The IRB has reviewed and approved procedures and information to be used when providing an opportunity for a family member to object to a subject's participation in the clinical investigation consistent with paragraph (a)(7)(v) of this section.

7. Additional protections of the rights and welfare of the subjects will be provided, including, at least: i. Consultation (including, where appropriate, consultation carried out by the IRB) with representatives of the communities in which the clinical investigation will be conducted and from which the subjects will be drawn; ii. Public disclosure to the communities in which the clinical investigation will be conducted and from which the subjects will be drawn, prior to initiation of the clinical investigation, of plans for the investigation and its risks and expected benefits; iii. Public disclosure of sufficient information following completion of the clinical investigation to apprise the community and researchers of the study, including the demographic characteristics of the research population, and its results; iv. Establishment of an independent data monitoring committee to exercise oversight of the clinical investigation; and v. If obtaining informed consent is not feasible and a legally authorized representative is

not reasonably available, the investigator has committed, if feasible, to attempting to contact within the therapeutic window the subject's family member who is not a legally authorized representative, and asking whether he or she objects to the subject's participation in the clinical investigation. The investigator will summarize efforts made to contact family members and make this information available to the IRB at the time of continuing review.

b. The IRB is responsible for ensuring that procedures are in place to inform, at the earliest feasible opportunity, each subject, or if the subject remains incapacitated, a legally authorized representative of the subject, or if such a representative is not reasonably available, a family member, of the subject's inclusion in the clinical investigation, the details of the investigation and other information contained in the informed consent document. The IRB shall also ensure that there is a procedure to inform the subject, or if the subject remains incapacitated, a legally authorized representative of the subject, or if such a representative is not reasonably available, a family member, that he or she may discontinue the subject's participation at any time without penalty or loss of benefits to which the subject is otherwise entitled. If a legally authorized representative or family member is told about the clinical investigation and the subject's condition improves, the subject is also to be informed as soon as feasible. If a subject is entered into a clinical investigation with waived consent and the subject dies before a legally authorized representative or family member can be contacted, information about the clinical investigation is to be provided to the subject's legally authorized representative or family member, if feasible.

c. The IRB determinations required by paragraph (a) of this section and the documentation required by paragraph (e) of this section are to be retained by the IRB for at least 3 years after completion of the clinical investigation, and the records shall be accessible for inspection and copying by FDA in accordance with Sec. 56.115(b) of this chapter.

d. Protocols involving an exception to the informed consent requirement under this section must be performed under a separate investigational new drug application (IND) or investigational device exemption (IDE) that clearly identifies such protocols as protocols that may include subjects who are unable to consent. The submission of those protocols in a separate IND/IDE is required even if an IND for the same drug product or an IDE for the same device already exists. Applications for investigations under this section may not be submitted as amendments under Secs. 312.30 or 812.35 of this chapter.

e. If an IRB determines that it cannot approve a clinical investigation because the investigation does not meet the criteria in the exception provided under paragraph (a) of this section or because of other relevant ethical concerns, the IRB must document its findings and provide these findings promptly in writing to the clinical investigator and to the sponsor of the clinical investigation. The sponsor of the clinical investigation must promptly disclose this information to FDA and to the sponsor's clinical investigators who are participating or are asked to participate in this or a substantially equivalent clinical investigation of the sponsor, and to other IRBs that have been, or are, asked to review this or a substantially equivalent investigation by that sponsor.

Sec. 50.25 Elements of informed consent.

a. Basic elements of informed consent. In seeking informed consent, the following information shall be provided to each subject:

1. A statement that the study involves research, an explanation of the purposes of the research and the expected duration of the subject's participation, a description of the procedures to be followed, and identification of any procedures which are experimental.

2. A description of any reasonably foreseeable risks or discomforts to the subject.

3. A description of any benefits to the subject or to others which may reasonably be expected from the research.

4. A disclosure of appropriate alternative procedures or courses of treatment, if any, that might be advantageous to the subject.

5. A statement describing the extent, if any, to which confidentiality of records identifying the subject will be maintained and that notes the possibility that the Food and Drug Administration may inspect the records.

6. For research involving more than minimal risk, an explanation as to whether any compensation and an explanation as to whether any medical treatments are available if injury occurs and, if so, what they consist of, or where further information may be obtained.

7. An explanation of whom to contact for answers to pertinent questions about the research and research subjects' rights, and whom to contact in the event of a research-related injury to the subject.

8. A statement that participation is voluntary, that refusal to participate will involve no penalty or loss of benefits to which the subject is otherwise entitled, and that the subject may discontinue participation at any time without penalty or loss of benefits to which the subject is otherwise entitled.

b. Additional elements of informed consent. When appropriate, one or more of the following elements of information shall also be provided to each subject:

1. A statement that the particular treatment or procedure may involve risks to the subject (or to the embryo or fetus, if the subject is or may become pregnant) which are currently unforeseeable.

2. Anticipated circumstances under which the subject's participation may be terminated by the investigator without regard to the subject's consent.

3. Any additional costs to the subject that may result from participation in the research.

4. The consequences of a subject's decision to withdraw from the research and procedures for orderly termination of participation by the subject.

5. A statement that significant new findings developed during the course of the research which may relate to the subject's willingness to continue participation will be provided to the subject.

6. The approximate number of subjects involved in the study.

c. The informed consent requirements in these regulations are not intended to preempt any applicable Federal, State, or local laws which require additional information to be disclosed for informed consent to be legally effective.

d. Nothing in these regulations is intended to limit the authority of a physician to provide emergency medical care to the extent the physician is permitted to do so under applicable Federal, State, or local law.

Sec. 50.27 Documentation of informed consent.

a. Except as provided in Sec. 56.109(c), informed consent shall be documented by the use of a written consent form approved by the IRB and signed and dated by the subject or the subject's legally authorized representative at the time of consent. A copy shall be given to the person signing the form.

b. Except as provided in Sec. 56.109(c), the consent form may be either of the following:

1. A written consent document that embodies the elements of informed consent required by Sec. 50.25. This form may be read to the subject or the subject's legally authorized representative, but, in any event, the investigator shall give either the subject or the representative adequate opportunity to read it before it is signed.

2. A short form written consent document stating that the elements of informed consent required by Sec. 50.25 have been presented orally to the subject or the subject's legally authorized representative. When this method is used, there shall be a witness to the oral presentation. Also, the IRB shall approve a written summary of what is to be said to the subject or the representative. Only the short form itself is to be signed by the subject or the representative. However, the witness shall sign both the short form and a copy of the summary, and the person actually obtaining the consent shall sign a copy of the summary. A copy of the summary shall be given to the subject or the representative in addition to a copy of the short form.

Form 1572

DEPARTMENT OF HEALTH AND HUMAN SERVICES PUBLIC HEALTH SERVICE FOOD AND DRUG ADMINISTRATION **STATEMENT OF INVESTIGATOR** *(TITLE 21, CODE OF FEDERAL REGULATIONS (CFR) PART 312)* (See instructions on reverse side.)	Form Approved: OMB No. 0910-0014. Expiration Date: September 30, 2002. *See OMB Statement on Reverse.*
	NOTE: No investigator may participate in an investigation until he/she provides the sponsor with a completed, signed Statement of Investigator, Form FDA 1572 (21 CFR 312.53(c)).

1. NAME AND ADDRESS OF INVESTIGATOR

2. EDUCATION, TRAINING, AND EXPERIENCE THAT QUALIFIES THE INVESTIGATOR AS AN EXPERT IN THE CLINICAL INVESTIGATION OF THE DRUG FOR THE USE UNDER INVESTIGATION. ONE OF THE FOLLOWING IS ATTACHED.

☐ CURRICULUM VITAE   ☐ OTHER STATEMENT OF QUALIFICATIONS

3. NAME AND ADDRESS OF ANY MEDICAL SCHOOL, HOSPITAL OR OTHER RESEARCH FACILITY WHERE THE CLINICAL INVESTIGATION(S) WILL BE CONDUCTED.

4. NAME AND ADDRESS OF ANY CLINICAL LABORATORY FACILITIES TO BE USED IN THE STUDY.

5. NAME AND ADDRESS OF THE INSTITUTIONAL REVIEW BOARD (IRB) THAT IS RESPONSIBLE FOR REVIEW AND APPROVAL OF THE STUDY(IES).

6. NAMES OF THE SUBINVESTIGATORS *(e.g., research fellows, residents, associates)* WHO WILL BE ASSISTING THE INVESTIGATOR IN THE CONDUCT OF THE INVESTIGATION(S).

7. NAME AND CODE NUMBER, IF ANY, OF THE PROTOCOL(S) IN THE IND FOR THE STUDY(IES) TO BE CONDUCTED BY THE INVESTIGATOR.

FORM FDA 1572 (8/01)   PREVIOUS EDITION IS OBSOLETE.   PAGE 1 OF 2

8. ATTACH THE FOLLOWING CLINICAL PROTOCOL INFORMATION:

☐ FOR PHASE 1 INVESTIGATIONS, A GENERAL OUTLINE OF THE PLANNED INVESTIGATION INCLUDING THE ESTIMATED DURATION OF THE STUDY AND THE MAXIMUM NUMBER OF SUBJECTS THAT WILL BE INVOLVED.

☐ FOR PHASE 2 OR 3 INVESTIGATIONS, AN OUTLINE OF THE STUDY PROTOCOL INCLUDING AN APPROXIMATION OF THE NUMBER OF SUBJECTS TO BE TREATED WITH THE DRUG AND THE NUMBER TO BE EMPLOYED AS CONTROLS, IF ANY; THE CLINICAL USES TO BE INVESTIGATED; CHARACTERISTICS OF SUBJECTS BY AGE, SEX, AND CONDITION; THE KIND OF CLINICAL OBSERVATIONS AND LABORATORY TESTS TO BE CONDUCTED; THE ESTIMATED DURATION OF THE STUDY; AND COPIES OR A DESCRIPTION OF CASE REPORT FORMS TO BE USED.

9. COMMITMENTS:

I agree to conduct the study(ies) in accordance with the relevant, current protocol(s) and will only make changes in a protocol after notifying the sponsor, except when necessary to protect the safety, rights, or welfare of subjects.

I agree to personally conduct or supervise the described investigation(s).

I agree to inform any patients, or any persons used as controls, that the drugs are being used for investigational purposes and I will ensure that the requirements relating to obtaining informed consent in 21 CFR Part 50 and institutional review board (IRB) review and approval in 21 CFR Part 56 are met.

I agree to report to the sponsor adverse experiences that occur in the course of the investigation(s) in accordance with 21 CFR 312.64.

I have read and understand the information in the investigator's brochure, including the potential risks and side effects of the drug.

I agree to ensure that all associates, colleagues, and employees assisting in the conduct of the study(ies) are informed about their obligations in meeting the above commitments.

I agree to maintain adequate and accurate records in accordance with 21 CFR 312.62 and to make those records available for inspection in accordance with 21 CFR 312.68.

I will ensure that an IRB that complies with the requirements of 21 CFR Part 56 will be responsible for the initial and continuing review and approval of the clinical investigation. I also agree to promptly report to the IRB all changes in the research activity and all unanticipated problems involving risks to human subjects or others. Additionally, I will not make any changes in the research without IRB approval, except where necessary to eliminate apparent immediate hazards to human subjects.

I agree to comply with all other requirements regarding the obligations of clinical investigators and all other pertinent requirements in 21 CFR Part 312.

INSTRUCTIONS FOR COMPLETING FORM FDA 1572
STATEMENT OF INVESTIGATOR:

1. Complete all sections. Attach a separate page if additional space is needed.

2. Attach curriculum vitae or other statement of qualifications as described in Section 2.

3. Attach protocol outline as described in Section 8.

4. Sign and date below.

5. FORWARD THE COMPLETED FORM AND ATTACHMENTS TO THE SPONSOR. The sponsor will incorporate this information along with other technical data into an Investigational New Drug Application (IND).

10. SIGNATURE OF INVESTIGATOR	11. DATE

(WARNING: A willfully false statement is a criminal offense. U.S.C. Title 18, Sec. 1001.)

Public reporting burden for this collection of information is estimated to average 100 hours per response, including the time for reviewing instructions, searching existing data sources, gathering and maintaining the data needed, and completing reviewing the collection of information. Send comments regarding this burden estimate or any other aspect of this collection of information, including suggestions for reducing this burden to:

Food and Drug Administration
CBER (HFM-99)
1401 Rockville Pike
Rockville, MD 20852-1448

Food and Drug Administration
CDER (HFD-94)
12229 Wilkins Avenue
Rockville, MD 20852

"An agency may not conduct or sponsor, and a person is not required to respond to, a collection of information unless it displays a currently valid OMB control number."

Please **DO NOT RETURN** this application to this address.

FORM FDA 1572 (8/01)   PAGE 2 OF 2

Directory of Health Associations

Use the following list to identify and contact health associations. These organizations often provide information and assistance for patients looking to participate in clinical trials. This list is updated frequently on the CenterWatch web site (www.centerwatch.com).

General

World Health Organization
Avenue Appia 20
1211 Geneva 27
Switzerland
+00 (41) 22-791-21-11
+00 (41) 22-791-31-11 fax
library@who.int
www.who.org

Cardiology/ Vascular Diseases

American Heart Association
National Center
7272 Greenville Ave.
Dallas, TX 75231-4599
(800) 242-8721
(214) 706-1341 fax
www.americanheart.org

Dermatology/ Plastic Surgery

The American Academy of Dermatology
930 N. Meacham Rd.
PO Box 4014
Schaumburg, IL 60168
(847) 330-0230
(847) 330-0050 fax
www.aad.org

National Psoriasis Foundation
6600 S.W. 92nd Ave.
Suite 300
Portland, OR 97223
(503) 244-7404
(503) 245-0626 fax
getinfo@npfusa.org
www.psoriasis.org

Endocrinology

American Diabetes Association
ATTN: Customer Services
1701 North Beauregard St.
Alexandria, VA 22311
(800) DIABETES
(703) 683-2890 fax
customerservice@diabetes.org
www.diabetes.org

Joslin Diabetes Center
One Joslin Place
Boston, MA 02215
(800) JOSLIN-1
(617) 732-2664 fax
www.joslin.harvard.edu

The Endocrine Society
4350 East West Hwy.
Suite 500
Bethesda, MD 20814-4426
(301) 941-0200
(301) 941-0259 fax
endostaff@endo-society.org
www.endo-society.org

Gastroenterology

**American Association for
the Study of Liver Diseases**
1729 King St.
Suite 100
Alexandria, VA 22314
(703) 299-9766
(703) 299-9622 fax
www.aasld.org

**American Board of
Colon and Rectal Surgery**
20600 Eureka Rd.
Suite 600
Taylor, MI 48180
(734) 282-9400
(734) 282-9402 fax
admin@abcrs.org
www.abcrs.org

**The American
Gastroenterological Association**
7910 Woodmont Ave.
Seventh Floor
Bethesda, MD 20814
(301) 654-2055
(301) 652-3890 fax
webinfo@gastro.org
www.gastro.org

American Liver Foundation
75 Maiden Lane
Suite 603
New York, NY 10038
(800) GO-LIVER (465-4837)
webmail@liverfoundation.org
www.liverfoundation.org

**Crohn's and Colitis
Foundation of America**
386 Park Ave. S.
17th Floor
New York, NY 10016
(800) 932-2423
(212) 779-4098 fax
info@ccfa.org
www.ccfa.org

Digestive Disease National Coalition
507 Capitol Court N.E.
Suite 200
Washington, DC 20002
(202) 544-7497
(202) 546-7105 fax

The Gastro-Intestinal Research Foundation
70 E. Lake St.
Suite 1015
Chicago, IL 60601-5907
(312) 332-1350
girf@girf.org
www.girf.org

Pediatric Crohn's and Colitis Association
PO Box 188
Newton, MA 02468
(617) 489-5854
http://pcca.hypermart.net

Gynecology

Endometriosis Association
8585 N. 76th Place
Milwaukee, WI 53223
(414) 355-2200
(414) 355-6065 fax
www.endometriosisassn.org

Hematology

National Heart, Lung, and Blood Institute
NHLBIinfo@rover.nhlbi.nih.gov
www.nhlbi.nih.gov

Sickle Cell Disease Association of America
200 Corporate Pointe
Suite 495
Culver City, CA 90230
(800) 421-8453

Immunology/ Infectious Diseases

American Academy of Allergy, Asthma, & Immunology
611 E. Wells St.
Milwaukee, WI 53202
(800) 822-2762
(414) 272-6071
(414) 272-6070 fax
info@aaaai.org
www.aaaai.org

American Autoimmune Related Diseases Association
22100 Gratiot Ave.
E. Detroit, MI 48021
(586) 776-3900
aarda@aol.com
www.aarda.org

American Foundation
for AIDS Research
120 Wall St.
13th Floor
New York, NY 10005-3902
(800) 39-amfAR
(212) 806-1601 fax
www.amfar.org

Musculoskeletal

National Osteoporosis Foundation
1232 22nd St. N.W.
Washington, DC 20037-1292
(202) 223-2226
www.nof.org

Arthritis Foundation
P.O. Box 7669
Atlanta, GA 30357-0669
(800) 283-7800
help@arthritis.org
www.arthritis.org

Nephrology/Urology

American Society of Nephrology
2025 M St. N.W., #800
Washington, DC 20036
(202) 367-1190
(202) 367-2190 fax
asn@dc.sba.com
www.asn-online.org

Neurology

Alzheimer's Association
919 North Michigan Ave.
Suite 1100
Chicago, IL 60611-1676
(800) 272-3900
(312) 335-1110 fax
info@alz.org
www.alz.org

American Academy of Neurology
1080 Montreal Ave.
St. Paul, MN 55116
(651) 695-1940
www.aan.com

United Cerebral Palsy Associations
1660 L St. N.W.
Suite 700
Washington, DC 20036
www.ucp.org

National Stroke Association
9707 E. Easter Lane
Englewood, CO 80112
(800) 787-6537
(303) 649-1328 fax
www.stroke.org

Oncology

National Cancer Institute
Bldg. 31, Rm. 10A31
31 Center Drive MSC 2580
Bethesda, MD 20892-2580
(800) 4-CANCER
www.nci.nih.gov

American Cancer Society
1599 Clifton Rd.
Atlanta, GA 30329
(800) ACS-2345
www.cancer.org

**The Leukemia and
Lymphoma Society**
1311 Mamaroneck Ave.
White Plains, NY 10605
(800) 955-4572
www.leukemia-lymphoma.org

Ophthalmology

The Glaucoma Foundation
116 John Street, Suite 1605
New York, NY 10038
(212) 285-0080
info@glaucoma-foundation.org
www.glaucoma-foundation.org

Otolaryngology

American Tinnitus Association
PO Box 5
Portland, OR 97207
(503) 248-9985
(503) 248-0024 fax
tinnitus@ata.org
www.ata.org

The Ear InfoSite
www.earinfosite.org

Pediatrics/Neonatology

March of Dimes
1275 Mamaroneck Ave.
White Plains, NY 10605
(888) MODIMES
www.modimes.org

National Children's Cancer Society
1015 Locust
Suite 600
St. Louis, MO 63101
(800) 532-6459
www.children-cancer.org

Pediheart
www.pediheart.org

Psychiatry/Psychology

**National Alliance
for the Mentally Ill**
1740 Broadway
New York, NY 10019
(212) 315-8700
info@lungusa.org
www.lungusa.org

**The Center for Mental
Health Services**
Colonial Place Three
2107 Wilson Blvd.
Suite 300
Arlington, VA 22201
(703) 524-7600
www.nami.org

Pulmonary/
Respiratory Diseases

American Lung Association
1740 Broadway
New York, NY 10019
(212) 315-8700
info@lungusa.org
www.lungusa.org

**National Heart, Lung,
and Blood Institute**
NHLBIinfo@rover.nhlbi.nih.gov
www.nhlbi.nih.gov

**Asthma and Allergy
Foundation of America**
1233 20th St. N.W.
Suite 402
Washington, DC 20036
(800) 7ASTHMA
(202) 466-8940 fax
info@aafa.org
www.aafa.org

**American Academy of Allergy,
Asthma, & Immunology**
611 E. Wells St.
Milwalkee, WI 53202
(800) 822-2762
(414) 272-6070 fax
info@aaaai.org
www.aaaai.org

Rheumatology

American College of Rheumatology
1800 Century Place
Suite 250
Atlanta, GA 30345
(404) 633-3777
(404) 633-1870 fax
acr@rheumatology.org
www.rheumatology.org

Arthritis Foundation
PO Box 7669
Atlanta, GA 30357-0669
(800) 283-7800
www.arthritis.org

Directory of Biotechnology and Pharmaceutical Companies

Use the list below to find clinical trials in your therapeutic area or to learn more about drugs in development at particular companies. Their web sites often have a section on clinical trials in progress.

This list of pharmaceutical companies is up to date as of the book's publication, but this is a dynamic industry. Please refer to the CenterWatch web site (www.centerwatch.com) for a current listing.

3M Pharmaceuticals
3M Center
Building 275-3W-01
St. Paul, MN 55144
(888) 364-3577
www.mmm.com

Aastrom Biosciences
24 Frank Lloyd Wright Dr.
PO Box 376
Ann Arbor, MI 48106
(734) 930-5555
(734) 665-0485 fax
www.aastrom.com

Abbott Laboratories
(847) 937-6100
(847) 937-1511 fax
www.abbott.com

Abgenix
6701 Kaiser Dr.
Fremont, CA 94555
(510) 608-6500
(510) 608-6511 fax
www.abgenix.com

Academic Pharmaceuticals
21 N. Skokie Valley Hwy.
Suite G3
Lake Bluff, IL 60044
(847) 735-1170
(847) 735-1173 fax

Acambis
38 Sidney St.
Cambridge, MA 02139
(617) 494-1339
(617) 494-1741 fax
www.acambis.com

Access Pharmaceuticals
2600 Stemmons Fwy.
Suite 176
Dallas, TX 75207
(214) 905-5100
(214) 905-5101 fax
axcs@accesspharma.com
www.accesspharma.com

Acorda Therapeutics
15 Skyline Dr.
Hawthorne, NY 10532
(914) 347-4300
(914) 347-4560 fax
info@acorda.com
www.acorda.com

Acusphere
500 Arsenal St.
Watertown, MA 02472
(617) 648-8800
(617) 926-4750 fax
www.acusphere.com

ADAC Laboratories
540 Alder Dr.
Milpitas, CA 95035
(800) 538-8531
(408) 321-9536 fax
www.adaclabs.com

Adolor
620 Pennsylvania Dr.
Exton, PA 19355
(484) 595-1500
(484) 595-1520 fax
adolor@adolor.com
www.adolor.com

Advanced Magnetics
61 Mooney St.
Cambridge, MA 02138
(617) 497-2070
(617) 547-2445 fax
info@advancedmagnetics.com
www.advancedmagnetics.com

Advanced Tissue Sciences
10933 N. Torrey Pines Rd.
La Jolla, CA 92037
(858) 713-7300
(858) 713-7400 fax
www.advancedtissue.com

Advanced Viral Research
200 Corporate Blvd. S.
Yonkers, NY 10701
(914) 376-7383
(914) 376-7368 fax
AGallantar@adviral.com
www.adviral.com

AEterna Laboratories
1405 Parc-Technologique Blvd.
Québec, QC
Canada G1P 4P5
(418) 652-8525
www.aeterna.com

Affymax Research Institute
4001 Miranda Ave.
Palo Alto, CA 94304
(650) 812-8700
(650) 434-0832 fax
www.affymax.com

AGI Dermatics
205 Buffalo Ave.
Freeport, NY 11520
(516) 868-9026
(516) 868-9143 fax
staff@agiderm.com
www.agiderm.com

Agouron Pharmaceuticals
10777 Science Center Dr.
San Diego, CA 92121
(858) 622-3000
(858) 678-8272 fax
www.agouron.com

Ajinomoto U.S.A.
Country Club Plaza
West 115 Century Rd.
Paramus, NJ 07652
(201) 261-1789
(201) 261-7343 fax
www.ajinomoto-usa.com

Akorn
2500 Millbrook Dr.
Buffalo Grove, IL 60089
(847) 279-6100
(847) 279-6123 fax
www.akorn.com

Alcon
6201 South Fwy.
Ft. Worth, TX 76134
(817) 293-0450
www.alconlabs.com

Alexion Pharmaceuticals
352 Knotter Dr.
Cheshire, CT 06410
(203) 272-2596
(203) 271-8198 fax
www.alxn.com

Alfacell
225 Belleville Ave.
Bloomfield, NJ 07003
(973) 748-8082
(973) 748-1355 fax
www.alfacell.com

Alkermes
64 Sidney St.
Cambridge, MA 02139
(617) 494-0171
(617) 494-9263 fax
www.alkermes.com

Allergan
2525 DuPont Dr.
PO Box 19534
Irvine, CA 92623-9534
(714) 246-4500
www.allergan.com

Alliance Pharmaceutical
3040 Science Park Rd.
San Diego, CA 92121
(858) 410-5200
(858) 410-5201 fax
www.allp.com

Allos Therapeutics
11080 CirclePoint Rd.
Suite 200
Westminster, CO 80020
(303) 426-6262
(303) 412-9160 fax
www.allos.com

Alpha Therapeutic
5555 Valley Blvd.
Los Angeles, CA 90032
(323) 225-2221
info@alphather.com
www.alphather.com

Alpharma USPD
7205 Windsor Blvd.
Baltimore, MD 21244
(800) 638-9096
(410) 298-6343 fax
www.alpharma.com

AltaRex
610 Lincoln St.
Waltham, MA 02451
(888) 801-6665
(781) 672-0142 fax
info@altarex.com
www.altarex.com

Alteon
170 Williams Dr.
Ramsey, NJ 07446
(201) 934-5000
(201) 934-8880 fax
www.alteonpharma.com

Alza
1900 Charleston Rd.
PO Box 7210
Mountain View, CA 94039-7210
(650) 564-5000
(650) 564-7070 fax
info@alza.com
www.alza.com

Amarillo Biosciences
Clinical Trials Area
800 W. Ninth Ave.
Amarillo, TX 79101
(806) 376-1741
(806) 376-9301 fax
www.amarbio.com

American Biogenetic Sciences
1375 Akron St.
Copiague, NY 11726
(631) 789-2600
(631) 789-1661 fax
info@mabxa.com
www.mabxa.com

American Home Products
5 Giralda Farms
Madison, NJ 07940
pr@ahp.com
www.ahp.com

Amerimmune
4236 Longridge Ave.
Unit #302
Studio City, CA 91604
(323) 525-0560
(323) 525-0870 fax
www.amerimmune.com

Amersham Biosciences
800 Centennial Ave.
PO Box 1327
Piscataway, NJ 08855-1327
(800) 526-3593
apbcsus@am.apbiotech.com
www.apbiotech.com

Amgen
Amgen Center
Thousand Oaks, CA 91320-1799
(805) 447-1000
(805) 447-1010 fax
www.amgen.com

Amide Pharmaceutical
101 E. Main St.
Little Falls, NJ 07424
(973) 890-1440
(973) 890-7980 fax
www.amide.com

Amylin Pharmaceuticals
9373 Towne Centre Dr.
Suite 250
San Diego, CA 92121
(858) 552-2200
(858) 552-2212 fax
www.amylin.com

Andrulis Pharmaceuticals
11800 Baltimore Ave
Beltsville, MD 20705
(301) 419-2400
(301) 419-3056 fax

Andrx
4955 Orange Dr.
Davie, FL 33314
(954) 584-0300
(954) 217-4327 fax
www.andrx.com

Anesta
4745 Wiley Post Way
Plaza 6, Suite 650
Salt Lake City, UT 84116
(800) 595-1405
(801) 595-1406 fax

Angelini Pharmaceuticals
70 Grand Ave.
Suite 109
River Edge, NJ 07661-1935
(201) 489-4100
(201) 489-9535 fax
www.angelinipharmaceuticals.com

Angiotech Pharmaceuticals
6660 N.W. Marine Dr.
Vancouver, BC
Canada V6T-1Z4
(604) 221-7676
(604) 221-2330 fax
www.angiotech.com

Angstrom Pharmaceuticals
10655 Roselle St.
Suite G
San Diego, CA 92121
(858) 350-1760
(858) 350-1761 fax
info@angstrominc.com
www.angstrominc.com

Anika Therapeutics
236 West Cummings Park
Woburn, MA 01801
(781) 932-6616
(781) 935-4120 fax
www.anikatherapeutics.com

Annovis
34 Mount Pleasant Dr.
Aston, PA 19014
(610) 579-1200
(610) 579-1201 fax
info@annovis.com
www.annovis.com

AnorMED
#200-20353 64th Ave.
Langley, BC
Canada V2Y 1N5
(604) 530-1057
(604) 530-0976 fax
info@anormed.com
www.anormed.com

Antex Biologics
300 Professional Dr.
Gaithersburg, MD 20879
(301) 590-0129
(301) 590-1251 fax
info@antexbiologics.com
www.antexbiologics.com

Anthra Pharmaceuticals
103 Carnegie Center
Suite 102
Princeton, NJ 08540
(609) 924.2680
(609) 924.3875 fax
www.anthra.com

Antigenics
630 Fifth Ave.
New York, NY 10111
(212) 332-4774
(212) 332-4778 fax
www.antigenics.com

Aphton Corporation
444 Brickell Ave.
Suite 51-507
Miami, FL 33131
(305) 374-7338
(305) 374-7615 fax
www.aphton.com

Apollo Biopharmaceutics
1 Broadway
Suite 600
Cambridge, MA 02142
(617) 621-7154

Aquila Biopharmaceuticals
175 Crossing Blvd.
Framingham, MA 01702
(508) 628-0100

Aradigm Corporation
3929 Point Eden Way
Hayward, CA 94545
(510) 265-9000
(510) 265-0277 fax
clinical@aradigm.com
www.aradigm.com

Arena Pharmaceuticals
6166 Nancy Ridge Dr.
San Diego, CA 92121
(858) 453-7200
(858) 453-7210 fax
www.arenapharm.com

Ariad Pharmaceuticals
26 Landsdowne St.
Cambridge, MA 02139
(617) 494-0400
(617) 494-8144 fax
www.ariad.com

Arkios BioDevelopment International
1093 Blackburn Ln.
Virginia Beach, VA 23454
(757) 228-3255
(757) 228-3256 fax
info@arkios.com
www.arkios.com

ArQule
19 Presidential Way
Woburn, MA 01801-5140
(781)-994-0300
info@arqule.com
www.arqule.com

Ascent Pediatrics
187 Ballardvale St.
Suite B-125
Wilmington, MA 01887
(978) 658-2500
(978) 658-3939 fax
www.ascentpediatrics.com

AstraZeneca
1800 Concord Pike
PO Box 15437
Wilmington, DE 19850
(800) 456-3669
(302) 886-2972 fax
www.astrazeneca.com

AtheroGenics
8995 Westside Parkway
Alpharetta, GA 30004
(678) 336-2500
(678) 336-2501 fax
www.atherogenics.com

Atlantic Technology Ventures
350 Fifth Ave.
Suite 5507
New York, NY 10118
(212) 267-2503
(212) 267-2159 fax
www.atlan.com

Atrix Laboratories
2579 Midpoint Dr.
Ft. Collins, CO 80525
(970) 482-5868
www.atrixlabs.com

AuRX, Inc
500 J McCormick Dr.
Glen Burnie, MD 21061
(410) 590-7610
(410) 590-2688 fax
www.aurx.com

AutoImmune Technologies
144 Elks Place
Suite 1402
New Orleans, LA 70112
(504) 529-9944
(504) 529-8982 fax
mailbox@autoimmune.com
www.autoimmune.com

AVANIR Pharmaceuticals
11388 Sorrento Valley Rd
Suite 200
San Diego, CA 92121
(858) 622-5200
(858) 658-7447 fax
www.avanir.com

AVANT Immunotherapeutics
119 Fourth Ave.
Needham, MA 02494-2725
(781) 433-0771
(781) 433-0262 fax
info@avantimmune.com
www.avantimmune.com

AVAX Technologies
9200 Indian Creek Parkway
Suite 200
Overland Park, KS 66210
(913) 693-8491
(913) 693-8497 fax
www.avax-tech.com

Aventis
300 Somerset Corporate Blvd.
Bridgewater, NJ 08807-2854
(800) 981-2491
www.aventis.com

AVI BioPharma
4575 S.W. Research Way
Suite 200
Corvallis, OR 97333
(541) 753-3635
www.AVIBIO.com

Avigen
1301 Harbor Bay Parkway
Alameda, CA 94502
(510) 748-7150
(510) 748-7155 fax
www.avigen.com

Aviron
297 N. Bernardo Ave.
Mountain View, CA 94043
(650) 919-6500
(650) 919-6610 fax
www.aviron.com

Axcan Pharma
597 Laurier Blvd
Mont-Saint-Hilaire, QC
Canada J3H 6C4
(450) 467-5138
(450) 464-9979 fax
axcan@axcan.com
www.axcan.com

Axonyx
825 Third Ave.
40th Floor
New York, NY 10022
(212) 688-4770
(212) 688-4843 fax
info@axonyx.com
www.axonyx.com

Bausch & Lomb Pharmaceuticals
8500 Hidden River Parkway
Tampa, FL 33637
Telephone: 813-975-7770
(800) 227-1427
www.bausch.com

Baxter Healthcare
One Baxter Parkway
Deerfield, Il 60015
(847) 948-2000
www.baxter.com

Bayer
100 Bayer Rd.
Pittsburgh, PA 15205
(412) 777-2000
www.bayerus.com

Bentley Pharmaceuticals
65 Lafayette Rd.
Third Floor
North Hampton, NH 03862
(603) 964-8006
(603) 964-6889 fax
www.bentleypharm.com

Berlex Laboratories
340 Changebridge Rd.
PO Box 1000
Montville, NJ 07045-1000
(973) 487-2000
www.berlex.com

Bertek
3711 Collins Ferry Rd.
Morgantown, WV 26505
(304) 285-6420
www.bertek.com

Bio-Technology General
Medical Affairs
70 Wood Ave. S.
Iselin, NJ 08830
(732) 632-8800
www.btgc.com

Biocodex
1910 Fairview Ave. E.
Suite 208
Seattle, WA 98102
(206) 322-5663
(206) 323-2968 fax

BioCryst Pharmaceuticals
2190 Parkway Lake Dr.,
Birmingham, AL 35244
(205) 444-4600
(205) 444-4640 fax
info@biocryst.com
www.biocryst.com

Biogen
14 Cambridge Ctr.
Cambridge, MA 02142
(617) 679-2000
(617) 679-2617 fax
www.biogen.com

BioKeys
9948 Hibert St.
Suite 100
San Diego, CA 92131
(858) 271-9671
(858) 271-9678 fax
info@biokeys.com
www.biokeys.com

Biomedical Frontiers
1095 10th Ave. S.E.
Minneapolis, MN 55414
(612) 378-0228

BioNumerik Pharmaceuticals
8122 Datapoint Dr.
Suite 1250
San Antonio, TX 78229
(210) 614-1701

Biopure Corporation
11 Hurley St.
Cambridge, MA 02141
(617) 234-6500
(617) 234-6505 fax
biopure@biopure.com
www.biopure.com

Biospecifics Technologies
35 Wilbur St.
Lynbrook, NY 11563
(516) 593-7000
www.biospecifics.com

BioStratum
4620 Creekstone Dr.
Suite 200
Durham, NC 27703
(919) 433-1000
(919) 433-1010 fax
info@biostratum.com
www.biostratum.com

Biosyn
1800 Byberry Rd., Building 13
Huntingdon Valley, PA 19006
(215) 914-0900
(215) 914-0914 fax
www.biosyn-inc.com

Biotherapies, Inc.
5692 Plymouth Rd.
Ann Arbor, MI 48105
(734) 996-9040
(734) 996-9024 fax
info@biotherapiesinc.com
www.biotherapiesinc.com

BioTime
935 Pardee St.
Berkeley, CA 94710
(510) 845-9535
www.biotimeinc.com

BioTransplant
Third Ave.
Building 75, Charlestown Navy Yard
Charlestown, MA 02129
(617) 241-5200
www.biotransplant.com

Biovail Corporation International
2488 Dunwin Dr.
Mississauga, ON
Canada L5L-1J9
(416) 285-6000
(416) 285-6499 fax
www.biovail.com

**Boehringer Ingelheim
Pharmaceuticals**
900 Old Ridgebury Rd.
Ridgefield, CT 06877
(203) 798-9988
www.boehringer-ingelheim.com

Bone Care International
1600 Aspen Commons
Middleton, WI 53562
(608) 662-7800
(608) 662-0032 fax
info@bonecare.com
www.bonecare.com

Boron Biologicals
1437 U.S. Hwy. 52 N.
Suite 195
Mt. Airy, NC 27030
(540) 728-0595
(540) 728-0315 fax
info@boronbiologicals.com
www.boronbiologicals.com

Boston Life Sciences
137 Newbury St.
8th floor
Boston, MA 02116
(617) 425-0200
(617) 425-0996 fax
IR@bostonlifesciences.com
www.bostonlifesciences.com

Bristol-Myers Squibb
345 Park Ave.
New York, NY 10154
(212) 546-4000
www.bms.com

Bryan Corporation
4 Plympton St.
Woburn, MA 01801
(800) 343-7711
(781) 935-7602 fax
www.bryancorporation.com

BSD Medical
2188 West 2200 S.
Salt Lake City, UT 84119
(801) 972-5555
(801) 972-5930 fax
info@bsdmc.com
www.bsdmc.com

BTG International
Five Tower Bridge
300 Barr Harbor Dr.
7th Floor
West Conshohocken, PA 19428
(610) 278-1660
(610) 278-1605 fax
info@btgplc.com
www.btgplc.com

Calyx Therapeutics
3513 Breakwater Ave.
Hayward, CA 94545
(510) 780-1020
(510) 780-1025 fax
info@calyxti.com
www.calyxtherapeutics.com

Cambridge NeuroScience
One Kendall Square
Building 700
Cambridge, MA 02139
(617) 225-0600
(617) 225-2714 fax

Carrington Laboratories
2001 Walnut Hill Lane
Irving, TX 75038
(800) 527-5216
(800) 358-5233
www.carringtonlabs.com

Cato Research
4364 S. Alston Ave.
Durham, NC 27713
(919) 361-2286
info@cato.com
www.cato.com

CEL-SCI Corporation
8229 Boone Blvd.
Suite 802
Vienna, VA 22182
(703) 506-9460
(703) 506-9471 fax
www.cel-sci.com

Celgene Corporation
7 Powder Horn Dr.
Warren, NJ 07059
(732) 271-1001
www.celgene.com

Cell Genesys
342 Lakeside Dr.
Foster City, CA 94404
(650) 425-4400
(650) 425-4457 fax
www.cellgenesys.com

Cell Pathways
702 Electronic Dr.
Horsham, PA 19044
(215) 706-3800
(215) 706-3801 fax
trials@cellpathways.com
www.cellpathways.com

Cell Therapeutics
501 Elliott Ave. West
Suite 400
Seattle, WA 98119
(800) 215-2355
www.cticseattle.com

Cellegy Pharmaceuticals
349 Oyster Point Blvd.
Suite 200
S. San Francisco, CA 94080
(650) 616-2200
(650) 616-2222 fax
www.cellegy.com

Centaur Pharmaceuticals
1220 Memorex Dr.
Santa Clara, CA 95050
(408) 822-1600
(408) 822-1601 fax
www.centpharm.com

Centocor
200 Great Valley Parkway
Malvern, PA 19355
(610) 651-6000
(610) 651-6100 fax
www.centocor.com

Cephalon
145 Brandywine Parkway
West Chester, PA 19380
(610) 344-0200
(610) 738-6590 fax
www.cephalon.com

Cerus Corporation
2411 Stanwell Dr.
Concord, CA 94520
(925) 288-6000
(925) 288-6001 fax
www.ceruscorp.com

Chiron Corporation
4560 Horton St.
Emeryville, CA 94608-2916
(510) 655-8730
(510) 655-9910 fax
communications@chiron.com
www.chiron.com

Chrysalis Bio Technology
2200 Market St.
Suite 605
Galveston, TX 77550
(409) 750-9251
www.chrysalisbio.com

Ciba Vision
11460 Johns Creek Parkway
Duluth, GA 30097
(770) 476-3937
www.cibavision.com

Coley Pharmaceutical
93 Worcester Rd.
Suite 101
Wellesley, MA 02481
(781) 431-6400
(781) 431-6403 fax
www.coleypharma.com

CollaGenex Pharmaceuticals
41 University Dr.
Suite 200
Newtown, PA 18940
(215) 579-7388
(215) 579-8577 fax
www.collagenex.com

Collateral Therapeutics
11622 El Camino Real
San Diego, CA 92130
(858) 794-3400
(858) 794-3440
info@collateralthx.com
www.collateralthx.com

Columbia Laboratories
www.columbialabs.com

Connetics Corporation
3290 West Bayshore Rd.
Palo Alto, CA 94303
(650) 843-2800
(650) 843-2899 fax
www.connetics.com

Corixa Corporation
1124 Columbia St.
Suite 200
Seattle, WA 98104
(206) 754-5711
(206) 754-5715 fax
info@corixa.com
www.corixa.com

Cortex Pharmaceuticals
15231 Barranca Parkway
Irvine, CA 92618
(949) 727-3157
(949) 727-3657 fax
info@cortexpharm.com
www.cortexpharm.com

Corvas International
3030 Science Park Rd.
San Diego, CA 92121
(858) 455-9800
(858) 455-7895 fax
info@corvas.com
www.corvas.com

Cubist Pharmaceuticals
65 Hayden Ave.
Lexington, MA 02421
(781) 860-8660
(781) 861-0566 fax
www.cubist.com

Curis
61 Moulton St.
Cambridge, MA 02138
(617) 503-6500
(617) 503-6501 fax
www.curis.com

CV Therapeutics
3172 Porter Dr.
Palo Alto, CA 94304
(650) 812-0585
(650) 858-0390 fax
www.cvt.com

Cygnus
400 Penobscot Dr.
Redwood City, CA 94063
(650) 369-4300
(650) 599-2503 fax
www.cygn.com

CytoDyn of New Mexico
4236 Longridge Ave., Unit #302,
Studio City, CA 91604
(323) 525-0560
(323) 525-0870 fax
cytodyn@cytodyn.com
www.cytodyn.com

Cytogen Corporation
600 College Rd. E.
Princeton, NJ 08540
(800) 833-3533
(609) 750-8123 fax
www.cytogen.com

CytRx Corporation
154 Technology Parkway
Suite 200
Norcross, GA 30092
(770) 368-9500
(770) 368-0622 fax
www.cytrx.com

Daiichi Pharmaceutical
11 Philips Parkway
Montvale, NJ 07645
(201) 573-7000
(201) 573-7650 fax
www.daiichius.com

Demegen
1051 Brinton Rd.
Pittsburgh, PA 15221
(412) 241-2150
(412) 241-2161 fax
info@demegen.com
www.demegen.com

Dendreon Corporation
3005 First Ave.
Seattle, WA 98121
(206) 256-4545
(206) 256-0571 fax
clinical@dendreon.com
www.dendreon.com

Diacrin
Building 96, 13th St., Charlestown,
MA, 02129
(617) 242-9100
(617) 242-0070 fax
clinicalinfo@diacrin.com
www.diacrin.com

Discovery Laboratories
350 S. Main St.
Suite 307
Doylestown, PA 18901
(215) 340-4699
(215) 340-3940 fax
www.discoverylabs.com

DOR BioPharma
28101 N. Ballard Dr.
Unit F
Lake Forest, IL 60045
(847) 573-8990
(847) 573-9285 fax
www.dorbiopharma.com

Draxis Health
6870 Goreway Dr.
Mississauga, ON
Canada L4V 1P1
(905) 677-5500
(905) 677-5502 fax
www.draxis.com

Du Pont
Barley Mill Plaza, P10
Wilmington, DE 19880
(800) 441-7515
www.dupont.com

Eli Lilly
Indianapolis, IN 46285
(800) 545-5979
www.lilly.com

EntreMed
9640 Medical Center Dr.
Rockville, MD 20850
(301) 217-9858
(301) 217-9594 fax
www.entremed.com

Entropin
45926 Oasis St.
Indio, CA 92201
(760) 775-8333
(760) 775-1224 fax
Entropin@aol.com
www.entropin.com

Enzo Biochem
527 Madison Ave
New York, NY 10022
(212) 583-0100
(212) 583-0150 fax
info@corp.enzobio.com
www.enzo.com

Enzon
20 Kingsbridge Rd.
Piscataway, NJ 08854
(732) 980-4500
(732) 980-5911 fax
www.enzon.com

Eon Labs
227-15 N. Conduit Ave.
Laurelton, NY 11413
(718) 276-8600
(718) 949-3120
www.eonlabs.com

Epic Therapeutics
220 Norwood Park S.
Norwood, MA 02062
(781) 440-0100
(781) 440-0111 fax

EpiGenesis Pharmaceuticals
7 Clarke Dr.
Cranbury, NJ 08512
(609) 409-6080
(609) 409-6126 fax
info@epigene.com
www.epigenesispharmaceuticals.com

Epix Medical
71 Rogers St.
Cambridge, MA 02142
(617) 250-6000
www.epixmed.com

Esperion Therapeutics
3621 S. State St.
695 KMS Place
Ann Arbor, MI 48108
(734) 332-0506
(734) 332-0516 fax
info@esperion.com
www.esperion.com

Essential Therapeutics
1365 Main St.
Waltham, MA, 02451
(781) 647-5554
(781) 647-5552 fax
info@essentialtherapeutics.com
www.essentialtherapeutics.com

Eukarion
Eukarion, Inc.
6F Alfred Circle
Bedford, MA 01730
(781) 275-0424
(781) 275-0752 fax
mail@eukarion.com
www.eukarion.com

Exocell
3508 Market St.
Suite 420
Philadelphia, PA 19104
(215) 222-5515
(215) 222-5325 fax
www.exocell.com

FibroGen
225 Gateway Blvd.
S. San Francisco, CA 94080
(650) 866-7200
(650) 866-7201 fax
www.fibrogen.com

Flemington Pharmaceutical
31 State Hwy. 12
Flemington, NJ 08822
(908) 782-3431
(908) 782-2445 fax
www.flemington-pharma.com

Fujisawa Healthcare
Three Parkway N.
Deerfield, IL 60015
(800) 727-7003
(847) 317-8229 fax
www.fujisawa.com

GelTex Pharmaceuticals
153 Second Ave
Waltham, MA 02451
(781) 290-5888
(781) 290-5890 fax
www.geltex.com

Genaera
5110 Campus Dr.
Plymouth Meeting, PA 19462
(610) 941-4020
(610) 941-5399 fax
info@genaera.com
www.genaera.com

Genelabs Technologies
505 Penobscot Dr.
Redwood City, CA 94063
(650) 369-9500
(650) 368-0709 fax
www.genelabs.com

Genentech
1 DNA Way
S. San Francisco, CA 94080
(650) 225-1000
(650) 225-6000 fax
webmaster@gene.com
www.gene.com

Genetix Pharmaceuticals
840 Memorial Dr.
Cambridge, MA 02139
(617) 491-5601
(617) 576-2421 fax
info@genetixpharm.com
www.genetixpharm.com

Genetronics
11199 Sorrento Valley Rd.
San Diego, CA 92121
(858) 597-6006
(858) 597-0119 fax
www.genetronics.com

Geneva Pharmaceuticals
2655 West Midway Blvd.
Broomfield, CO 80038
(303) 438-2400
(303) 438-4464 fax
www.genevarx.com

Genitope Corporation
525 Penobscot Dr.
Redwood City, Ca 94063
(650) 482-2000
(650) 482-2002 fax
Clinicalinfo@genitope.com
www.genitope.com

Genta
Two Oak Way
Berkeley Heights, NJ 07922
(908) 286-9800
info@genta.com
www.genta.com

GenVec
65 W. Watkins Mill Rd.
Gaithersburg, MD 20878
(240) 632-0740
(240) 632-0735 fax
www.genvec.com

Genzyme Corporation
One Kendall Square
Cambridge, MA 02139
(617) 252-7500
(617) 252-7600 fax
www.genzyme.com

Geron Corporation
230 Constitution Dr.
Menlo Park, CA 94025
(650) 473-7700
(650) 473-7750
info@geron.com
www.geron.com

Gilead
333 Lakeside Dr.
Foster City, CA 94404
(650) 574-3000
(650) 578-9264 fax
www.gilead.com

GlaxoSmithKline
5 Moore Dr.
PO Box 13398
Research Triangle Park, NC 27709
(888) 825-5249
www.gsk.com

Gliatech
23420 Commerce Park Rd.
Cleveland, OH 44122
(216) 831-3200
(216) 831-4220 fax
www.gliatech.com

Glyko
11 Pimentel Court
Novato, CA 94949
(800) 334-5956
(415) 382-3511 fax
thelab@glyko.com
www.glyko.com

Guilford Pharmaceuticals
6611 Tributary St.
Baltimore, MD 21224
(410) 631-6300
(410) 631-6338 fax
www.guilfordpharm.com

Gynetics
(800) 311-7378
info@gynetics.com
www.gynetics.com

Halsey Drug Company Inc.
(800) 336-2750
general@halseydrug.com
www.halseydrug.com

Hauser Inc.
5555 Airport Blvd.
Boulder, CO 80301
(303) 443-4662
(303) 441-5801 fax
corpcomm@hauser.com
www.hauser.com

Healthspan Sciences
4953 Smith Canyon Court
San Diego, CA 92130
(760) 497-5614
info@healthspansciences.com
www.healthspansciences.com

Hemosol USA
8 Wood Hollow Rd.
Suite 301
Parsippany, NJ 07054
(973) 781-0200
(973) 781-9840 fax
hml@hemosol.com
www.hemosol.com

Hi-Tech Pharmacal
369 Bayview Ave.
Amityville, NY 11701
(631) 789-8228
(631) 789-8429 fax
www.hitechpharm.com

Hoffmann-La Roche
340 Kingsland St.
Nutley, NJ 07110
(973) 235-5000
www.rocheusa.com

Hollis-Eden Pharmaceuticals
9333 Genesee Ave.
Suite 200
San Diego, CA 92121
(858) 587-9333
(858) 558-6470 fax
www.holliseden.com

Human Genome Sciences
9410 Key West Ave.
Rockville, MD 20850
(301) 309-8504
(301) 309-8512 fax
www.hgsi.com

Hybridon
345 Vassar St.
Cambridge, MA 02139
(617) 679-5500
(617) 679-5592 fax
www.hybridon.com

ICN Pharmaceuticals
3300 Hyland Ave.
Costa Mesa, CA 92626
(714) 545-0100
(714) 641-7223
www.icnpharm.com

ICOS Corporation
22021 20th Ave. SE
Bothell, WA 98021
(425) 485-1900
info@icos.com
www.icos.com

ID Biomedical
1510-800 West Pender
Vancouver, BC
Canada V6C 2V6
(604) 431-9314
(604) 431-9378 fax
info@idbiomedical.com
www.idbiomedical.com

IDEC Pharmaceuticals
3030 Callan Rd.
San Diego, CA 92121
(858) 431-8500
(858) 431-8750 fax
www.idecpharm.com

IDUN Pharmaceuticals
9380 Judicial Dr.
San Diego, CA 92121
(858) 623-1330
www.idun.com

ILEX Oncology
4545 Horizon Hill Blvd.
San Antonio, TX 78229
(210) 949-8200
(210) 949-8210 fax
www.ilexoncology.com

ImaRx Pharmaceutical
1635 E. 18th St.
Tucson, AZ 85719
(520) 770-1259
(520) 791-2437 fax
www.imarx.com

ImClone Systems
180 Varick St.
New York, NY 10014
(212) 645-1405
(212) 645-2054 fax
www.imclone.com

Immune Network, Ltd.
3650 Wesbrook Mall
Vancouver, BC
Canada V6S 2L2
(604) 222-5541
(604) 222-5542 fax
info@immunenetwork.com
www.immunenetwork.com

Immune Response Corporation
5935 Darwin Court
Carlsbad, CA 92008
(760) 431-7080
(760) 431-8636 fax
www.imnr.com

Immunex Corporation
51 University St.
Seattle, WA 98101
(206) 587-0430
(206) 587-0606 fax
www.immunex.com

ImmunoGen
128 Sidney St.
Cambridge, MA 02139
(617) 995-2500
(617) 995-2510 fax
www.immunogen.com

Immunomedics
300 American Rd.
Morris Plains, NJ 07950
(973) 605-8200
(973) 605-8282 fax
www.immunomedics.com

Immusol
10790 Roselle St.
San Diego, CA 92121
(858) 824-1100
(858) 824-1112 fax
info@immusol.com
www.immusol.com

Incyte Pharmaceuticals
3160 Porter Dr.
Palo Alto, CA 94304
(650) 855-0555
(650) 855-0572 fax
www.incyte.com

Inex Pharmaceuticals
100-8900 Glenlyon Parkway
Burnaby, BC
Canada V5J 5J8
(604) 419-3200
(604) 419-3201 fax
info@inexpharm.com
www.inexpharm.com

Inflazyme Pharmaceuticals
5600 Parkwood Way
Suite 425
Richmond, BC
Canada V6V 2M2
(604) 279-8711 fax
info@inflazyme.com
www.inflazyme.com

Inhale Therapeutic Systems
150 Industrial Rd.
San Carlos, CA 94070
(650) 631-3100
(650) 631-3150 fax
inhale@inhale.com
www.inhale.com

Inhibitex
8995 Westside Parkway
Alpharetta, GA 30004
(678) 336-2600
(678) 336-2626 fax
www.inhibitex.com

Inkine Pharmaceutical Company
1787 Sentry Parkway West
Building 18, Suite 440
Blue Bell, PA 19422
(215) 283-6850
(215) 283-4600 fax
www.inkine.com

InSite Vision
965 Atlantic Ave.
Alameda, CA 94501
(510) 865-8800
(510) 865-5700 fax
www.insitevision.com

Insmed Pharmaceuticals
4851 Lakebrook Dr.
Glen Allen, VA 23060
(804) 565-3000
(804) 565-3500 fax
www.insmed.com

Inspire Pharmaceuticals
4222 Emperor Blvd.
Suite 470
Durham, NC 27703
(919) 941-9777
www.inspirepharm.com

Interferon Sciences
783 Jersey Ave.
New Brunswick, NJ 08901
(888) 728-4372
(732) 249-6895 fax
www.interferonsciences.com

Interneuron Pharmaceuticals
99 Hayden Ave.
Suite 200
Lexington, MA 02421
(781) 861-8444
(781) 861-3830 fax
www.interneuron.com

IntraBiotics Pharmaceuticals
1245 Terra Bella Ave.
Mountain View, CA 94043
(650) 526-6800.
www.intrabiotics.com

Introgen Therapeutics
2250 Holcombe
Houston, TX 77030
(713) 797-9960
(713) 797-9913 fax
www.introgen.com

Iomed
2441 South 3850 West
Suite A
Salt Lake City, UT 84120
(801) 975-1191
(801) 972-9072 fax
info@iomed.com
www.iomed.com

Isis Pharmaceuticals
2292 Faraday Ave.
Carlsbad, CA 92008
(760) 931-9200
(760) 931-9639 fax
info@isisph.com
www.isip.com

Ivax Corporation
4400 Biscayne Blvd.
Miami, FL 33137
(305) 575-6000
www.ivax.com

Janssen Pharmaeutica
1125 Trenton-Harbourton Rd.
Titusville, NJ 08560
(609) 730-2000
(609) 730-2323 fax
cacteam@janus.jnj.com
www.us.janssen.com

Johnson & Johnson
One Johnson & Johnson Plaza
New Brunswick, NJ 08933
(732) 524-0400
www.jnj.com

King Pharmaceuticals
501 Fifth St.
Bristol, TN 37620
(423) 989-8000
www.kingpharm.com

La Jolla Pharmaceutical
6455 Nancy Ridge Dr.
San Diego, CA 92121
(858) 452-6600
(858) 452-6893 fax
www.ljpc.com

Layton Bioscience
709 E. Evelyn Ave.
Sunnyvale, CA 94086
(408) 616-1000
(408) 616-1005 fax
www.laytonbio.com

Ligand Pharmaceuticals
10275 Science Center Dr.
San Diego, CA 92121
(858) 550-7500
(858) 550-7506 fax
www.ligand.com

Lorus Therapeutics Inc.
2 Meridian Rd.
Toronto, ON
Canada M9W 4Z7
(416) 798-1200
(416) 798-2200 fax
www.lorusthera.com

MacroChem Corporation
110 Hartwell Ave.
Lexington, MA 02421-3134
(781) 862-4003
(781) 862-4338 fax
www.macrochem.com

Mallinckrodt
675 McDonnell Blvd.
Hazelwood, MO 63042
(314) 654-2000
www.mallinckrodt.com

Maret Pharmaceuticals
4041 MacArthur Blvd.
Suie 375
Newport Beach, CA 92660
(949) 225-0005
(949) 225-0006 fax
maret@maretpharma.com
www.maretpharma.com

Matritech
330 Nevada St.
Newton, MA 02460
(617) 928-0820
(617) 928-0821 fax
www.matritech.com

Matrix Pharmaceutical
34700 Campus Dr.
Fremont, CA 94555
(510) 742-7700
(510) 742-0632 fax
www.matx.com

Maxim Pharmaceuticals
8899 University Center Lane
Suite 400
San Diego, CA 92122
(888) 562-4040
www.maxim.com

McGhan Medical
700 Ward Dr.
Santa Barbera, CA 93111
(805) 683-6761
(805) 967-5839 fax
www.mcghan.com

Medarex
707 State Rd.
Princeton, NJ 08540-1437
(609) 430-2880
(609) 430-2850 fax
information@medarex.com
www.medarex.com

MediChem Research
2501 Davey Rd.
Woodridge, IL 60517
(630) 783-4600
(630) 783-4909 fax
internet@medichem.com
www.medichem.com

MedImmune
35 W. Watkins Mill Rd.
Gaithersburg, MD 20878
(301) 417-0770
info@medimmune.com
www.medimmune.com

Medinox
11575 Sorrento Valley Rd.
Suite 201
San Diego, CA 92121
(858) 793-4820
(858) 793-4823 fax
info@medinox.com
www.medinox.com

Merck & Co.
1 Merck Dr.
PO Box 100
Whitehouse Station, NJ 08889
(800) 422-9675
(908) 735-1253 fax
www.merck.com

Merrimack Pharmaceuticals
50 Church St.
5th Floor
Cambridge, MA 02138
(617) 441-1000
(617) 491-1386 fax
www.merrimackpharma.com

Merz
4215 Tudor Lane
Greensboro, NC 27410
(800) 334-0514
(336) 856-0107 fax
infor@merzusa.om
www.merzusa.com

Metabolex
3876 Bay Center Place
Hayward, CA 94545
(510) 293-8800
(510) 293-9090 fax
info@metabolex.com
www.metabolex.com

MGI Pharma
5775 W. Old Shakopee Rd.
Suite 100
Bloomington, MN 55437
(952) 346-4771
www.mgipharma.com

Mikart
1750 Chattahoochee Ave.
Atlanta, GA 30318
(404) 351-4510
(404) 350-0432 fax
www.mikart.com

Milkhaus Laboratory
70 Elm St.
Providence, RI 02903
(401) 273-4555
(401) 273-8555 fax
info@milkhaus.com
www.milkhaus.com

Millenium Pharmaceuticals
75 Sidney St.
Cambridge, MA 02139
(617) 679-7000
(617) 374-7788 fax
info@mlnm.com
www.mlnm.com

Miravant
336 Bollay Dr.
Santa Barbara, CA 93117
(805) 685-9880
(805) 685-7981 fax
www.miravant.com

Mission Pharmacal
10999 IH-10 W.
Suite 1000
San Antonio, TX 78230
(800) 531-3333
www.missionpharmacal.com

Molecumetics
2023 120th Ave. N.E.
Bellevue, WA 98005
(425) 646-8865
(425) 646-8890 fax
www.molecumetics.com

Monsanto
800 N. Lindbergh Blvd.
St. Louis, MO 63167
(314) 694-1000
www.monsanto.com

Mylan Pharmaceuticals
781 Chestnut Ridge Rd.
PO Box 4310
Morgantown, WV 26505
www.mylan.com

Myriad Genetics
320 Wakara Way
Salt Lake City, UT 84108
(801) 584-3600
www.myriad.com

Nabi
5800 Park of Commerce Blvd. N.W.
Boca Raton, FL 33487
(561) 989-5800
www.nabi.com

Nastech Pharmaceutical
45 Adams Ave.
Hauppauge, NY 11788
(631) 273-0101
(631) 273-0252 fax
www.nastech.com

NeoRx Corporation
410 West Harrison St.
Seattle WA 98119
(206) 281-7001
(206) 284-7112 fax
www.neorx.com

Neose Technologies
102 Witmer Rd.
Horsham, PA 19044
(215) 441-5890
info@neose.com
www.neose.com

NeoTherapeutics
157 Technology Dr.
Irvine, CA 92618
(949) 788-6700
(949) 450-6706 fax
www.neotherapeutics.com

Neurobiological Technologies
3260 Blume Dr.
Suite 500
Richmond, CA 94806
(510) 262-1730
(510) 262-0204 fax
www.ntii.com

Neurocrine Biosciences
10555 Science Center Dr.
San Diego, CA 92121
(858) 658-7600
(858) 658-7601 fax
www.neurocrine.com

Neurogen Corporation
35 N.E. Industrial Rd.
Branford, CT 06405
(203) 488-8201
(203) 481-8683 fax
www.neurogen.com

Nexell Therapeutics
9 Parker
Irvine, CA 92618
(949) 470-9011
(949) 586-2420 fax
www.nexellinc.com

NexMed
350 Corporate Blvd.
Robbinsville, NJ 08691
(609) 208-9688
www.nexmed.com

NitroMed
12 Oak Park Dr.
Bedford, MA 01730
(781) 275-9700
www.nitromed.com

Northfield Laboratories
1560 Sherman Ave.
Suite 1000
Evanston, IL 60201-4800
(847) 864-3500
www.northfieldlabs.com

Northwest Biotherapeutics
21720 23rd Dr. S.E.
Suite 100
Bothell, WA 98021
(425) 608-3000
(425) 608-3026 fax
www.nwbio.com

Novavax
8320 Guilford Rd.
Suite C
Columbia, MD 21046
(301) 854-3900
(301) 854-3901 fax
www.novavax.com

Novelos Therapeutics
255 Washington St.
Suite 150
Newton, MA 02458
(617) 244-1616
(617) 964-6331 fax
www.novelos.com

Noven Pharmaceuticals
11960 S.W. 144th St.
Miami, FL 33186
www.noven.com

NPS Pharmaceuticals
420 Chipeta Way
Salt Lake City, UT 84108
(801) 583-4939
www.npsp.com

Nymox Pharmaceutical
9900 Cavendish Blvd.
Suite 306
St.-Laurent, QC
Canada H4M 2V2
(800) 936-9669
(514) 332-2227 fax
www.nymox.com

Oculex Pharmaceuticals
601 W. California Ave.
Sunnyvale, CA 94086
(408) 481-0424
(408) 481-0662 fax
www.oculex.com

Ontogen Corporation
6451 El Camino Real
Carlsbad, CA 92009
(760) 930-0100
(760) 930-0200 fax
www.ontogen.com

Ontogeny
45 Moulton St.
Cambridge, MA 02138-1118
(617) 876-0086
(617) 876-0866 fax
www.ontogeny.com

OraPharma
730 Louis Dr.
Warminster, PA 18974
(215) 956-2200
www.orapharma.com

Organogenesis
150 Dan Rd.
Canton, MA 02021
(781) 575-0775
(781) 575-0440 fax
www.organogenesis.com

Orphan Medical
13911 Ridgedale Dr.
Suite 250
Minnetonka, MN 55305
(888) 867-7426
www.orphan.com

Ortho-McNeil Pharmaceutical
(800) 682-6532
www.orthomcneil.com

OrthoLogic
1275 W. Washington
Tempe, AZ 85281
(800) 937-5520
www.orthologic.com

OSI Pharmaceuticals
106 Charles Lindberg Blvd.
Uniondale, NY 11553
(516) 222-0023
(516) 222-0114 fax
www.osip.com

Osiris Therapeutics
2001 Aliceanna St.
Baltimore, MD 21231
(410) 522-5005
(410) 522-6999 fax
osiris@osiristx.com
www.osiristx.com

Otsuka America Pharmaceuticals
2440 Research Blvd.
Rockville, MD 20850
(301) 990-0030
(301) 212-8647 fax
clinicalinquiries@otsuka.com
www.otsuka.com

OXiGENE
321 Arsenal St.
Watertown, MA 02472
(617) 673-7800
(617) 924-9229 fax
www.oxigene.com

OXIS International
6040 N. Cutter Circle
Suite 317
Portland, OR 97217
(800) 547-3686
(503) 283-4058 fax
info@oxis.com
www.oxis.com

OXO Chemie
601 Gateway Blvd.
Suite 450
S. San Francisco, CA 94080
(650) 246-2200
(650) 246-2222 fax
www.oxochemie.com

Paddock Laboratories
3940 Quebec Ave. N
Minneapolis, MN 55427
(763) 546-4676
(763) 546-4842 fax
info@paddocklabs.com
www.paddocklabs.com

Palatin Technologies
103 Carnegie Center
Suite 200
Princeton, NJ 08540
(609) 520-1911
(609) 452-0880 fax
www.palatin.com

Par Pharmaceutical
One Ram Ridge Rd.
Spring Valley, NY 10977
(800) 727-0923
www.parpharm.com

Paracelsian
95 Brown Rd, #1005
Ithaca, NY 14850
(888) 689-4224
(607) 257-2734 fax
www.paracelsian.com

Parnell Pharmaceuticals
PO Box 5130
Larkspur, CA 94977 USA
(415) 256-1800
(415) 256-8099 fax
mail@parnellpharm.com
www.parnellpharm.com

Pediatric Pharmaceuticals
120 Wood Ave. S.
Suite 300
Iselin, NJ 08830
(732) 603-7708
pedpharm@worldnet.att.net
www.pediatricpharm.com

Penwest Pharmaceuticals
2981 Route 22
Patterson, NY 12563
(845) 878-3414
www.penwestpharmaceuticals.com

Peregrine Pharmaceuticals Inc.
14272 Franklin Ave.
Suite 100
Tustin, CA 92780
(714) 508-6000
(714) 838-5817 fax
www.peregrineinc.com

Perrigo
515 Eastern Ave.
Allegan, MI 49010
(800) 719-9260
(616) 673-9128 fax
www.perrigo.com

Pfizer
235 E. 42nd St.
MS 11-22
New York, NY 10017
(212) 573-2323
(212) 573-7851 fax
www.pfizer.com

Pharm-Eco Laboratories
25 Patton Rd.
Devens, MA 01432
(978) 784-5000
(978) 784-5500 fax
main@pharmeco.com
www.pharmeco.com

**Pharmaceutical Product
Development (PPD)**
3151 S. 17th St.
Wilmington, NC 28412
(910) 251-0081
(910) 762-5820 fax
www.ppdi.com

Pharmacia Corporation
100 Rte. 206 N.
Peapack, NJ 07977
(908) 901-8000
(908) 901-8379 fax
www.pharmacia.com

Pharmacyclics
995 E. Arques Ave.
unnyvale, CA 94085
(408) 774-0330
(408) 774-0340 fax
info@pcyc.com
www.pcyc.com

Pharmadigm
2401 Foothill Dr.
Salt Lake City, UT 84109
(801) 464-6100
(801) 464-6116 fax
info@pharmadigm.com
www.pharmadigm.com

Pharmascience
6111 Avenue Royalmount
Suite 100
Montreal, QC
Canada H4P 2T4
(514) 340-9800
(514) 342-7764 fax
info@pharmascience.com
www.pharmascience.com

Pharmos Corporation
99 Wood Ave. S.
Suite 301
Iselin, NJ 08830
(732) 452-9556
(732) 452-9557 fax
info@pharmos-us.com
www.pharmoscorp.com

Pherin Pharmaceuticals
350 N. Bernardo Ave.
Mountain View, CA 94043
(650) 903-7100
(650) 903-7101 fax
www.pherin.com

Phytera
377 Plantation St.
Worcester, MA 01605
(508) 792-6800
(508) 792-1339 fax
www.phytera.com

Polydex Pharmaceuticals
421 Comstock Rd.
Scarborough, ON
Canada, M1L 2H5
(416) 755-2231
www.polydex.com

PowderJect Vaccines
585 Science Dr.
Madison, WI 53711
(608) 231-3150
(608) 231-6990 fax
www.powderject.com

Praecis Pharmaceuticals
830 Winter St.
Waltham, MA 02451
(781) 795-4100
info@praecis.com
www.praecis.com

Procter & Gamble Pharmaceuticals
PO Box 599
Cincinnati, OH 45201
(800) 836-0658
www.pgpharma.com

Procyon Biopharma
1650 Trans-Canada
Dorval, QC
Canada H9P 1H7
(514) 685-9283
(514) 685-5138
info@procyonbiopharma.com
www.procyonbiopharma.com

Progenics Pharmaceuticals
777 Old Saw Mill River Rd.
Tarrytown, NY 10591
(914) 789-2800
(914) 789-2817 fax
info@progneics.com
www.progenics.com

Protarga
2200 Renaissance Blvd.
Suite 450
King of Prussia, PA 19406
(610) 592-4000
www.protarga.com

Protein Design Labs
34801 Campus Dr.
Fremont, CA 94555
(510) 574-1400
(510) 574-1500 fax
www.pdl.com

Protein Sciences
1000 Research Pkwy.
Meriden, CT 06450
(800) 488-7099
(203) 686-0268 fax
www.proteinsciences.com

Protherics
5214 Maryland Way
Suite 405
Brentwood, TN 37027
(615) 327-1027
(615) 320-1212 fax
www.protherics.com

Purdue Pharma L.P.
201 Tresser Blvd.
Stamford, CT 06901
(203) 588-8000
(203) 588-8850 fax
www.pharma.com

QLT Phototherapeutics Inc.
887 Great Northern Way
Vancouver, BC
Canada V5T 4T5
(604) 707-7000
(604) 707-7001 fax
www.qlt-pdt.com

Questcor
3260 Whipple Rd.
Union City, CA 94587
(510) 400-0700
(510) 400-0799 fax
www.questcor.com

R.P. Scherer
645 Martinsville Rd.
Suite 200
Basking Ridge, NJ 07920
(888) 636-1919
information@rpscherer.com
www.rpscherer.com

Redox Pharmaceuticals
100 Forest Dr.
Greenvale, NY 11548
(516) 625-2906
(516) 621-7944 fax
info@redoxpharm.com
www.redoxpharm.com

Regeneron Pharmaceuticals
777 Old Saw Mill River Rd.
Tarrytown, NY 10591
(914) 345-7400
(914) 347-2113 fax
info@regeneron.com
www.regeneron.com

Repligen Corporation
117 Fourth Ave.
Needham, MA 02494
(800) 622-2259
(781) 453-0048 fax
info@repligen.com
www.repligen.com

ReProtect, LLC
703 Stags Head Rd.
Baltimore, MD 21286
(410) 337-8377
www.reprotect.com

Research Corporation Technologies
101 N. Wilmot Rd.
Suite 600
Tucson, AZ 85711
(520) 748-4400
(520) 748-0025 fax
info@rctech.com
www.rctech.com

Rhone-Poulenc Rorer
500 Arcola Rd.
PO Box 1200
Collegeville, PA 19426-0107
(800) 727-6737
www.rhone-poulenc.com

Ribozyme Pharmaceuticals
2950 Wilderness Pl.
Boulder, CO 80301
(303) 449-6500
www.rpi.com

Roche Bioscience
3401 Hillview Ave.
Palo Alto, CA 94304
(650) 855-5050
http://paloalto.roche.com

Romark Laboratories
6200 Courtney Campbell Causeway
Suite 880
Tampa, FL 33607
(813) 282-8544
(813) 282-4910 fax
www.romarklabs.com

Roxane Laboratories
PO Box 16532
Columbus, OH 43216
(800) 962-8364
www.roxane.com

SangStat Medical
6300 Dumbarton Circle
Fremont, CA 94555
(888) 764-7828
(510) 789-4400 fax
www.sangstat.com

Sanofi-Synthelabo Pharmaceuticals
90 Park Ave.
New York, NY 10016
(212) 551-4000
www.sanofi-synthelaboUS.com

Santarus Inc.
10590 West Ocean Air Dr.
Suite 200
San Diego, CA 92130
(858) 314-5700
(858) 314-5701 fax
contacts@santarus.com
www.santarus.com

Schering-Plough Corporation
2000 Galloping Hill Rd.
Kenilworth, NJ 07033
(908) 298-4000
www.sch-plough.com

Schwarz Pharma
PO Box 2038
Milwaukee WI 53201
(800) 558-5114
www.schwarzusa.com

SciClone Pharmaceuticals
901 Mariner's Island Blvd.
Suite 205
San Mateo, CA 94404
(650) 358-3456
(650) 358-3469 fax
www.sciclone.com

Scios
820 West Maude Ave.
Sunnyvale, CA 94085
(408) 616-8200
(408) 616-8206 fax
www.sciosinc.com

Seattle Genetics
21823 30th Dr. S.E.
Bothell, WA 98021
(425) 527-4000
(425) 527-4001 fax
contact@seagen.com
www.seattlegenetics.com

Selective Genetics
11035 Roselle St.
San Diego, CA 92121
(858) 625-0100
(858) 625-0050 fax
www.selectivegenetics.com

Sepracor
111 Locke Dr.
Marlborough, MA 01752
(508) 481-6700
info@sepracor.com
www.sepracor.com

Serono Laboratories
One Technology Place
Rockland, MA 02370
(781) 982-9000
(781) 871-6754 fax
www.serono.com

Sicor
19 Hughes
Irvine, CA 92618
(800) 729-9991
(949) 855-8210 fax
www.gensiasicor.com

Sidmak Laboratories
17 West St.
East Hanover, NJ 07936
(800) 922-0547
(800) 572-9014 fax
administrator@sidmaklab.com
www.sidmaklab.com

SIGA Technologies
420 Lexington Ave.
Suite 620
New York, NY 10170
(212) 672-9100
(212) 697-3130 fax
info@siga.com
www.siga.com

Sigma-Tau Pharmaceuticals
800 S. Frederick Ave.
Suite 300
Gaithersburg, MD 20877
(800) 447-0169
www.sigmatau.com

Solvay Pharmaceuticals
901 Sawyer Rd.
Marietta, GA 30062
(800) 354-0026
www.solvay.com

Sonus Pharmaceuticals
22026 20th Ave. SE
Bothell, WA 98021
(425) 487-9500
(425) 489-0626 fax
www.sonuspharma.com

Stiefel Laboratories
255 Alhambra Circle
Coral Gables, FL 33134
(888) 784-3335
www.stiefel.com

StressGen
10241 Wateridge Circle Dr.
Suite C200
San Diego, CA 92121
(858) 202-4900
(858) 450-6849 fax
www.stressgen.com

Stryker Corporation
2725 Fairfield Rd..
Kalamazoo, MI 49002.
(616) 385-6600
www.strykercorp.com

Synsorb Biotech
410, 1167 Kensington Crescent N.W.
Calgary, AB
Canada T2N 1X7
(403)283-5900
(403)283-5907 fax
www.synsorb.com

Synthetic Blood International
3189 Airway Ave.
Building C
Costa Mesa, CA 92626
(714) 427-6363
(714) 427-6361 fax
info@sybd.com
www.sybd.com

**Takeda Pharmaceuticals
North America**
475 Half Day Rd.
Suite 500
Lincolnshire, IL 60069
(847) 383-3000
www.takedapharm.com

Tanox Biosystems
10301 Stella Link
Houston, TX 77025
(713) 578-4000
(713) 578-5002 fax
info@tanox.com
www.tanox.com

Targeted Genetics
1100 Olive Way
Suite 100
Seattle, WA 98101
(206) 623-7612
(206) 223-0288 fax
www.targen.com

Telik
750 Gateway Blvd.
S. San Francisco, CA 94080
(650) 244-9303
(650) 244-9388 fax
inquiry@telik.com
www.telik.com

Teva Pharmaceuticals USA
1090 Horsham Rd.
PO Box 1090
North Wales, PA 19454
(215) 591-3000
www.tevapharmusa.com

Texas Biotechnology
7000 Fannin
20th Floor
Houston, TX 77030
(713) 796-8822
(713) 796-8232 fax
www.tbc.com

Theragenics Corporation
5203 Bristol Industrial Way
Buford, GA 30518
(770) 271-0233
www.theragenics.com

Theratechnologies
2310 Alfred-Nobel Blvd.
St. Laurent, QC
Canada H4S 24A
(514) 336-7800
(514) 336-7242 fax
www.theratech.com

Therion Biologics
76 Rogers St.
Cambridge, MA 02142
(617) 876-7779
(617) 876-9391 fax
www.therionbio.com

Titan Pharmaceuticals
400 Oyster Point Blvd.
Suite 505
S. San Fransisco, CA 94080
(650) 244-4990
(650) 244-0715 fax
www.titanpharm.com

Transkaryotic Therapies
195 Albany St.
Cambridge, MA 02139
(617) 349-0200
www.tktx.com

Triangle Pharmaceuticals
4 University Place
4611 University Dr.
Durham, NC 27707
(919) 493-5980
www.tripharm.com

Trimeris
3578 Westgate Dr.
3rd Floor
Durham, NC 27707
(919) 419-6050
(919) 419-1816 fax
info@trimeris.com
www.trimeris.com

Tularik
2 Corporate Dr.
S. San Francisco, CA 94080
(650) 825-7000
(650) 825-7303 fax
www.tularik.com

Unimed Pharmaceuticals
4 Parkway N.
2nd floor
Deerfield, IL 60015
(847) 282-5400
(847) 374-8480 fax
www.unimed.com

United Therapeutics
1110 Spring St.
Silver Spring, MD 20910
(301) 608-9292
(301) 608-9291 fax
www.unither.com

Upsher-Smith Laboratories
13700 First Ave. N.
Minneapolis, MN 55441
(800) 654-2299
www.upsher-smith.com

Valentis
863A Mitten Rd.
Burlingame, CA 94010
(650) 697-1900
(650) 652-1980 fax
info@valentis.com
www.valentis.com

Vasogen
2155 Dunwin Dr.
Suite 10
Mississauga, ON
Canada L5L 4M1
(905) 569-2265
(905) 569-9231 fax
www.vasogen.com

VaxGen
1000 Marina Blvd.
Suite 200
Brisbane, CA 94005
(650) 624-1000
(650) 624-1001 fax
www.vaxgen.com

Versicor
34790 Ardentech Court
Freemont, CA 94555
(510) 739-3000
(510) 739-3003 fax
info@versicor.com
www.versicor.com

Vertex Pharmaceuticals
130 Waverly St.
Cambridge, MA 02139
(617) 444-6100
(617) 444-6680 fax
www.vpharm.com

Vical
9373 Towne Centre Dr.
Suite 100
San Diego, CA 92121
(858) 646-1100
(858) 646-1150 fax
info@vical.com
www.vical.com

Vion Pharmaceuticals
4 Science Park
New Haven, CT 06511
(203) 498-4210
(203) 498-4211 fax
www.vionpharm.com

Viragen
865 S.W. 78th Ave.
Suite 100
Plantation, FL 33324
www.viragen.com

ViroPharma
405 Eagleview Blvd.
Exton, PA 19341
(610) 458-7300
www.viropharma.com

Vitex
134 Coolidge Ave.
Watertown, MA 02472
(617) 926-1551
info@vitechnologies.com
www.vitechnologies.com

Vivus
545 Middlefield Rd.
Suite 200
Menlo Park, CA 94025
(650) 934-5200
www.vivus.com

Warner Chilcott Laboratories
80 Corporate Center
100 Enterprise Dr.
Suite 280
Rockaway, NJ07866
(973) 442-3200
(973) 442-3283 fax
www.wclabs.com

Watson Pharmaceuticals
311 Bonnine Circle
Corona, CA 92880
(909) 270-1400
www.watsonpharm.com

WE Pharmaceuticals
PO Box 1142
Ramona, CA 92065
(760) 788-9155
www.weez.com

Wyeth
5 Giralda Farms
Madison, NJ 07940
pr@wyeth.com
www.wyeth.com

Xcyte Therapies
1124 Columbia St.
Suite 130
Seattle, WA 98104
(206) 262-6200
(206) 262-0900 fax
info@xcytetherapies.com
www.xcytetherapies.com

XOMA Corporation
2910 Seventh St.
Berkeley, CA 94710
www.xoma.com

Yamanouchi Pharmaceutical
www.yamanouchi.com

YM Biosciences
5045 Orbitor Dr.
Building 11, Suite 400
Mississauga, ON
Canada L4W 4Y4
(905) 629-9761
(905) 629-4959 fax
www.ymbiosciences.com

Zenith Goldline Pharmaceuticals
4400 Biscayne Blvd.
Miami, FL 33137
(305) 575-6000
www.ivax.com

Zonagen
2408 Timberloch Place, B-4
The Woodlands, TX 77380
(281) 719-3400
(281) 719-3446 fax
faxwww.zonagen.com

Zycos Inc.
44 Hartwell Ave.
Lexington, MA 02421
(781) 274-6500
(781) 274-0839 fax
www.zycos.com

ABOUT THE AUTHORS

Kenneth A. Getz is the publisher, president and CEO of CenterWatch, which he co-founded in 1994. Ken is a well-known speaker at conferences and serves on several boards, including the Institute of Medicine's Clinical Research Roundtable, the Drug Information Association's Steering Committee for North America, the Association for Clinical Research Professional's Future Trends Committee and the Doris Duke Foundation's Consortium to Examine Clinical Research Ethics. Ken is a widely known author of articles and chapters in scholarly and trade journals and books. He has appeared on major national radio and television programs to speak with patients and their advocates about the clinical trial process. Ken holds an MBA from the J.L. Kellogg Graduate School of Management at Northwestern University and an undergraduate degree from Brandeis University. He lives with his wife Debra and their three children in southern Massachusetts.

Deborah Borfitz has written for numerous health and business periodicals throughout her 20-year career and now contributes regularly to several of the nation's best-in-class publications, including *Medical Economics Magazine*, the *CenterWatch Newsletter*, *Strategic Health Care Marketing*, and *eHealthcare Strategy & Trends*. Deborah was born and raised in Norwich, NY and attended the state's universities in Cortland and Oneonta. She now resides in Florida with her husband, Dale Armstrong, and their two children.